7.50

WITHDRAWN BY
WHITMAN COLLEGE LIBRARY

DJUKA SOCIETY AND SOCIAL CHANGE

Dr. SILVIA W. de GROOT

DJUKA SOCIETY AND SOCIAL CHANGE

History of an attempt to develop a Bush Negro
community in Surinam 1917-1926

ASSEN, 1969

VAN GORCUM & COMP. N.V. - DR. H. J. PRAKKE & H. M. G. PRAKKE

© 1969 by Koninklijke Van Gorcum & Comp. N.V., Assen, The Netherlands

No parts of this book may be reproduced in any form, by print, photoprint, microfilm or any other means without written permission from the publisher

Printed in the Netherlands by Royal VanGorcum Ltd.

to S.R.

CONTENTS

INTRODUCTION XI

CHAPTER I HISTORICAL SURVEY 1

§ 1 THE SETTING 1
§ 2 ORIGIN AND ORGANIZATION OF THE COLONY 1
§ 3 THE SLAVES AND THEIR OWNERS 4
§ 4 THE RUNAWAYS AND THE PEACE TREATIES 5

CHAPTER II THE DJUKA SOCIETY 12

§ 1 INTRODUCTION 12
§ 2 THE ESTABLISHMENT OF THE DJUKA SOCIETY 13
§ 3 ORGANIZATION OF THE DJUKA SOCIETY 17
a Political structure 17 / *b Civil administration* 18 / 1 Form 18 / 2 Possibilities of coercion 18 / 3 Emoluments 20 / *c The priesthood* 20 / 1 The hierarchy of priests 20 / 2 Definition of duties 21 / 3 Funeral priests 23 / 4 The *obiaman* (medicine-man) 23 / 5 The *wisiman* (witch) 24 / *d The supernatural world* 26 / 1 Divinities and oracles 26 / 2 The *jorkas* (ancestors) 27 / 3 Avenging gods and avenging spirits 28 / *e Forms of kinship* 29 / *f Some characteristics of the Djukas* 30 / *g Means of living* 34 / 1 Agriculture, hunting, fishing 34 / 2 Income from trade and services 36

CHAPTER III THE COLONIAL ADMINISTRATION 39

§ 1 THE DUTCH GOVERNMENT 39
§ 2 THE GOVERNOR 43
§ 3 THE COLONIAL STATES 45
§ 4 RENEWED INTEREST IN THE BUSH NEGROES 47
§ 5 NOTES ON THE DESIGN OF AN 'EXPERIMENT' 51

CHAPTER IV DESIGN OF A DEVELOPMENT PLAN, 1918-1919 . . . 55

§ 1 ELECTION AND APPOINTMENT OF A POSTHOLDER 55

§ 2 THE POSTHOLDER WILLEM FREDERIK VAN LIER 56
a Biographical data 56 / *b Van Lier and the Surinam community* 58 / *c Van Lier as amateur ethnographer* 61 / *d Appreciation and criticism by contemporaries* 63 / *e Van Lier's attitude to the Djukas* 65 / 1 His attitude as colonial official 65 / 2 His attitude as 'educator' 66
§ 3 THE DEVELOPMENT PLAN. 68
a The notes 68 / 1 Education 68 / 2 Agriculture and cattle-breeding 70 / 3 Medical aid 73 / *b The plan of work* 75 / 1 Education 75 / 2 Agriculture and cattle-breeding 76 / 3 Medical aid 77
§ 4 ASSESSMENT OF THE DEVELOPMENT PLAN 78
a Expected results 78 / *b The education plan* 78 / *c Agriculture, cattel-breeding and fisheries* 81 / *d Medical aid* 83
§ 5 THE INSTALLATION OF THE POSTHOLDER 85
a Acceptance under coercion 85 / *b The Governor's point of view* 86 / *c The postholder's point of view* 87 / *d The Djuka point of view* 88
§ 6 THE ATTITUDE OF THE DJUKAS; RESISTANCE AGAINST WESTERNIZATION 89
a Historically conditioned distrust 89 / *b Contacts with western civilization* 90 / 1 The Government 90 / 2 Catholic and Protestant mission work 91 / 3 Medical aid 91 / 4 Economic contacts 92 / *c Degree of social control* 93 / *d Degree of social stratification* 93

CHAPTER V PERIOD 1919-1921 97

§ 1 FIRST STAY IN THE TAPANAHONI, 11 DECEMBER 1919 - 26 JUNE 1920 97
a Reception and installation among the Djukas 97 / *b The choice of a dwelling-place* 99 / *c Medical aid* 101 / *d Education* 110 / *e The Governor refuses to appoint Kanapé as Head Chief* 112 / *f Van Lier decides to go on leave* 113
§ 2 SECOND STAY IN THE TAPANAHONI, 29 OCTOBER 1920 - 22 MAY 1921. 116
a Medical aid 116 / *b Agriculture* 118 / *c Education* 120 / *d The strike* 120 / *e Request for financial aid to start a boarding-school; plan for extension of forestry* 123

CHAPTER VI PERIOD 1921-1924. 126

§ 1 THIRD STAY IN THE TAPANAHONI, 21 NOVEMBER 1921 - 22 JUNE 1922. 126
a Agriculture, cattle-breeding and forestry 126 / *b Meeting at Drietabbetje* 128 / *c Notes on the meeting* 230 / *d The population census and the survey of health conditions among the Djukas* 131 / *e The Colonial State refuse a grant for a boarding-school* 134 / *f Van Lier leaves for Paramaribo* 135 / *g The loan is granted* 137 / *h Notes on the matter of the grant* 140
§ 2 FOURTH STAY IN THE TAPANAHONI, 26 AUGUST 1923 - 15 MARCH 1924 141
a Fresh difficulties 141 / *b The controversy between High Priest Kanape and Chief Popo* 144 / *c Death of Chief Popo* 148 / *d Notes on a complicated accusation of witchcraft* 156 / *e Medical aid* 151 / *f Education* 152 / *g Notes on the educational work* 155 / *h Agriculture and cattle-breeding* 155
§ 3 NOTES ON A REPORT BY THE POSTHOLDER. 156
a On the relations between government and postholder 157 / *b On criticism and slander* 157 / *c On agriculture and forestry* 159 / *d On the continuity of the educational work* 160

CHAPTER VII PERIOD 1924-1926. 162

§ 1 FIFTH STAY IN THE TAPANAHONI, 18 JULY 1924 - 18 NOVEMBER 1925 162
a Education 162

§ 2 VAN LIER IN ALBINA; TROUBLES WITH THE DISTRICT COMMISIONER. 165
§ 3 BACK IN GRANMAN STAALKONDRÉ. 168
a Education 168 | *b Governor and States decide to discontinue the boarding-school* 169 | *c The school* 181 | *d Agriculture, cattle-breeding and fishing* 185 | *e Medical aid* 185 | *f More disagreement with the District Commissioner* 185 | *g Abolishment of boarding-school and postholdership* 188
§ 4 NOTES ON THE FIFTH STAY IN THE TAPANAHONI. 195
a The influence of the power tactics 195 | *b The role of the District Commissioner* 197 | *c The abolishment of boarding-school and postholdership* 200 | 1 The role of the Government 200 | 2 The reactions of the Djukas 201 | *d Notes on the project* 202

CHAPTER VIII SHORT SURVEY OF THE EVENTS AFTER 1926 206
§ 1 BROTHER ZANGEN AT GRANMAN STAALKONDRÉ 206
§ 2 ESTABLISHMENT AND GROWTH OF THE MISSION POST AT SAJÉ 209
§ 3 LISIEUX, A CATHOLIC DAY-AND BOARDING-SCHOOL ON THE TAPANAHONI. 212
§ 4 STOELMAN'S ISLAND. 216
§ 5 DRIETABBETJE 217

CHAPTER IX CONCLUSION. 219
§ 1 VIEWS OF THE PARTIES CONCERNED; A SUMMARY. 219
a The Government's view 219 | *b The postholder's view* 220 | *c The view of the Djuka community* 220
§ 2 VIEWS HELD BY CONTEMPORARIES 221
a Father Morssink 221 | *b The press* 226
§ 3 THE VIEW OF A DJUKA PRIEST 227
§ 4 THE DEVELOPMENT PROJECT OF THE DJUKA COMMUNITY WAS NOT A 'COMMUNITY DEVELOPMENT' PROJECT 234
§ 5 CONCLUDING REMARKS 237
a The design of the development plan 237 | *b The policy of the employers* 238 | *c The capacities of the executor* 239 | 1 Technical skill 239 | 2 Belief in mission 240 | 3 Cultural empathy 241 | 4 A sense of politics 241 | 5 Organization ability 242 | *d The reactions of the Djukas* 242 | *e The influence of 'chance events'* 243 | 1 The strike 243 | 2 The death of Chief Popo and other chance events 244 | *f Final assessment* 244

LIST OF WORKS CONSULTED 246

BIBLIOGRAPHY OF WILLEM FREDERIK VAN LIER'S WRITINGS 251

GLOSSARY OF DJUKA WORDS APPEARING IN THE TEXT. 253

MAPS. 256

INTRODUCTION

This study deals with a period in the history of the Djukas, one of the Bush Negro tribes of Surinam. It concerns the period of 1917 to 1926, which has particular significance because during that time the first systematic effort was made to bring about social change and to draw them more fully into the whole of the Surinam community. This development plan was initiated by the Colonial Administration and its execution was assigned to an official specially appointed for the purpose, called a postholder.

During the first quarter of the twentieth century Dutch politics was in a stage of transition from the 'Liberal period' to the so-called 'Ethical period', designated by Furnivall (1956, p. 288) as the 'new constructive policy'. Whereas the aim during the Liberal period was to increase the prosperity of the colonized population by allowing free play to economic forces, it was pursued during the Ethical period by means of intervention in the colonial economy, 'even at the expense of freedom' (Furnivall 1956, p. 288). This state intervention had certain financial consequences for the motherland. In the case of Surinam the Dutch Government was daunted by these consequences and preferred to leave the financial risks to private investors. With a few exceptions, however, the latter did not come forward: investment in the Dutch East Indies promised richer rewards. The colony of Surinam had to cope with a chronic shortage of field-labourers (as the result of the abolition of slavery in 1863). Immigration of contract labourers from China, India and Indonesia was not sufficient to meet this shortage. The Bush Negro groups living in the interior (numbering at least 20,000) constituted a potential supply of labour.

The Surinam Bush Negroes form an exceptional group on the American continent: they are descended from slaves imported from West Africa since the early seventeenth century, who escaped from their masters and from the plantations. They kept themselves alive in the jungle and banded together in groups, making up a society with a cultural pattern that contained many West African elements. Their self-chosen freedom, its defence by means of a century-long guerilla struggle against the slave-colony, their consequent distrust of the colonists, all this heightened their isolation. All efforts at breaking down this isolation met with resistance. Contacts between Bush Negroes and coast-dwellers remained casual and brief (cf. de Groot, 1963).

During the period in question the Government attempted to persuade a group of Bush Negroes to establish contact with western civilization by offering them education, agricultural instruction and medical aid. If this attempt should prove fruitful, it could bring about the integration of the jungle-dwellers into the colonial scheme and thereby enlarge the number of potential labour recruits.

W. F. van Lier, the postholder who took this task upon himself, had shown in a series of newspaper articles prior to his appointment that he had a thorough ethnographic knowledge of the Djukas and, moreover, had ideas on how to carry out the proposed plan.

Proceeding from the 'case-history' set forth here, an analysis is given of the social process that took place in the Djuka community as a result of the attempted introduction of western culture. That is to say: an analysis of the attitudes of the parties concerned, the reactions to their reciprocal mode of action, and of the conflict situations arising from the clash of separate cultures (cf. Van Velsen, 1967, p. 148). This also necessitates an ethnographic knowledge of the society in question. In this case the knowledge has been obtained from, among other sources, the writings of the ethnographer-postholder W.F. van Lier as well as from present-day investigations (Chapter II §§ 1, 2).

The processes described unfold within a definite, clearly restricted period but cannot be observed outside its historical context (cf. Gluckman, 1967, p. 15). Hence this history is briefly set forth in Chapters I, II and VIII. The analysis includes contemporary opinions of the development project, as well as the view of a Djuka spokesman who offered me his commentary forty years later (Chapter IX §§ 3, 4).

The Djuka conflicts which played an important role during the given period are discussed in Chapter VI § 2 and Chapter VII § 4. Unforeseen events which influenced the course of the project and forced the parties concerned to revise their position, as for instance a strike (Chapter V § 2b), an internal struggle for power and a number of deaths (Chapter VI § 2b, c, d) are analyzed in Chapter IX § 6c. The attempt to modify the traditional social structure of the Djuka society by means of the introduction of western civilization encountered strong opposition. The moving forces behind this opposition may be divided into a number of internal and external factors which exerted a powerful mutual influence upon each other (cf. Köbben, 1968a, p. 56). In Chapter IV § 6 these factors are discussed.

The attempt, treated in this study, to develop a traditional society differs in a political, ideological and technical sense from Community Development as carried out after the second world war, the principles of which were evolved by organs of the United Nations. But there are also certain similarities between the two. Thus it appears possible to compare the capacities and attitudes of the executor of the project and of his employers with the standards that are laid down in modern development planning (Chapter IX § 6).

By means of the adopted method I hope to provide further insight into the functioning of the Djuka society. Moreover I hope to show in the light of this concrete project which forces were operating in Surinam colonial politics in the nineteen-twenties. Hence the detailed account of the deliberations on this topic in the Colonial States and the discussion of the attitude of the colonial Government (Chapter III).

A study of this development project has been made feasible by the fact that there is extensive documentation on the subject in the Central Archives of Paramaribo. The considerations leading up to the decision to tackle the project, the critical discussion of the course along which it developed and the eventual decision to abandon the experiment are contained in the 'Minutes of the Colonial States'. The details of the project are accurately described in journals and reports by the executor; the correspondence on the subject, as well as these journals and reports, have been preserved in the files of the 'Government Resolutions' and 'Secretarial Agendas'.

The ethnographic knowledge of the executor of the development project, W.F. van Lier, has to a large extent been recorded in print. A list of his writings has been added to the general bibliography.

ACKNOWLEDGMENTS

At the completion of this study I should like to thank all those who helped me with it. In the first place Prof. Dr. A. J. F. Köbben, for his invaluable and deeply appreciated criticism, from which the design and the composition derived so much benefit. Furthermore Prof. Dr. W. F. Wertheim who was willing to go over the manuscript with critical interest.

Prof. Dr. R.A.J. van Lier drew my attention to eighteenth and nineteenth century Surinam archives, thus setting me on the track of the present subject, as well as others. He put at my disposal the printed and typed ethnographic writings of his uncle, W. F. van Lier, which have been left in his possession. I greatly appreciate his kind interest.

I thank the Surinam Government for the obliging manner in which they enabled me to carry out my investigation in Paramaribo and in the interior.

The Central Archives in Paramaribo under the directorship of Miss E. Themen rendered me excellent service; so did the Archives of the Moravian Brothers and the Episcopal Archives. I am much indebted to Mr. J. M. L. Th. Cals for the important manuscripts I was able to consult by favour of his cooperation.

The friendly and sympathetic manner in which I was received by the Djukas impressed me deeply. I should like to mention, with special gratitude, the priest Da Kodjo Kanapé who set forth his views to me most helpfully.

I owe a great deal to the stimulating discussions on my work I was able to have with Dr. H. U. E. Thoden van Velzen, Drs. W. van Wetering, Drs. H. P. A. van Roosmalen, Prof. Dr. S. W. Mintz, Prof. Dr. A. H. Niehoff, Drs. Ch. H. Eersel, Dr. Ir. F. E. Essed and others. I am grateful to Miss Elisabeth Eybers for her conscientious and skilful translation of the manuscript. Miss U. M. Lichtveld, from whom I had lessons in the Surinam language, was also of great assistance in the compiling of a bibliography.

My investigation was made financially possible by means of subsidies from WOTRO (Netherlands Foundation for the Advancement of Tropical Research), from the Z.W.O. (Netherlands Organisation for the Advancement of Pure Research) and from STICUSA (The foundation for cultural cooperation with Surinam and the Netherlands Antillas). I was likewise aided by the International Federation of University Women, who gave me the *Winifred Cullis Award* 1965 for an earlier piece of research.

CHAPTER I

HISTORICAL SURVEY

§ 1 THE SETTING

Surinam, situated on the north-east coast of South America, between 2° and 6° north latitude and 54° and 58° west longitude, covers an area of a good 142,822 km² (55,167 square miles). The western frontier is formed by the Corantijn River, the eastern frontier by the Marowijne River. In the south the country borders on Brazil, in the north on the Atlantic Ocean. The border rivers Corantijn and Marowijne, like the rivers Surinam and Coppename, run from south to north; the Cottica, the Commewijne, the Saramacca and the Nickerie run more or less parallel to the coastline. The upper reaches of the south-north running rivers are difficult to navigate because of the many rapids and can only be attempted by dug-outs (*corjalen*). The coastal fringe consists of heavy sea-clay, criss-crossed by strips of sand and shell, and is 50 to 100 km wide. This is the agricultural region, traditionally the plantation area, made suitable for this purpose by reclamation. Here the majority of the inhabitants of Surinam live, with Paramaribo as capital and focal point. To the south of this area there is a wide belt of savanna and secondary woods, beyond which the primeval forest starts and the territory becomes hilly, with several mountain ranges with peaks rising to a height of twelve hundred meters. In the immense forest the Bush Negroes and Indians live. The former have settled along the rivers, the latter lead a nomadic or semi-nomadic existence.

§ 2 ORIGIN AND ORGANIZATION OF THE COLONY

Although the coast of Guyana was discovered in 1499 by two of Amerigo Vespucci's captains (Alonso de Ojeda and Juan de la Cosa), it was not until 1630 that an appreciable number of immigrants came to settle in Surinam: sixty British, under direction of a Captain Maréchal. After a number of others had tried in vain to make a living there, another Englishman, Willoughby, Earl of Parham, succeeded in 1650 in founding a permanent colony, the ownership of which was presented to him by the King of England in 1662. In 1664 the number of colonists was augmented by a group of Portuguese Jews. In the second war against England (1665-1667) the Zealander Abraham Crijnssen managed to capture the colony from Willoughby.

A period of confusion, during which the States of Zealand as well as the States General claimed to have sovereign powers in Surinam, came to an end in 1682, when Zealand sold the colony to the West India Company (for Fls. 260,000) which, together with the city of Amsterdam and Cornelis van Aerssen van Sommelsdijk, formed a 'triumvirate'. This triumvirate, under the name of the *Geoctroyeerde Societeit van Suriname* (Chartered Society of Surinam) administered the colony. The Chartered Society, supervised by the States General – who offered its protection when Surinam had to be defended against enemies inside and outside the country – remained in existence until 1795, when the administration of Surinam was taken over by a "Committee for Colonies and Possessions on the coast of Guinea and in America" until 1801, and from 1801 to 1816 by an "American Colonies and Possessions Council".

The administrative conditions laid down in the Charter of the Surinam Society in 1682 were carried out by the first Governor, Cornelis van Aerssen van Sommelsdijk, who worked out further details in Surinam itself.

The Governor, who was the highest official in the colony, was appointed by the W.I.C., subject to the approval of the States General and the Prince of Orange. He administered the colony, assisted by the Political Council ("selected from the most prominent, wise and moderate colonials"). The First Councillor was the Commandant, who was in command of the fortifications and the troops. A Fiscal sat on the Council in an advisory capacity. The Political Council was split into two Councils in 1764: a Police Council and Criminal Law Council. The Council of Civil Justice was a separate body. The members of the Council were selected by the Governor from double lists drawn up by the colonists. This arrangement remained essentially the same until 1816.

From 1799 to 1814 Surinam was – apart from a short interval – a British protectorate, the only change being that the Governor was appointed by England.

In 1816 this system of administration was supplanted by a new one, which remained in force until 1828. The Governor General, appointed by the King, had the greatest executive power; he was assisted by a Police and a Criminal Law Court, nine members of which were appointed by the Governor as before and were nominated by the colonists, i.e. by those who owned plantations, "consequently by those who are most concerned with the welfare of the country". However, the final authority was the mother country, which ruled the colony through the Colonial Department.

In almost every respect the colony fared badly from the end of the eighteenth century: the new administrative system, for instance, was unsatisfactory, complaints poured in and in 1828 J. van den Bosch, who had been sent to the West Indies as Chief Commissioner to inspect the situation, drafted a new administrative system. This also proved to be unsatisfactory and had to be revised as early as 1832. The High Court was converted into a Colonial Council, composed of the Attorney General, who was also Administrator of Finance, and six of the most prominent residents, so that the colonists were given somewhat more say, at any rate in executive matters. These members of the Council could be selected in the old way from "owners of plantations resident in the colony, or agents of owners". As most plantations at that time were mortgaged by their owners in the Netherlands, they were run by agents of the mortgage banks. Consequently only a few members of the Colonial Council were plantation owners, most of them being agents. Although this system of administration had an adverse effect on the colony – this 'plantocracy' of absent, conservative interested parties was opposed to all changes in existing conditions – it was not until the abolition of slavery in 1863 that any appreciable change came about. The slave owners were granted an indemnity of approximately Fls. 10,000 (Fls. 300 per slave), three-quarters of which was paid out in the Netherlands. The number of plantations rapidly decreased, but all the same there was a tremendous labour shortage. The former slaves, after being held for ten years under contract on the plantations as 'free labourers', refused to continue doing this work. The shortage was somewhat relieved by the immigration of new contract labourers: Chinese, Hindustani and Javanese.

In 1865 new Governmental Regulations came into operation. Surinam was granted a system of limited autonomy. This remained valid until 1937, with repeated modifications which, as a rule, imposed further limitations on the autonomy. The period of 1917 to 1926, treated in the present study, thus fell under the governmental regulations of 1865 (see Chapter III § 1).[1]

§ 3 THE SLAVES AND THEIR OWNERS

Ever since 1650 plantations were the most important source of income in Surinam. The labour needed for large-scale cultivation of staples like sugar in the beginning and, later on, coffee, cacao, cotton, tobacco and indigo, was supplied by slaves since whites – non-slaves – had proved from the start to be unsuitable for this heavy work, both in Surinam and other subjugated tropical territories. In the beginning Indians were used for the plantation work, but in the long run they also proved to be not very suitable. However, in the 16th century an enormous reservoir of potential slaves was discovered in West Africa that could be tapped comparatively easily and cheaply.

The Dutch West India Company, established in 1621, provided the region from Brazil to the southern part of North America with this kind of labour. In November 1668, when Surinam was taken over by Abraham Crijnssen of Zealand, he reported 714 slaves, not counting women and children.

The importation of slaves from West Africa was carried on legally until 1814, when the trade was prohibited[2], and illegally until 1823, when an end could be put to the contraband traffic by means of a strict registration system. It is not known exactly how many slaves were imported between the beginning of the trade and 1823; the estimates are between 300,000 and 350,000. The meagre data, likewise estimated, concerning the number of slaves in the colony present the following picture:

Year	Number of slaves	Number of whites	Number of plantations
1738	57000	2100	400
1786	50000	3350	500
1791	53000	3300	591
1830	53000	8500	451
1863	33600	16500	162

To these numbers should still be added the 6 to 8000 runaways and 1 to 2000 Indians in order to arrive at the total population.

In 1863 there were, moreover, 5607 manumitted slaves.

A population register in 1924 (Almanac of Surinam 1925) gives the following figures:

112,800 whites, Creoles, British Indians and Javanese

18,163 Bush Negroes and 2580 Indians.

It may be said that the most important factors determining the character of the colony of Surinam are: firstly, that it was regarded as a possession to be exploited, secondly that it was a slave colony. For the acceptance of slavery as an institution, i.e. the use of men as 'instruments of production'[3] arguments were needed. The main rationalizations were:
1. Slavery is not contradictory to Christian doctrines.
2. The Negro is inferior to the white. This could be inferred from many of his characteristics: his customs were 'barbarian' (i.e. not Christian), he only worked if forced to do so, he was vindictive, slow of understanding and sexually promiscuous.

Armed with a feeling of superiority that was justified by these convictions, the plantation manager was confronted by a slave population outnumbering the whites by 25 to 1 in 1738, 15 to 1 in 1786 and 6 to 1 in 1830. The slaves had to be coerced into working and were furthermore mostly hostile, either overtly or covertly, towards their masters. In spite of his ideology and cultivated feelings of superiority, the slave owner lived in constant fear of slave risings that was far from groundless.

In a society of this kind, in which the white masters were subject to great tension, it is not surprising that "unstable, quick-tempered, easily offended persons with maniacal tendencies"[4] developed. On the plantations these tendencies often enough took the form of arbitrary treatment and atrocities.

§ 4 THE RUNAWAYS AND THE PEACE TREATIES

The slaves of Surinam never united to carry out a large-scale rising, as happened elsewhere in the Caribbeans (Berbice, Haiti, etc.). Nevertheless large groups threw off the yoke of slavery by running away. The rising, however, occurred mostly on one or two plantations at a time and the groups gathered in the forest. The enormous and – for whites – almost impenetrable forest area favoured these escapes. The runaways fled into the forest or up the rivers and creeks and built villages and cultivated the land. But this was not enough: necessity and the thirst for revenge drove them back to the inhabited colony to attack plantations and carry off women, food, implements and weapons.

At the time of Lord Parham and his successors (1650-1667) the running away of slaves had already been reported, and when Indian slaves were used, these also escaped into the forest or up the rivers (the Surinam, Saramacca and Coppename). Both Negroes and Indians harrassed the plantations. During this period a group of runaways, who had settled at the Para Creek and later at the Coppename, already numbered several hundred.

The number, estimated at as many as 6000 in 1738, gradually rose and came to approximately 7000 in 1786; when slavery was abolished in 1863 there were about 8000.

Governor van Sommelsdijk, who arrived in Surinam in 1683, made peace with the Indians and henceforth the latter no longer bothered the colony. A year later, in 1684, peace was concluded with the Negroes at Coppename, and of this group, too, nothing more was heard. But the number of slaves who ran away mounted, thus heightening the unrest in the colony.

After a rising in 1690 on a Jewish plantation, in the course of which the owner was killed and all the slaves escaped into the forest, the colony was forced to take more effective measures against the loss of valuable slaves and the plundering by the runaways.

Many attempts in this direction were made. During the governorship of Van Sommelsdijk an armed civilian guard had been formed. Consisting of eleven companies (one of which was Jewish) in the outlying districts and three to five in Paramaribo, it undertook patrols against runaways, but without much success, so that from 1730 onwards soldiers were also used. The penalties for running away were made more severe: after 1721 it was punished by death. The rewards for the apprehension of runaways were regularly increased. Wolbers[5] states that "the rewards for apprehending and returning a runaway slave was fixed at 5 florins in 1685; in 1687 it was increased to 300 lbs. of sugar if the slave was expressly hunted down, otherwise only 100 lbs; in 1698 it was increased to 25 florins... and 50 florins...".

But all these measures proved unavailing and the number of slaves who ran away kept mounting, especially after 1712, when a panic among the colonists during the invasion by the French Admiral Jacques Cassard caused them to send their wives and children, accompanied by their slaves, into the forest. The women and children returned, but a large number of slaves chose to stay in the forest and joined the existing groups. At that time there were about 400 plantations, about 50,000 slaves and 2000 whites! More than 10% of the slaves had run away. This percentage remained more or less constant until about 1830, after which the number of plantations and slaves diminished.

In 1730, after the plantations had suffered many attacks, a number of expeditions were undertaken, which resulted in the discovery and destruction of the notorious Klaas and Pedro villages on the Saramacca River.

However, the "expeditions, not having had the intended effect, did more damage than good; while they increased the arrogance not only of the runaways, but even of the slaves, and made the paths through the forest leading to the Marroons known to them",[6] Governor Mauricius, who had been in Surinam since 1742, decided to take other measures in 1749. He examined the possibility of making peace or in some way negotiating with the runaways (as Van Sommelsdijk had done with the Indians and the Coppename Negroes during his term of office, and as the English had made peace with the so-called chiefs of the runaway Negroes in 1739, after the island of Jamaica had been exposed to the same danger as Surinam through the impudence of the runaways).

In spite of opposition of the members of the Council, who did not see the good of making peace at all and shrank from the expenses of the vast expedition, Mauricius persisted and effected his immediate purpose. After an expedition to the Saramacca with 1000 soldiers under the command of Commander Carel Otto Creutz, resulting in the destruction of three villages and cultivated lands, contact was made with Chief Adu and his roughly 1800 subjects. The negotiations were successful and the peace was based on the treaty of 1739 with the runaways in Jamaica. Creutz departed, after promising that gifts would be sent to ratify the peace. But now the members of the Council, who in any case had been opposed to the conclusion of peace, objected to the plan of sending Louis Nepveu and thirty soldiers with gifts to Adu. They found it too expensive and thought that a few whites under a certain Picolet (a member of the Council) and twenty carriers would be sufficient. The result was disastrous: the group was attacked by a dissatisfied chief, Zam Zam, and all were massacred. Adu, who waited in vain for the presents and had concluded from rumours about the disagreement in Paramaribo that the peace was a ruse to attack him again, resumed the war and attacks on the plantations continued undiminished. Inside the plantations themselves it also came to bloody risings. The area around the Commewijne and its tributaries, the Cottica, Perica and Tempati, was a centre of unrest. In 1757 there was a big rising in Tempati: all the slaves of the timber plantations next to the river refused to be transferred to a different kind of plantation, and escaped into the forest.

They joined a group of Negroes that had already run away to the Djuka Creek, a tributary of the Marowijne. Together they formed a group of about six hundred, who regularly attacked plantations, carrying off weapons, implements and women, but at the same time leaving letters signed by a certain Boston at every plantation to indicate that they were prepared to make peace.

In 1760 Governor Crommelin decided to react to the offer of peace from the runaways along the Djuka Creek. After first sending two trusted Negro slaves to them to find out whether the Bush Negroes were sincere, James Abercrombie and J. Rudolph Zobre left with gifts and a draft of peace conditions.

They were received with great solemnity. The two delegates had to stomach a number of reproaches on account of the misbehaviour of the whites on the plantations, and also because the presents included no powder and shot, for which the Djukas had asked specially. Furthermore the remarkable bravery with which the Bush Negroes had defended themselves was pointed out to them. This was followed by an acceptance of the peace treaty in principle. A new list of presents, to be sent a year later when the peace would be confirmed on oath, was drawn up. In April 1761 the same two delegates duly headed for the Djuka terrain, accompanied by nine or ten soldiers and sixty carriers. On 22 May peace was concluded officially and confirmed on oath according to the Negro[7] as well as the white custom, on which occasion Boston begged the Governor to have the slaves treated better as it would be difficult to send maltreated slaves back. At last, in October 1761, Major Meyer was sent to the Djukas to re-confirm the peace officially with Arabi and Pamo, the two most important chiefs, and present gifts again.

The peace treaty was again based on the treaty concluded with the runaways in Jamaica in 1739. The most important terms of the peace treaty were that the Bush Negro groups were declared free and that they were to surrender runaways who joined them. Moreover, they were to undertake patrols, either by themselves or together with the whites, in order to track down, capture and hand over runaways. The expenses connected with the expeditions would be refunded, rewards would be given for the captured slaves. The Government undertook to send gifts regularly in order to meet their need for implements, clothing, etc. Without special leave the Bush Negroes were not to come closer than two days or ten hours by boat to the inhabited part of the colony. The number of men allowed to navigate the lower part of the river to trade and to visit Paramaribo was put at ten or twelve at a time. A pass system was introduced in order to make it possible to supervise the number of men and the imported and exported goods. A 'Postholder' would see to it that all these stipulations were observed. His status was both that of a Government official and a military man, and he was to live among the Bush Negroes, together with two assistants, preferably in the village of the Granman (Paramount Chief), who undertook to send some of his closest relatives as *ostagiers* (hostages) to Paramaribo. After the succes of these peace negotiations, the Saramaccaners who had meanwhile moved from the Saramacca River to the upper Surinam River, also proved to be prepared to try again. A few Saramaccaners who desired peace presented themselves in the main village of the Djukas, Bongo Dotti, outside their own area, and discussions about the possibility of coming to an agreement under the same conditions took place. Louis Nepveu, a brother of Jan Nepveu, who was to become Governor, played an important part in the talks, first in Bongo Dotti and later at the Sara Creek (a tributary of the Surinam River), where peace was made with the Saramaccaners in the same way as with the Djukas on 18 September, 1762. The same Negro Chief, Zam Zam, who was responsible for the failure of the attempts at peacemaking in 1750, interfered with the distribution of the presents, causing Chief Musinga to be passed over. Musinga was furious and, convinced that the whites were partly to blame, attacked some plantations, carried off 150 slaves and repelled a patrol sent after him. But eventually he concluded a separate peace in 1767, together with his co-chief Becu. This group, the Becu-Musinga or Matuari Negroes, remained at the Saramacca. They obtained free passage through the Wanica Creek for the transportation of their products.

Peace had been made. The colonists rejoiced. In Paramaribo days of prayer and thanksgiving were held, Governor Crommelin was praised and congratulated by the directors of the Society and those who had contributed to the conclusion of peace were rewarded with money and gifts.

However, the problems of the colony were by no means solved yet: soon the conclusion of peace with the three Bush Negro groups proved to be no guarantee that the slaves' running away would stop. This group – with much reluctance and passive resistance – more or less kept to the terms of the treaty and surrendered some of the runaways, but this did not prevent the slaves, who saw no improvement in their treatment on the plantations, from revolting, running away and forming new centres of unrest, endangering the colony and creating an atmosphere of panic. Many new measures were taken. Governor Nepveu, who was appointed in 1770, took great pains to solve the problem. He had a military cordon built round the cultivated part of the colony, consisting of a connecting road and military posts at regular intervals[8], created the 'Free Corps', composed of manumitted Negroes and mulattos who were used in expeditions against runaways, and applied for another reinforcement of twelve hundred men. In 1773 eight hundred men under the command of Colonel Fourgeoud arrived from the Netherlands.

The newly formed groups of *marroons* attacked the plantations in the Commewijne and Cottica areas fiercely, successfully repulsed patrols and took some of the military posts of the cordon. Their chiefs, Bonni, Baron and Joli Coeur, were good fighters, fearless and revengeful. It cost the colony and the forces brought from the Netherlands years of tremendous exertion before these 'Bonni Negroes' were driven out of their villages, which had been converted into fortresses. They fled far into the interior, where they were placed under control of the Djukas along the Upper Marowijne. This war, varying in intensity but never really ceasing, lasted from 1769 to 1789.

When the Peace Treaty with the three Bush Negro tribes (the Saramaccaners, Djukas or Aucaners, and Matuaris or Becu-Musinga Negroes) was renewed in a 'Political Contract' in 1835, 1837 and 1838, its most important part was again those measures that protected the colony: the fixing of the boundaries the Negroes were not allowed to pass, the prevention of attacks from men travelling down the river to the town by means of a pass system, and the stipulation concerning the capture and surrender of runaways.

The postholder was made responsible for supervising the observance of the new contract to a greater extent than previously in 1761. It was his duty to observe all movements of the Bush Negroes on his outpost and to report them regularly. The postholder's activities had less positive results than had been expected, as regular reprimands and irritated letters from Paramaribo to the different postholders showed. This can be partly explained by the fact that the relation between the Bush Negroes and the Government was regarded completely onesidedly. There was, for instance, no understanding of the way the Bush Negroes looked at their relationship with the Government and the contracts they concluded with it. The attitude of the Government and of the entire colony was that the peace conditions had been forcibly imposed on the Bush Negroes, and were intended to prevent them from endangering the colony once more by attacking the plantations and harbouring the runaways. (Supervision was necessary, for they were not to be trusted!) The Bush Negroes, on the other hand, thought that, even though the whites had strengthened their position by the use of armed forces, they had not succeeded in vanquishing them and had, for that reason, been obliged to offer a peace treaty. It was true that the conditions of the treaty restricted their movements and that they were bound to hand over runaways, but they had obtained their freedom as well as their sovereignty in the area they inhabited without help from outside. Their voluntary isolation protected them from the whites (these were never to be trusted), while they made their wishes known to the postholder who, in their view, exercised very little authority. The gifts offered to them every four years they regarded as a sort of tribute.

NOTES

[1] For the history of Surinam see e.g. Hartsinck, 1770, Nassy, 1788, Stedman, 1799, Van Heeckeren, 1826, Teenstra, 1842, Wolbers, 1861, Kappler, 1881, amongst others.
[2] In England this prohibition had already been enforced in 1808.
[3] R.A.J. van Lier, 1949, p. 64.
[4] R.A.J. van Lier, 1949, pp. 62, 63. This applied especially to the plantation slaves, to a lesser extent to the domestic slaves, among whom the 'slave conduct pattern' (indicated by Hoetink, 1958, p. 124 et seq.) was more commonly found.
[5] Wolbers, 1861, pp. 138, 139.
[6] Hartsinck, 1770, p. 767.
[7] Part of which was that "Each of the delegates was obliged to sleep with one of the most prominent Negro women during their stay, in order to be more assured of the Peace, and because their confidence in the white men would thus be considerably increased." (Hartsinck, 1770, p. 798).
[8] "It ran from the Jews' Savanna to the Surinam River approximately westward up to the Imotappi post on the Upper Commewijne; from there it turned straight north along this river up to the l'Espérance post and from there it ran from east to west, passed the Perica up to Willemsbrug, and then north to the coast". Enc. N.W.I., 1917, pp. 127-128.

CHAPTER II

THE DJUKA SOCIETY

§ 1 INTRODUCTION

The following survey describes certain aspects of the Djuka society with which one should be familiar in order to gain an insight into the development project treated in this study.

The history of the Djukas is based on a description of the origin and development of the Djuka society compiled by Wong (1938), from archive documents, historical writings and data recorded among the Djukas themselves; from a study of the archives made by the author[1]; and from brief data drawn from other historical writings.

The facts concerning the organization of the Djuka society are derived from various sources. W.F. van Lier collected, in his capacity of amateur ethnographer before and during his term as official postholder among the Djukas, numerous and valuable data which were published later (see Bibliography). Furthermore, use has been made of the results of modern investigation by professional ethnologists carried out among the Djukas, particularly the excellent study by H.U.E. Thoden van Velzen (1966): *Political Control in the Djuka Society*. Proceeding from the civil and church administrative groups that exerted an influence on the functioning of the Djuka society, an analysis is made of the structure of the political, religious and social pattern of the Djuka community along the Tapanahoni River as revealed in the various and frequent activities of these groups.

Other sources of information are:

H.U.E. Thoden van Velzen's study (1967): *Belief in the Avenging Spirits*, which describes how such a spirit, present as a curse in practically every matrilineage, can have a binding or disrupting function, depending on the role it plays in various conflict situations.

The oracle god from Granbori visiting Drietabbetje. He is wrapped up in a bundle of many cloths, presented to him by devotees. (photograph by the author)

A.J.F. Köbben (1967): *Unity and Disunity*, in which the Djuka society, settled on the banks of the Cottica River since the beginning of the 19th century, is analysed as kinship system. Köbben proceeds from the hypothesis that kinship forms the basis of legal, political, economic and religious relations in a Bush Negro village.

A.J.F. Köbben (1968a): *Continuity in Change*.

A.J.F. Köbben (1968b): *Law at Village Level* (also dealing with the Djukas along the Cottica River).

W. van Wetering: *Djuka Witchcraft Beliefs*, a sociological approach (forthcoming).

W. van Wetering (1967): *Conflicts between co-wives among the Djukas*.

Jean Hurault (1961): *Les Noirs Refugiés Boni de la Guyane Française*. Although this fine and comprehensive study does not deal with the Djukas, aspects of Bush Negro religion are treated which throw light on similar aspects of the Djuka society when studied for comparative purposes.

§ 2 THE ESTABLISHMENT OF THE DJUKA SOCIETY

The written history of the Djuka society dates from the beginning of the peace negotiations in 1758. Neither from literature, nor from unpublished documents, nor from the Djuka traditions handed down by word of mouth is it possible to ascertain from which African tribes the Djuka society (or other Bush Negro communities) is derived. This is not surprising. When they came to Surinam the slaves were rarely sold in groups of one tribe or put to work on the same plantation. Families were usually separated, too, when sold. After their escape the runaways grouped themselves in settlements in the dense forest. These groups consisted, on the one hand, of those who were newly arrived from Africa, the so-called saltwater Negroes, and, on the other hand, of those who had spent some time on the plantations and who, if possible, fled together with family and friends.

The Bush Negroes, in the organization of their new society, did not proceed on the basis of their West African tribal connections but formed clans composed according to the plantations from which the fugitives came. Nearly all the names of these matrilinear clans or *los*[2] are derived from the names of the plantations or their owners.

So, although the Bush Negroes were well aware of their African descent, they were no longer conscious of the difference between the original tribes. Hence their oral tradition starts with the *loweten* (Sur.: time of escape).

Investigation has revealed that the Djukas believe Avo Abenkina to be their eldest ancestress, who fled with her son Pamo and her two daughters from the plantation Adrichem on the upper Surinam, probably in 1712. She is the foundress of the most important clan from which the Paramount Chiefs and priests were chosen, the Oto-*lo*.

The regular arrival of fresh groups of runaways forced the Djukas to keep on adapting their newly formed tribal structure. In the process a struggle for supremacy and clashes about the successional rights were inevitable.

The Negroes from the Tempati area under leadership of Arabi (belonging to the Dikan-*lo*) arrived at the Djuka Creek in 1757 and founded eight villages, among which Bongo Dotti, where Arabi had his seat.

The peace negotiations were conducted by Arabi in the first place, but when it came to the final ratification it appeared that Pamo's sanction was required after all. This could indicate a conflict of power, just as the wording which occurs in the peace contract does: "Pamo to whom the Country belongs, Araby who lives in Djuka." Pamo deprived Arabi of his position in 1762 (and not, as Wong (1938) believes, in 1766, when Arabi died) and was recognized as Granman by the Government. This appears from letters written by the postholder, who lived at Bongo Dotti. Partly as a result of the quarrels about the carrying out of the peace contracts (regarding the handing over of runaways, the Government's failure to send shot, gunpowder and rifles, the fact that the women did not turn up who were to have been bought by the Government from a 'shipload of Loanga slaves', and other grievances), Arabi had to surrender all authority and a number of influential followers to Pamo. And so the power remained in the hands of those who had been the first to arrive at the Djuka Creek. This conflict of power seems to have led to a division into two main groups which was maintained after the Djukas had settled along the Tapanahoni during the course of years: along the upper part of the river the *Opo-Ningre* (Upper Negroes) live, and along the lower part the *Bilo-Ningre* (Lower Negroes).[3] The *lo* from which the Paramount Chief was elected, the Oto, settled along the upper Tapanahoni.

The conflict of power was resumed after Pamo's death, this time between Pamo's Oto-*lo* and the Missidjan-*lo*, who were closely related by family ties. Bambey, of Pamo's *lo*, was proclaimed Paramount Chief,

The High Priest Arabi left Drietabbetje after a quarrel with Granman Oseisie (1865-1915) and founded a new religious centre in Granbori. After the two rulers had been reconciled, the oracle god of Granbori 'visited' Drietabbetje on special occasions and 'stayed' in the house of Arabi. This is still the case. The photograph was taken on the occasion of such a visit in 1965. (photograph by the author)

but Tonnie of the Missidjan-*lo* pleaded his claim with the Government, who eventually appointed them both: Bambey was 'charged with defence' and Tonnie with 'civil administration'. Up till 1839 the Missidjans remained in power, but in that year Bijman's appointment effected a return of the Granmanship to the Oto-*lo*, where it has remained to this day.

Meanwhile Bambey has become a national hero among the Djukas on account of his struggle (on the side of the Government) against the Bonni's whom he helped to defeat.

In 1801 the number of Djukas along the Tapanahoni was estimated at 2488.

Troubles kept recurring with regard to the succession of deceased head chiefs. The Paramount Chief-High Priest had the right to designate and educate his successor, but occasionally another leader was appointed. Paramount Chief Bijman held office from 1838 to 1865.[4] He was in fairly close contact with the Government, although this was often accompanied by clashes.[5] Bijman educated his nephew (on his sister's side) to succeed him. The latter, Oseisie, was not yet of age when Bijman died and Blijmoffo acted as regent, now training his own nephew Arabi (or Aguma Sakka). At Blijmoffo's death the chiefs decided, however, that Oseisie should become Paramount Chief after all (1888), while Arabi became High Priest. A bitter conflict arose between the two of them, though both were members of the Oto-*lo*. Eventually Arabi and his entourage moved further up the river and founded a religious centre there. Oseisie, well versed in matters of priesthood by reason of the education he had received from Bijman, declared that he was High Priest as well as Granman and would serve the Oracle-god, Grantata.

Oseisie was generally regarded as a good Paramount Chief who governed his people justly and liberally, in spite of internal troubles: the struggle against Arabi and his conservative following, which also contributed to the failure of two efforts at establishing a school in his residential village, Drietabbetje. He was also well thought of by the Government, although they reproached him for sabotaging the school he had asked for.

Oseisie, as well as Arabi, took the education of a chosen successor in hand. But Arabi's protégé did not come in for consideration at all. When Oseisie died in 1915, lengthy negotiations followed with a view to the choice of a successor. In this instance, too, the preference of a deceased Granman was disregarded and the group wielding the greatest political were able to force a decision. Another cousin of Oseisie, Amakti ('the mighty'), seemed more tractable to the leading political faction of the moment than Oseisie's protégé Kanapé, with his self-assured conduct and outspoken opinions. Amakti, who had had no training whatsoever in the esoteric profession of High Priest, contented himself with the Granmanship, while Kanapé became High Priest, something which even his opponents could not prevent.

In 1921 Kanapé was nominated Head Chief by the Government, thus sharing the responsibility for the administration with Amakti, and his vigorous personality enabled him to make his influence felt on all sorts of occasions in the Tapanahoni. This was also apparent after Amakti's death in 1931. The latter had educated and designated his sister's son, Amatodja, to succeed him, and although he was accepted as Paramount Chief when Amakti died, Kanapé managed to have his actual installation postponed for six years. Amatodja refused to rule jointly with Kanapé. He wanted to be Granman, without having Kanapé as salaried Head Chief at his side. In 1937 he succeeded, aided by the Government, to get Kanapé out of the way. The ambitious Head Chief was deposed, "while retaining part of his allowance. This was intended to sugar the pill of his dismissal somewhat".[6] Amatodja had educated Gazon to succeed him. In 1951, however, his maternal uncle, Akontu Felanti, came into power as Gazon, feeling too young for such a demanding and responsible position, chose to withdraw. Akontu Felanti also became High Priest. He died in 1964 and was succeeded the following year by Gazon. Gazon has a High Priest at his side: Asinfu (Amerkan). The gradually increasing influence which the Government endeavoured to exert was also apparent in its attempt to have Granman Gazon's appointment by the Surinam Government take place at his headquarters in Drietabbetje. This attempt failed because of internal troubles and probably also as a result of the protest by a number of prominent Djukas against what they regarded as overt interference in their affairs. The pledging of the official oath which is part of the nomination ceremony took place in Paramaribo, as formerly, although under the auspices of the Prime Minister and not of the Governor.[7]

Amakti, seated among his village headmen, 'chiefs', was Paramount Chief of the Djukas from 1916 to 1931. The official uniform was supplied by the Government. The silver collar with inscription and the silvertopped cane were presented as gifts to the paramount chief and chiefs during and shortly after the peace, concluded in 1761, as insignia of their official rank.

§ 3 ORGANIZATION OF THE DJUKA SOCIETY

a Political structure

The Djuka tribe is subdivided into matrilinear, exogamous clans, named *los*. Its origin has been discussed in § 1 of the present chapter. The hierarchy within the clans, as well as between the various clans, is a determining factor in the hierarchy in the Djuka political structure. There are twelve clans, the one from which the Granman is chosen, the Oto-*lo*, being the most important, followed immediately by the Missidjan-*lo*. The *los* are separated into those inhabiting the upper part of the river (who regard themselves as the élite) and those inhabiting the lower part. The twelve *los* are:

Upper (*Opo*)	Lower (*Bilo*)
1. Oto	6. Pulugudu or Ledimusu
2. Missidjan	7. Pedri
3. Dju	8. Dika
4. Pinasi	9. Bray
5. Pata	10. Njafaai
	11. Compagnie
	12. La Pay.

As a rule the *los* live together in one village, sometimes there are two or more *los* in the same village, sometimes the members of one *lo* inhabit several villages. When a single *lo* inhabits a village, the number of functionaries usually depends on the size of the *lo*. If there are more than one *lo* in a village, each *lo* has its own leader.

In the course of years very little has been altered in the composition of the Djuka administrative system. The hierarchy of functions in force during the period of 1918-1928 was as follows:

At the head of all the Djukas there is the Granman, a member of the Oto-*lo*, whose seat is in Drietabbetje. His representative is the *Granfiskari*[8] (formerly there were two), not always chosen from the same *lo*. The function of this official is not clearly defined.

At the head of each *lo* there is the Grand Chief, *Gran-kaptèn* or *Ledidiakti* (red-jacket from the colour of the coat trimmings of his uniform). His co-administrator and understudy is the vice-chief, *Kaptèn* or *Blakadjakti* (black-jacket). Under them there are the forest-chiefs, *Boesi-kaptèn* or *Bassias*[9], who regulate the day-to-day affairs of the community.

The matrilineages of each *lo* (families regarding themselves as descended from the same ancestress) also have a representative who exercises authority within this group. As a rule it is the oldest male member of the lineage.

The changes to be noted as compared to the situation today (1969) are that the office of *Granfiskari* has disappeared, but the Granman is aided by two Head Chiefs. A village is usually governed by two chiefs, the function of vice-chief and forest-chief has lapsed. But every official has two *Bassias* and vice-*Bassias* at his disposal[10] and there are usually one or more female *Bassias* in every village who occupy themselves with village domestic matters, supervising the preparation of meals and religious ceremonies and assisting at the reception of prominent members of the community.

In § 2 of the present chapter the procedure governing the succession of Paramount Chiefs has been described. Chiefs, just like Granmans are chosen from the matrilineage of their predecessors, but the number of relatives from whom the Granman may be chosen seems less restricted than in the case of a chief: the latter is usually succeeded by a son of his mother's brother's son.[11] The choice made by the village and the *lo* has to be sanctioned by the Granman.

The *Bassias* are elected by the chiefs, as a rule one of his matrilinear relatives and one from the other groups inhabiting the village in question.

b Civil administration

1 Form

For the exercise of their administrative task the village worthies regularly assemble in a *krutu*. It depends on the nature and magnitude of the matter to be discussed whether the meeting is held *en famille*, within the *lo*, the village, by a number of villages, or at Drietabbetje, the Granman's residential seat. In difficult matters one can always take one's case to a court of appeal.

Matters of policy, conflicts, offences and crimes – also depending on gravity – can be settled out of court, or by the verdict of higher authorities, and by the infliction of punishment. When decisions have to be taken, the pronouncements made by elders present at the meeting are always listened to.

2 Possibilities of coercion

It depends on various factors wheter the exercise of power, the execution of decisions that have been taken or punishments that have been imposed is successfully carried out – in the first place on the personality of the administrator himself.¹² Vigorous Granmans like, for instance, Bijman, Oseisie, Akontu Felanti, governed with much more efficiency than someone like Amakti who could not hold his own, even *vis-à-vis* his subjects, without support of the powerful High Priest Kanapé.

Furthermore, much depends on the political or historical power group to which one belongs, or, in other words, whether one has gathered enough faction members round one who can add their support. In this way a chief of the lower Tapanahoni, i.e. a member of the politically less important group, could, by gaining influence with the priests of the second important God of the Djukas, also resident in the *Bilo* area, oppose weighty decisions of the – *Opo* – High Priest (Chapter VI § 2).

Political manoeuvres to obtain an increase in power are closely connected with this forming of factions. A Granman will try to gather the largest possible following by granting favours or putting people into a position of dependence on him.

Another aid to the exercise of power is an appeal, or a threat of appeal, which is usually enough, to the Surinam Government, which could cause the loss of a salary or favours bestowed by the Government. A Granman would, however, make very limited use of this measure, since loyalty to his people demands that he should draw the Government as little as possible into internal matters. During the period under discussion, when only the Granman and Head Chief received an allowance, it happened still more rarely than during the past fifteen years, since all the chiefs and *Bassias* are now also being paid a salary.

To some extent the fact that Granman and chiefs were (and are) usually the only persons to have direct contact with government officials caused a condition of monopoly. The gaining or refusal of favours always had to be conducted through them.¹³ As the Djuka society does not possess a police force or any other body that can enforce the carrying out of decisions with powerful means, it is clear that one can speak of an 'insufficient ascendency'.¹⁴

Conflicts will preferably be settled inside the family, or between families. Village conflicts, too, are usually settled by the chiefs themselves, by his *Bassias* or others. Only for complicated cases, serious offences or crimes, is the Granman's arbitration invoked. However, there are cases which the chiefs always have to bring to the Granman's attention. These include: murder, manslaughter and violent physical aggression; all deaths (except those of children under ten), and the cause of death as established by the priests; the desire expressed by fellow villagers to receive the 'sacraments of the church'; every absence of the chief of a village [15]. In some cases and only to a limited, predetermined extent, an injured person or group may take the law into their own hands: in the case of adultery the offended husband may give his wife's seducer a thrashing; the conflict should preferably be settled by the infliction of punishment (usually by imposing some task or other) or fines (the payment of a quantity of money, drink, food, clothes, a boat). Serious offences called for grave physical punishment in former days, when they were not yet brought to court: death by hanging or being burnt alive (abolished by Granman Blijmoffo 1865-1882), and flogging (still practised forty years ago). Today the following are considered to be severe punishments: exile, stiff fines (which go to swell the pockets of the judges), humiliating tasks, forced labour (as a rule for the Granman), compulsory unemployment or having to sit in the sun for one or several days.

3 Emoluments

In addition to a salary and an official uniform (nowadays also an outboard motor) which the Granman and the Head Chief receive from the Government, the administrators have other sources of income. Primarily the Granman, of course, who receives the largest share of the fines imposed, who benefits from the unpaid labour (the clearing of ground for cultivation, building of huts and boats, etc), who receives some of the spoils of the chase, the best part of the food for sacrificial feasts and part of the appropriated inheritance of witches and others whom the Great God has punished with death. Moreover, visitors and friends offer him gifts. To a much lesser extent chiefs and *Bassias* profit from these services and donations.

c The priesthood

1 The hierarchy of priests

A permanent group of active priests are found in those villages where a permanent oracle-god resides, namely in Drietabbetje, Granbori (Upper Tapanahoni), Tabbetje, Fisiti and Malobbi (Lower Tapanahoni). In principle these oracles may always be consulted through the priests, also by inhabitants of other villages. Each village has, moreover, a number of personal minor oracles – derived from the major oracles – who have no significance outside the village.

Among the permanent oracles the hierarchy of priests attached to the most inportant oracle, at Drietabbetje, will probably serve as a typical example of the graded priesthood; it is the best-known, for the other important centres, Granbori and Tabbetje, firmly repulse all interest from outside. It may be taken for granted that conditions elsewhere, *mutatis mutandis*, will not differ essentially. At the head of the hieratic staff we have the High Priest, a function either combined with or independent of the Granmanship. He directs the chief religious ceremonies and acts as spokesman when the oracle of the Great Divinity is consulted. He has been educated by his predecessor. After his period of training, at the most suitable stage, he usually becomes the second priest of the hierarchy. He is elected from the Oto-*lo* and is a sister's son or a classificatory sister's son of the Granman. The High Priest chooses his closest collaborating co-chiefs, observing the rule that the first priest is generally chosen from the Missidjan-*lo* and the second priest, as has been mentioned, from his nearest matrilinear relatives. They will have followed a long course of training to become thoroughly versed in oracular jurisprudence, liturgy, ritual and medicine, prior to being brought beforet he Great Divinity and are, with his approval, dedicated to the priesthood.

Other members of the oracle's staff are the front and hind bearers. The hind bearer is a pupil of the front bearer. The bearers have, firstly, to learn to reply correctly to the questions put by the priest to the oracle who is carried on a plank on their heads; or rather, to interpret correctly the answer given by the god to the questions, by letting the oracle move his head in affirmation or negation. The bearer-priests are usually chosen from the sons of the High Priest or of the first priest, or from persons dependent on them.

2 Definition of duties

The duties of the High Priest and his staff are so comprehensive as to keep them occupied practically every day and for the best part of their time. Then it must be remembered that they often take over part of the task of civil government when religious aspects are involved.

The priests give help to those who, for one reason or another, come to ask assistance from the oracle. In the first place they may want to know the cause of illness or death. These causes could be: crisis conditions[16], witchcraft, sins against some command of the Great God, or natural causes.[17] As to the cause of death: usually this will have been verified in the village of the deceased, but it may be necessary to consult the oracle so as to have the human verdict confirmed.

The administering of the 'sacraments' is a second duty of the priests.

This is supposed to produce effects of healing and safeguarding. Various sacraments are known: the benediction, during which the oracle, the Great God, is passed across the patient's body; the ritual cleansing, when the patient is washed with beer or with an infusion of medicinal leaves; or one can have a special talisman manufactured as a protection against witchcraft. If a person fears that he is possessed by a witch or by an avenging spirit, he could have it exorcized by the pronouncement of a magic formula, by receiving ritual cleansing or praying to the influential ancestors. Finally one can also gather in groups to be exonerated from the suspicion of being a witch by attending the annual ceremony where one swears an oath in the presence of the Great God declaring that this is not the case. On this occasion an innocuous liquid is drunk from a calabash and if the suspected person dies or falls ill within three months, this is accepted as proof that he is guilty of witchcraft. The contrary does not necessarily demonstrate his innocence: the proof may manifest itself only after a long period. The Djukas as well as other Bush Negro tribes perform this ritual several times during the course of their life.[18]

A third duty of the priest is the carrying out of special purification rites. These rites are related to the estate left behind by someone who has been put to death by the Great God because the deceased was a witch or committed some other offence against one of the divine laws. All his possessions have to be brought to Drietabbetje. A witch's entire estate reverts to the church of the Great God, the inheritance left by others goes partly to the Great God, partly to the High Priest and his staff. The part that is given back by the priests to the next of kin is taken home after the purification rites. For all the inhabitants of the Tapanahoni these rites are performed in Drietabbetje. The fear of divine punishment is too great for any of the relatives to attempt to evade them.

A task to be performed by the priest after each performance of the purification rites is the sacrifice to the 'deceased servitors of the church', the prominent ancestors or *Granjorkas*. Sacrificial feasts are celebrated, prayers are offered to them, a nocturnal dance-festival is held. The Great Divinity is informed of the forthcoming sacrificial feast and gives it his approval. Votive offerings are also brought to the *Granjorkas* on other important occasions: the ancestors' blessing is implored, for instance, on an intended visit by the Paramount Chief. Finally prayers are offered once every three weeks, on Sunday night, to the Great God as well as to the *Granjorkas* asking them to guard the people from transgressing against their laws and to prevent the minor gods from punishing the people too severely for their sins.

The priests have no fixed income. Their emoluments depend on the services they render. Thus they receive part of the completely or partly confiscated effects of the deceased. The payment for cases treated by them varies, also depending on what the patient or the penalized wrong-doer is regarded as being capable of paying (or rather, what the members of his lineage will probably be able to raise). Part of the payment demanded consists of *tafia* (a kind of rum) most of which, however, is employed for the ritual, furthermore of cloth, bottled beer, the performing of commissions, and once in a while a money fine. For the furnishing of a talisman payment (in money and in kind) is demanded.

3 Funeral priests

As has already been mentioned, every death occurring among the Djukas in the Tapanahoni must be reported to the Granman, as well as the cause of the death. The latter is ascertained by the funeral priests who are present in every village. They form a separate category in the hierarchy of priests. Together with the coffin-makers (*kisiman*) and grave-diggers (*oroman*) they constitute a society of trained and initiated members, the only kind of organized society existing in the Bush Negro community. Besides ascertaining the cause of death whenever someone dies, they attend to the relationship between the living and the dead (the *jorkas*), arrange the funeral and perform the prescribed rites during the period of mourning. To ascertain the cause of death the corpse is placed in a coffin supported on the heads of two bearers and interrogated by two priests. The funeral priests receive, by way of reward for their services, part of the goods (especially cloth) donated to the deceased. During the funeral proceedings and while they are carrying out the necessary rites, they are supplied with food and *tafia* by the relatives.

4 The *obiaman* (medicine-man)

The medicine-man also occupies a position of authority in the religious life of the Djukas. Their remedies are of a natural, but also and above all of a supernatural kind and are intended to combat the causes of the disease as well as the disease itself. In a certain sense these *obiamans* are rivals of the priests, because those who become ill are not obliged to turn to the priests, but may make a choice, or consult both authorities. (Another alternative is recourse to western medical aid.)

The word *obia* signifies the magical and remedial capacities possessed by a number of gods. The god transfers the knowledge of these gifts to a person by taking possession of him, that is to say, he becomes the 'bearer', the 'steed' of the god. When the bearer conjures up the god in himself by means of dancing, singing, ablutions and other rites, he becomes possessed, falls into a trance, and the god speaks through the possessed person, uttering medical and religious advice. To be able to communicate the language of the god intelligibly requires a long period of training. As a rule a full-fledged *obiaman* has a number of apprentices who learn from him the language, the dance, the rites, a knowledge of herbs and other remedies, natural or supernatural. The apprentice has to pay handsomely for his training, submit himself to all sorts of restrictions (sexual intercourse is forbidden) and undergo penance.

Besides supplying medicine, the *obiaman* also provides remedies against supernatural dangers, in the first place against witchcraft. It depends on the reputation of the *obiaman* whethr he is considered capable of doing this. He also provides remedies against the vengeance of the gods and ancestors who can punish a person with illness or other misfortune for offences committed against them.

For the purpose of diagnosis and deciding on a course of therapy, the *obiaman* also employs mediums: Djukas who are mediums of a god – and there are a great many of them[19], both men and women – are put into a trance and then convey the utterances of the god to the *obiaman*. The *obiaman* is also paid for his services in kind: with cloth, *tafia*, foodstuffs, while separate gifts should be brought for the god he consulted.

5 The *wisiman* (witch)

Although the *wisiman*[20] does not belong to the priesthood any more than the *obiaman*, it seems fitting to devote some attention to the subject here, firstly because one of the most important functions of the priests of the Great God is to repress *wisi*, secondly because the *wisiman* may be called the *obiaman's* opposing force. While the *obiaman* applies his supernatural gift beneficently, the *wisiman* is supposed to do the same with evil intent. Witchcraft is the worst crime that could be perpetrated against a fellow human being. It evokes great terror, also on account of its indefinable aspects: every illness, every accident, every failure may be the result of witchcraft. Whether or no a suspected person is a witch cannot be ascertained until after his death. Witches turn upon their prey from jealousy, vindictiveness or hatred: thus it may be dangerous to enjoy happiness, a good income, a prosperous harvest, attractive children, valuable possessions like a shop or an outboard motor.

The possession of wealth may also give rise to the suspicion of witchcraft: it may have been acquired with the aid of malignant occult practices and at the cost of others.

There are very few counter-measures: an *obiaman* will have to be capable of manufacturing an extremely potent talisman if it is to safeguard one against *wisi*. The most powerful protection is given by the Great God in Drietabbetje. The victim of *wisi* can have the evil influences exorcized by the priests of the Great God, who offer prayers and sacrifices to him and to the prominent ancestors, and perform the ritual ablutions to cleanse the victim.

When it has been established after his death that a person was a witch, no customary burial with accompanying rites is held, the corpse is flung into the forest (or shovelled there, without ceremony, into the earth, something on which the Government has insisted all along). The whole estate, everything the deceased possessed, accrues to the Great God in Drietabbetje. A witch's death may not be mourned, it should be looked upon as an occasion for rejoicing. The treatment meted out to witches has undergone considerable change in the course of time. Before the abolition of capital punishment by Granman Blijmoffo (1865-1882), a person could be labelled a witch while still alive and be tortured to death on the grill. (The body was then disposed of in the manner described above.) When *wisimans* were no longer put to death, this may have prompted the lynching of suspects by those who regarded themselves as his victims. In order to prevent such acts of aggression (which might have led to governmental interference) it was ordained, probably by Oseisie (1889-1915) that *wisi* could be proved only after death. I have made this deduction because it was Oseisie who instituted the cult of Grantata (the Great God) and, in particular, his opposition to *wisi* in its still existing form.

The proof that a deceased person was a *wisiman* is furnished by himself. Every corpse is carried by funeral priests, as described in § 3c, and interrogated about the cause of his death. When the corpse, laid in a coffin and carried on the heads of two bearers, sets out at the command of the funeral priests directly towards the mortuary after having circled thrice round the village prayer-pole, has given satisfactory replies concerning the cause of death and has moreover managed to indicate the hiding-place of three persons concealed beforehand, then it has been proved that he is not a *wisiman*. The contrary is the case if the bearers make for the wood, give incorrect answers and cannot find the hidden persons. The questioning is kept up until the deceased at long last 'admits' that he was a *wisiman*.

Even after the death of a *wisiman* his spirit may continue to torture the living: it has then joined the evil *jorkas*.

d The supernatural world

1 Divinities and oracles

The Djuka gods also constitute a hierarchy. They are, moreover, supposed to be endowed with human characteristics and habits, with the probable exception of the Supreme God, who, although he is the 'creator', does not concern himself with the conflicts of earthdwellers. This Supreme God: Nana, or Nana Kediampon, or Nijankapon, keeps guard over the human race in an aloof, indirect manner. He has no special priests, a prayer-pole in only a few villages, and very few sacrifices or prayers for protection are offered to him.[21]

The chief Djuka gods are Grantata or Gran Gadu (also known as Sweli Gadu) whose sacral name is Gwangwella, and Gedeunsu. Both are oracle-gods; Gran Gadu has his seat in Drietabbetje and is served by Oto-*lo* priests, Gedeunsu has his seat in Tabbetje and has members of the Pedi-*lo* for priests (and priestesses). Both gods played their part in the running away period and are supposed to have been 'brought along' from Africa by priestesses, also ancestresses of the *los* to which the gods belong.

Gwangwella has a chequered past. His power was established at the time of Granman Oseisie (1888-1915) in the form in which it still exists at present: the oracle-god employed by the Granman-High Priest and the priesthood of Drietabbetje in the exercise of their authority. The various accounts of his 'career', as told to investigators, broadly correspond to each other, but differ in a number of details. They all mention the fact that the ancestress Avo Abenkina gave the god to her daughters Kato and Musato to take along when they fled into the forest. He was a martial god and protected his adherents in the guerilla war and against witchcraft. When peace had been concluded in 1761 the Djukas moved up the Tapanahoni and a rift was established between the Upper and Lower *los*. Gwangwella's role as battle-god receded into the background.

The Gran Gadu cult was revived by Granman Oseisie. Oseisie had not been trained as High Priest when he became Granman. Arabi (or Aguma Sakka) had received this training. Between these two a conflict of power erupted since Oseisie wanted to be, in accordance with tradition, High

Priest as well as Granman. Arabi moved to Granbori, a village situated higher up on the Tapanahoni, taking the bundle containing Grantata along with him. Oseisie, however, instituted a fresh Gran Gadu cult and proclaimed himself to be its High Priest. Subsequently peace was restored between the two opponents. Gadu-Gwangwella was now considered to be 'fully present' in a bundle in both places.[22] All the same, the oracle-god of Drietabbetje, as described in § 2 of this chapter, plays the major role through the administrative, religious and medical power his 'servitors' are able to exercise. The activities of High Priest Kanapé, during Amakti's Granmanship (1916-1931) and later, were especially favourable to the consolidation of this power.

Little is known about Gedeunsu. As has been mentioned in § 3, the priests of this god are not communicative and repel the inquisitiveness of investigators. This oracle-god is supposed to be a patron of agriculture, hunting and fishing, also of children and of parturition. His relationship to the oracle-god of Drietabbetje may be described as 'well-disposed but aloof'. Gedeunsu visits his colleague once every couple of years, the Granman occasionally pays a visit to Gedeunsu. His authority extends itself particularly within the area of the Lower Tapanahoni. Drietabbetje is the only place where aid can be sought in case of witchcraft.

After these two major gods a number of minor gods follow, each of whom plays an important role in the life of the Djukas. Although they may be divided into benevolent and malevolent gods, one should not forget that benevolent gods can be angered if the rites owing to them are neglected, and that malevolent gods may be appeased by means of many and assiduous votive offerings. This favourable or unfavourable mood, however, is usually only directed to the person bringing offers and the members of his lineage. Most of these minor gods are capable of manifesting themselves in human beings, and someone who is possessed by a god may be consulted while in a trance. The oracle-god communicates through his medium, man or woman, the cause of the accident, illness or other troubles, and the appropriate cure (sacrifices, medicines, purifying baths). Thus the *obiamans* (discussed in § 3) are not the only ones to be consulted about illness, etc., although they are regarded as being specialized in the art of healing. Other mediums are consulted incidentally and in accordance with their reputation.

2 The *jorkas* (ancestors)

Another group playing an important role as go-between with the supernatural are the spirits of the deceased, the *jorkas*. They are capable of functioning as intermediaries between living persons and the gods. The place occupied by these spirits in the life of the Djukas is partly dependent on their status and the sort of life they led while on earth. The spirit leaving the body after burial (during the death rites the *jorka* can be questioned, especially about the cause of his death) retains the characteristics of the deceased. They are divided as follows:

i. The *Granjorkas*, those who played a prominent part during life, did great deeds, led an exemplary existence. They include those 'praised by the gods' (*Gado bresi*) who are supposed to dwell in close vicinity to the gods and whose prayers on behalf of human beings are always heard by the gods. A more important role is played by those who participate in the assemblies and councils of the gods to discuss the fate of mankind: *a de krutu na gado kondre* (they come together in the land of the gods).

ii. The *jorkas*, the spirits of those who did not distinguish themselves particularly whilst alive, but behaved like virtuous people.

iii. The evil (*takru*) *jorkas*, the wrongdoers in the community, who continue to do their bad deeds in the spirit world and keep on pestering the living.

The *jorka* is closely connected with the lineage to which the deceased belonged. Every lineage, every *lo* has a separate altar or prayer-pole where votive offerings are brought and prayers said to the ancestors. The rites are conducted by the head of the lineage. The *jorkas*, like the gods, can also take possession of a human being and through him utter warnings against dangers or indicate remedies for illnesses. On the other hand it is also possible that the spirit of the deceased feels offended or neglected, in which case he can punish the lineage with illness and death.

3 Avenging gods and avenging spirits

The power of revenge which may be exercized by gods or spirits (of the dead), called *kunu*, plays a terrifying role in the lives of the Djukas. Contrary to *wisi* (witchcraft) it cannot be practised by the living. In most lineages one or more *kunus* occur. In case of illness or trouble brought to Drietabbetje for consultation, the priests will first investigate this before they go further into the matter.

Various minor gods are capable of persecuting human beings because of their revengefulness. They are particularly offended when their dwelling-place is destroyed. Papagadu, who has chosen the sacred snake as his domicile, lays a curse on man when this snake is killed; Ampuku, who lives in the cotton-tree, is enraged when this tree is felled without the required offerings; and Kantamasu when his seat, the termite-hill, is disturbed.

The spirit of the deceased can also act as a *kunu*. An offence which, above all, arouses their desire for vengeance is incest (sexual intercourse between matrilinear relatives). This may affect all the members of the lineage of both the man and the woman, as well as the culprits themselves. Other sins which may precipitate *kunu* are breach of faith, infidelity, perjury, malicious gossip (particularly against members of one's own lineage).

The punishments likely to strike the culprit are, apart from illness and death, insanity, the loss of a child, crop failure, accidents while felling trees etc. A special way of calling down *kunu* on someone is by committing suicide: the person who drove the victim to this desperate deed will be pursued by his curse. It is possible to escape the curse of the avenging spirit "by regular offerings and supplications and by showing gratitude as long as all goes well".[23]

e Forms of kinship

The Djuka family ties are determined matrilinearly. The tribe is divided in clans, or *los*, the members of which regard themselves as being descendants of one or more ancestresses. (It should be remembered that these tribal ancestresses usually came from the plantation from which the *lo* escaped as a group.) The number of *los* have remained more or less constant through the centuries. Wong (1938) mentions fourteen, Van Lier twelve[24], and Thoden van Velzen thirteen.[25] These variations are probably the result of fusion or secession, or the fact that a *lo* has become extinct.[26] The names of the *los* have not been altered, except for their spelling.

As has been indicated in the history of their origin, the division between *Opo* (upper river) and *Bilo* (lower river) groups has politico-historical grounds. There is still some animosity between the two groups although it has subsided somewhat in the course of time, but "the Upper group regards itself as being superior to the Lower group and each group applies derogatory epithets to the other."[27] The fact that the *Bilo* Negroes possess an important god, Gedeunsu, has probably helped them to hold their own with ease in spite of the fact that they are governed by a Granman-High Priest of the *Opo* Negroes.

The *los* are divided into matrilineages, the *beres* (bellies) bound together by a demonstrable matrilineal relationship usually going back not more than a couple of generations. A *bere* consists of a number of matrisegments having, in their turn, a stronger sense of interrelationship. [28]

The sense of relationship between members of a matrilineage is very strong and expresses itself in the acceptance of responsibility for everything happening within the lineage and in solidarity towards those outside the lineage.

The lineage atones for or profits by the deeds of fellow-members. Thus an avenging spirit not only strikes the person guilty of an offence, but all the members of his lineage. Similarly the lineage will contribute to pay fines, obligations and votive offerings inside and outside the group.

f Some characteristics of the Djukas

To throw some light on the personality of the Djukas as revealed to investigators who occupied themselves, for longer or shorter periods, with the pursuit and collection of facts concerning this Bush Negro community, here is a comparative description of the findings of some of them, namely W.F. van Lier, H.U.E. Thoden van Velzen and the missionary I.G. Spalburg. Van Lier's views occur throughout his writings and letters (1918-1942), those of Thoden van Velzen in his doctoral thesis (1966) and those of Spalburg in the small book he wrote during his stay at Drietabbetje as a teacher in the Moravian Brothers school (1899).

Van Lier, for a start, finds that the Djukas have 'sound moral principles'. He does not specify this pronouncement, but from the context it appears that by this he means a moral attitude towards social relationships as a whole, which he himself regards as correct.

Thoden van Velzen says that there exists a broad ideal of 'mutual co-operation and the peaceful and generally acceptable way of solving differences'. Which does not mean that the people adhere to this moral attitude, this ideal: Van Lier calls them avaricious and unhelpful amongst each other while Thoden van Velzen remarks that there is little mutual help and that payment is asked for every service rendered.

Van Lier believes that the Djuka's entire life is controlled by his religion, his faith in the power of the oracle (Gran Gadu) and the spirits of the deceased.

In this connection Thoden van Velzen states that the church of the Great Divinity (i.e. Gran Gadu) represents the real power of organization in the Tapanahoni, on which the faithful are dependent. Although that is,

Prayer-pole, probably belonging to the clan of the present Granman Gazon. The (half decayed) cloths are gifts of relatives to the ancestors. The bottles, filled with *tafia* (rum), gin or beer, are used for the pouring of libations during prayers.

(photograph by the author)

generally speaking, the case, there is undoubtedly a difference between the religious feelings of individuals. Van Lier differentiates between the 'orthodox' and the 'modern'.

The Djukas are proud, Van Lier says, and their pride is partly based on the fact that they gained their freedom from the whites by fighting for it. As an example of their pride he mentions the fact that they will never beg from one another. However, they have no objection to begging from whites and from urban Negroes and they hold that *Lanti* (the Government) is obliged to support them. The Djukas do not suffer from an inferiority complex, Thoden van Velzen says, and are only too conscious of their worth. Towards foreigners[29], however, the Djuka clearly feels that he is the weaker party. Consequently he believes that it is the duty of the powerful foreigner to render assistance to the weak Bush Negro. One and all they display a 'great frankness' in the 'asking for favours' and regard free medical aid, for instance, as a matter of course.

All the same, Van Lier says that they display 'a submissiveness bordering on toadyism' towards the Granman, the elders, the foreigner. Another aspect of this tendency is probably what he calls their furtiveness and cowardice, their reluctance to speak the truth. Thoden van Velzen calls them 'extremely courteous'. Especially the Granman enjoys great esteem and the people 'outdo themselves to overwhelm him with extravagant praise and declarations of loyalty'.

This extreme obsequiousness causes repressed aggression which finds an indirect outlet in backbiting. Van Lier says that the 'class feeling' is highly developed: this is most apparent in the differences that are felt in the status of the upper-river Djukas and the lower-river Djukas. In the eyes of the *Opo Ningre* themselves they are the 'patricians' and the *Bilo Ningre* the 'plebeians.'

Thoden van Velzen remarks with regard to the existing controversies between *Opo* and *Bilo* that the *Opo* regard themselves as being superior and believe that more witchcraft and more incest occur among the *Bilo*, while the *Bilo* believe that the *Opo* behaviour toward the Granman is too servile.

Van Lier and Thoden van Velzen both give examples of – sometimes violent – clashes between the two groups.

The foreigner is regarded with suspicion: one can never be sure what his motives are when he makes overtures. Van Lier finds the chief cause of this in the fact that they have not forgotten that the whites enslaved them, and are not convinced that the whites will not try to do so (in another form) once more. Thoden van Velzen also mentions the fact that it is difficult for a Djuka to develop a satisfactory relationship with a foreigner: he feels that he should be kept at a distance. Too close contacts are considered as 'having truck with the enemy' and this is a serious crime – probably the most serious after witchcraft.

Nonetheless both authors point out that it is regarded as of utmost importance to entertain a friendly superficial contact with this same foreigner. Van Lier believes that they are, after all, 'attached' to the white man and receive him well: whoever visits a Bush Negro village is always offered a well-cleaned lodging-place and drink. But at the same time one does expect *quid pro quo* in the shape of foodstuffs, medicine, tobacco. Thoden van Velzen, too, remarks that one is supposed to show hospitality to the foreigner: by assuming a hostile attitude to him (stealing from him or, even worse, killing him) one invites serious supernatural dangers that could strike, not only the offender and his nearest relatives, but also his fellow tribesmen.

Although there is also a certain degree of mutual distrust among the Djukas themselves (too intimate relations with – especially – someone outside the lineage would give the other a chance of applying witchcraft), both investigators remark that they are friendly and sociable and have a sense of humour.

Van Lier finds that they do not harbour grievances and quickly forget the injustices they have suffered. Thoden van Velzen says that they do not drive matters to extremes when conflicts arise, and are glad to make compromises.

Finally some remarks about the Djukas' view of education.

Van Lier says: "There is not a Bush Negro nowadays who does not hanker after education." They believe that a knowledge of reading and writing will bring them material advantage in their contact with the world of foreigners. But a concern for their 'spiritual welfare' surpasses all desire for material gain. By this Van Lier means that every effort to inculcate the Christian doctrine in addition to pure book-learning will come up against opposition.

Thoden van Velzen, too, believes that the Djukas are well aware of the benefits of education and are particularly eager to learn arithmetic. But they have an outspoken aversion to Christian education and efforts in that direction will always meet with passive resistance.

Others who recorded their impressions also gave, briefly, their view on the Djuka personality. One of them, the missionary I.G. Spalburg, taught for a while at a small school in Drietabbetje. Because he also tried to impart a knowledge of Christianity (he belonged to the Moravian

Brothers) his efforts were doomed to failure. He lived among the Djukas from 1896 to 1900. In his booklet *A Sketch of Marowijne and its Inhabitants* (1899) he wrote (pp. 31, 32): It is difficult to name definite characteristics of the Aucaners. On the one hand they are hospitable, they are easily attracted to strangers, they are mutually helpful in their work and – however strange it may sound – of a forgiving nature. But on the other hand there is reason enough to call the Aucaner mean and avaricious.... To extort as much as possible from the white man is a maxim with which even the youngest is acquainted. They have no scruples about lying and cheating. They are very insolent towards the whites, on the other hand they are the greatest cowards amongst one another and lack the moral courage to speak their mind openly. They have a tendency to flatter and butter each other up. An object, no matter how hideous, only has to belong to the Granman in order to be called fine and beautiful. They have great respect for the Dutch tricolour and for official communications."

Spalburg's opinion coincides to some extent with the previously quoted critics, but in other respects it is less favourable. As regards the teaching he was trying to do in Drietabbetje, Granman Oseisie's residential village at the time of writing the said booklet, he records (p. 43): "The work progresses slowly and demands much patience. Also, the greatest caution has to be preserved so as not to force religion upon the children and adults. The priests are powerful and it may be that they are watching the teacher's activity with suspicion."

As for the latter: Spalburg actually had to leave because the priests would not tolerate his (cautious?) attempts at converting the people.

Finally an example of an 'unenlightened' colonial official as postholder among the Djukas from 1846-1857, a predecessor of W.F. van Lier, Ch. L. Dhondt. He did not have a good word to spare for the Djukas and felt that he was "exiled in a sort of wilderness, among capricious Negroes that are called human beings". He complained about their unruliness, recalcitrance and insolence, he wrote with horror about their religion and ceremonial rites. "The outrageous, terrifying things the Negroes do are extraordinarily savage and idolatrous." He believed that the Government treated them with too much tolerance; and only extreme severity would "make them improve their ways, for as soon as any favours are bestowed upon these people, who, in spite of their godless way of life are not stupid, they immediately suppose that the Government needs them and were forced to do it".[30]

g Means of living

1 Agriculture, hunting, fishing

The Bush Negro provides in his daily needs by means of agriculture, hunting and fishing. To supplement what he collects in this way he makes use of the – very scarce – small shops run by Creoles, Chinese or Bush Negroes along the Marowijne, or he shops in Albina or Paramaribo. This supplementation with rice, flour, biscuits, salt, sugar, strong drink and tinned foodstuffs was necessary, not only because the Bush Negroes themselves did not have a supply of these things, but because the fairly frequent crop failures caused a real food shortage. This was the case in Van Lier's time and even today it still occurs. Not much has changed during the past fifty years. There are more shops along the Marowijne and the Tapanahoni where they can obtain their additional requirements. Albina and Paramaribo have become more accessible because of the increased use of outboard motors and the construction of a few small airfields, and migratory labour has expanded.

The Bush Negro farms on small plots that have been cleared and where shifting cultivation is practised. The soil in the interior of Surinam, partly hilly, is rich in kaolinite which has a low base exchange capacity. The presence of dense primeval forests is no indication of a fertile soil, but supplies humus with a slightly higher base exchange capacity cations. After the deforestation the humus forms the base of fertility for about two crops. Although valuable agricultural soil can be developed with the aid of chemical fertilizers and erosion control in parts where the slope is not too steep and where there are no other obstructions besides ferrite caps, rockiness or concretion layers, there is, of course, no question of this in the agricultural practice of the Bush Negro. The clearing of the plots is done by the menfolk. They chop down the trees during the 'long dry season' in October and November. After the wood has been left for some weeks to dry out, it is burnt. Large tree-trunks are left lying, branches are cleared away. The soil is not cultivated further and during the 'short rainy season' (December and January) the women do the planting. The various crops are planted in a medley: the chief crop is bitter cassava, the second most important (unirrigated) rice, then bananas and bacoven, root-crops, maize, groundnuts, sugar-cane, tobacco, pepper, gourds. (Fruit-trees are usually planted in or round the villages.) The plot, planted with annuals and biennials, yields all the year round but has to be abandoned after two or three crops because it cannot produce any longer after this exhaustive cultivation. The soil recovers fairly slowly. The layer of humus has been partly destroyed by burning and the soil is impoverished too by the method of tilling.

Another reason for seeking fresh soil is the ant plague. The parasol ant (especially *atta sexdens*) attacks the crops, settles in the exploited terrain and travels along to the next plot, which is near the previous one.

Obviously this method leads to a continuous extension of soil made unfit for agricultural purposes. Moreover, the area available for cultivation is limited, in spite of the apparently immense region at the disposal of the Bush Negro. The distance between provision plot and dwelling-place should not be too great. The parts that are suitable for cultivation have definite bounds: along the Tapanahoni arable land is available from the village of Granbori (the forest further south is the Granman's hunting-ground) up to the confluence of the Marowijne: from the point where the Lawa flows into the Marowijne up to the territory of the Bonnis. Then, too, the plots should not lie too far from the river or a creek, otherwise the problem of transport becomes too difficult. Many Bush Negroes are obliged to pitch temporary camps at provision grounds situated far from their villages.

The choice of a plot is further restricted by the method of land division: each village and each family is allocated a definite area. The distribution of the provision grounds is promoted by the fact that the man clears a plot for his wife (or wives) in the terrain of her lineage, and for himself in the terrain of his matrilineage.

All these factors combine to make the provision of food a precarious matter which is directly threatened by crop failure. Ever since the eighteenth century periods of famine have occurred. Although the number of Djukas has been steadily on the increase, the shortage has not grown progressively worse: the likewise increased opportunities of additional earning and communication have improved their chance of procuring additional foodstuffs from the coastal parts.

The food produced in the Bush Negro provision ground is onesided and insufficient: they get a surplus of carbohydrates, too little fat, vitamins (especially of the B-complex) and (animal) proteins. This lack is partly compensated for by hunting and fishing. Hunting is done with guns and hunting-dogs (bought from and trained by Indians, the Oajanas and the Trios). Hunting is not subject to any rules and the unlimited shooting of game and wildfowl during the course of centuries has disturbed the natural balance. Consequently the inhabited parts are poorly stocked and dependent for supplies on the surrounding virgin forest. Hunting is a favourite sport and the men are prepared to set out on expeditions lasting days and weeks (for instance to the area along the Upper Tapanahoni set aside as hunting-ground by the Granman). Monkeys, sloths, tapirs, wild-boar, deer, rabbits, hares are hunted. (Shooting the panther is taboo.) Birds and reptiles (wood-tortoise, leguan) are considered game, while most snakes and the cayman are taboo.

Fishing offers the same picture as hunting: as a result of unlimited fishing the Tapanahoni, although containing a large variety of kinds, has become, as far as numbers go, 'exhausted'. Fishing seasons, as legally regulated in the coastal parts of Surinam, cannot be enforced here, nor are hunting restrictions acknowledged. "In the upper parts the people consider themselves above the laws made in the lower parts."[31]

Fishing is done with the aid of traps, bow-and-arrow, rod-and-line, spears for stabbing by lantern-light, and with poison. The last method is particularly harmful for the fish supply, since young fish are killed as well as full-grown and spawning fish. Fishing with poison, called *ponsu*, is forbidden (Police Penal Regulations 1915, Art. 45), but this prohibition, too, is not *de rigueur*. Holding a *ponsu* is a special event in which all the surrounding villages take part. The poison, collected from the *neku*-lian (*Lonchocarpus sp.*) or the *bumbi*-root (*Thephrosia toxicania syn.*) is dropped into the water in a dammed-up part of the river and when the doped fish rise to the surface the fishing starts. Most of the catch is barbecued.

2 Income from trade and services

From the above it is clear that the Djuka, if he were to depend entirely on what his own territory yields by way of provision, would eke out a scanty livelihood. Even the supply of primary necessities is insufficient. Consequently the Djukas have always had to rely on their contact with the coastal area to procure additional provisions. As a result of this the population, especially the male part of it, was mobile; and money – for making the supplementary purchases – has always played a role. The part played by money *within* the Djuka society is small, but not negligible. If provision grounds produce more than is needed for the owner's family, the surplus is sold. When the oracle, village priests, funeral priests, *obiamans* or mediums are consulted, payment is made partly in kind (with goods that have to be imported: *tafia*, beer, cloth), partly in food, partly in money. If there is no husband to help and others have to be asked to clear a provision ground, make a dug-out or build a hut, their services must be paid for. Hunters sell the spoils of the chase. A man who takes one or more wives has to supply her, in addition to things he can provide personally like a house, provision ground, a dug-out, hand-carved wooden utensils, with objects costing money: pots and pans, cloth and trinkets.

At the end of the nineteenth century the possibilities of freight-carrying on the Marowijne and Lawa opened up, and have, ever since, been busily exploited. Since about 1870 gold-mining was developed between the Lawa and the Tapanahoni; concessions were granted by both the Dutch and the French authorities to companies as well as to private gold-seekers. All these were dependent on river transport by dug-out, and the only people capable of manoeuvring a boat through the dangerous rapids and rocky stretches were the Bush Negroes. Besides gold-seekers, balata-gatherers also made use of these cargo-carriers. During the time that gold was still found in sufficient quantities (up to about 1910), these services brought regular and quite considerable returns. When the gold became depleted, river transport dwindled and difficulties arose in connection with prices and conditions of payment, sometimes leading to strikes.

Not until after the second world war did the practice of hiring one's services as – unskilled – paid labourer develop as a result of the opening up of the interior as well as the increased opportunities of employment in the city and in the coastal districts.[32]

NOTES

[1] De Groot, 1963.
[2] These clans or *los* grew out of the villages where groups who felt drawn to one another came together. Probably *lo* is an African word. In Ibo and Yoruba dialects it means house, village, agglomeration; in Ewe: to join together (G. Lindblom, 1924, pp. 19, 20).
[3] Part of the Djuka tribe later on emigrated to the area of the Cottica and Commewijne Rivers (De Groot, 1964), while a small number settled along the Sara Creek.
[4] Van Lier believes, mistakenly, that Bijman was the first Paramount Chief known to and installed by the Government (1919, p. 39).
[5] De Groot, 1963.
[6] Note for the Governor (12 September 1948) by the official land-surveyor A. Currie, temporarily at the Governor's disposal preparatory to provisions of General Administration.
[7] Thoden van Velzen, 1966, pp. 301-318.
[8] *Granfiskari* is derived from 'Grand Fiscal', a judicial function in the administration of Surinam before 1863.
[9] *Bastia* or *Bastiaan* was the name given to an overseer of the slaves.
[10] Thoden van Velzen, 1966, p. 69.
[11] Thoden van Velzen, 1966, p. 69.
[12] Köbben , 1966, p. 25.

[13] Köbben, 1966, p. 27: "Djuka law is less perfect than western law and the order it creates is a precarious order... But in this society law *can* be imperfect because the groups are small and the social structure is simple."

[14] Thoden van Velzen, 1966.

[15] Thoden van Velzen, 1966, p. 81.

[16] This means the disturbance of relations between different people or between a person and supernatural forces due to negligence, reckless or evil behaviour, which may evoke supernatural punishment (Thoden van Velzen, 1966, p. 98).

[17] The reasons mentioned are derived from Thoden van Velzen (1966, p. 146 et seq.) who gives the diagnosis of 204 cases with the percentages they represent, viz. respectively 49, 18, 16 and 7%.

[18] That the Gran Gadu of the Djukas also played an important role with the Saramaccaners, among others, is made clear by Junker (1925, p. 156).

[19] Thoden van Velzen found 42%, Köbben (along the Cottica) at least 20%.

[20] A woman can also be a *wisiman*, just as the word 'witch' is applied to both men and women.

[21] This is according to Thoden van Velzen (1966, p. 11). According to Van Lier, 1919, p. 180, sacrifices are never offered to him.

[22] The god is furthermore 'present' in a bundle on the Cottica and in another on the Sara Creek. He can also be consulted in those places.

[23] Köbben, 1967, p. 19.

[24] Van Lier (1919, p. 38) believes that there are seven *los*; he changes this in a lecture (undated, but probably delivered after 1930) on: How a Djuka dies and is buried.

[25] Thoden van Velzen, 1966, p. 32.

[26] De Groot, 1963, pp. 52-55.

[27] Thoden van Velzen, 1966, p. 9.

[28] Thoden van Velzen, 1966, p. 34.

[29] Thoden van Velzen describes the concept 'foreigner' as follows on p. 26: "The inhabitants of the coastal plain of Surinam are called *Bakaa* (*bakra*) by the Djukas. In earlier times this term was applied only to whites, nowadays the Bush Negroes also use it for other population groups on the coastal plain. *Bakaa* is a cultural concept; it can be translated as 'foreigner' because it has the emotional association of being uninitiated in the way of life and religion of the Bush Negroes". J.G. Spalburg (1899, op. 37) says that "by whites or *bakra* the Aucaners actually mean all civilized people, no matter how dark-complexioned, and especially those who can read and write".

[30] De Groot, 1963, pp. 31-39.

[31] Geyskes, 1954, p. 61.

[32] The data contained in § 3g are derived from:
Enc. van Nederlands-West-Indië, 1917
Suriname Studie Syndicaat, 1919
Stahel, 1933, p. 158, et seq.
Geyskes, 1954, p. 61 et seq.
Geyskes 1955, p. 135 et seq.
Bakker, 1955.
Nationaal Ontwikkelingsplan (National Development Project), 1965, Part II, p. 458
Van der Kuyp, 1962, p. 205 et seq.

CHAPTER III

THE COLONIAL ADMINISTRATION

§ 1 THE DUTCH GOVERNMENT

The periode of Surinam prosperity lasted, with brief lapses, from its conquest in 1667 up to 1773.

This prosperity carried with it: increase in the number of plantations, sufficient import of slaves and investment of profits in the mother country. A combination of factors caused a gradual deterioration of the colony after 1773: the growing absenteeism of plantation owners, the raising of exorbitant loans (leading to a crisis on the Amsterdam exchange), the guerila war of the runaway slaves which cost large sums of money, the liquidation of the West Indian Company in 1795, one of the results of which was the dwindling import of African hands; the French Revolution and the Napoleonic wars. The changed European attitude towards the slave trade first resulted in its prohibition and later on in the abolition of slavery. This led to further undermining of the Surinam plantation system. The shortage of hands could not be compensated speedily and sufficiently by the immigration of labourers. The Dutch government took measures to reanimate the colony, e.g. by the repeated introduction of new administrative systems (1816, 1828, 1832, 1865 and 1901).

However, as J. A. Polak remarked in his article on administrative schemes in the *Encyclopedie van Nederlandsch West-Indië* (1917, p. 127): "the best administrative scheme is incapable of improving a country's economical situation".

The mother country was obliged to grant subsidies and to continue doing so to an increasing degree.

The following brief statement[1] gives the amounts after the governmental regulations of 1865 came into force:

1867-1870	average per annum Fls.				350,000
1871-1880	,,	,,	,,	,,	356,000
1881-1890	,,	,,	,,	,,	106,000
1891-1900	,,	,,	,,	,,	160,000
1901-1910	,,	,,	,,	,,	207,000
1911-1920	,,	,,	,,	,,	1,373,000
1921-1930	,,	,,	,,	,,	3,660,000
1931-1940	,,	,,	,,	,,	2,869,000

This annual blood-letting caused considerable discomfort to the Dutch government and constant efforts were made to improve Surinam's economic position and financial independence as well as to curtail the expenses of the mother country: two incompatible aims which gave rise to a series of new and inexpedient plans, or to sensible plans which demanded financial sacrifice and were not carried out.

The Idenburg plan (1908) is an example of the former: it envisaged an annual saving on the Surinam budget of Fls. 30,000, with the understanding that:

a. the colony was to meet the costs of administration and other direct expenses from its own resources;

b. the costs of economic development would, for the time being, be paid by the mother country but Surinam would gradually take over the responsibility;

c. the costs of special undertakings would be met with short-time loans.[2]

This plan was drawn up at the prompting of the Socialist member of the Second Chamber, H. van Kol, and was named after the Minister of Colonies, A.W.F. Idenburg (1902-1905).

In 1900, when the budget was under discussion, the position of Surinam was described as 'not unfavourable' in the Preliminary Report of the Second Chamber. Following this up, Van Kol[3] found that the time had arrived to start decreasing the subsidy, arguing that "subsidy serves as a pretext for enforcing reactionary measures and depriving the colony of a large part of its autonomy."[4] The gradual decrease of subsidy was worked out in the Idenburg plan. In spite of the retrenchment in expenditure (even before the plan came officially into action in 1908) the annual subsidies rose continually and in 1908 the same Van Kol[5] proposed that the colony should be told: "You will get a subsidy for another ten years, and after that nothing more." In 1914[6] Van Kol proposed taking over Surinam's existing debts and letting the colony manage its own domestic affairs after that, without further support. These proposals were not accepted.

Meanwhile more and more objections were being raised to the drastic application of the Idenburg plan by the Government. In 1916 Van Kol also joined in the chorus of protest, despite the fact that he was the progenitor of the plan, as he put it. "But the way they are now carrying out the Idenburg plan I originally defended, makes me feel like a white father who is admitted to the lying-in room and is there confronted with a Negro baby"[7].

Governor van Asbeck (1911-1916) handed in his resignation and declared that he was doing it "because of the demand for severe application of the Idenburg plan under present circumstances."[8]

The Minister of Colonies, Pleyte (1913-1918), stated that the mother country would spend more on the colony, but that he wished to adhere to the Idenburg plan, "even if less rigorously than during the past years." During a discussion of the budget for 1918 in the Second Chamber, however, a motion to abolish the Idenburg plan was passed.[9]

Although H. van Kol had initially been a supporter of the plan to pursue economy for the above reasons, he was nevertheless one of the most active advocates on behalf of Surinam. He was regarded as an adherent of the 'ethical period'[10] following upon the period of 'liberalism' which dominated colonial politics from about 1870 to 1900.[11] Van Kol's many pleas for deeper understanding and knowledge of the colony and the improvement of social and economic care indicate this, even though these pleas gave no direct results.

The two following plans, briefly discussed here, point to the growing 'ethical' sense of colonial responsibility which the government was not able to keep pace with:

1. The plan of the so-called 'Bos Welfare Commission'. On the instructions of the Minister of Colonies this commission was appointed in 1911 under the leadership of Dr. D. Bos, a member of the Second Chamber. Its aim was to investigate "the economic and financial situation of the colony of Surinam" and to give advice as to the means of improving this situation. The commission's conclusions were not pessimistic and their recommendations for the improvement of education (technical instruction), infrastructure (road-builing), soil-research and the increase of labour productivity by means of higher wages and better social services pointed the way to a genuine advance. In order to carry out the plan the Dutch government would, however, have to invest large sums of money. This they dared not do. They waited for private invest-

ment but it did not materialize: "all eyes were turned toward the East."[12]

2. The plan of the 'Surinam Study Syndicate' of 1919. This was not a government commission but was set up in 1916 by the newly appointed Governor G.J. Staal (former Secretary General of the Minister of Colonies) and financed by members of the Syndicate, amongst others the large East-Indian plantation associations. Its leader was J.S.C. Kasteleyn. They arrived at approximately the same conclusions and made similar recommendations as the Bos Commission. The Study Syndicate also hoped to make Surinam in the long run financially independent of the mother country. Since it was a private undertaking this commission could afford to be more critical. Thus they believed that "such a defective economic policy is evidently being followed with regard to Surinam that there can never be any prospect of a rapid economic development of the colony."[13] And "Just as the raising of children does not consist in the prevention of their death by starvation... one cannot expect a colony to be independent as long as the help it received from the mother country amounted merely to the provision of what is indispensable for the immediate future and no opportunity has been created for the development of its natural resources."[14]

In spite of this criticism and that of a number of members of the First and Second Chambers, the various ministers and their adherents attributed the failure of many administrative and financial measures to the residents of the colony. In 1915 the acting Minister of Colonies, Rambonnet, complained: "During the past fifty years we have spent Fls. 32,000,000 on Surinam and we have not advanced an inch" and he pointed out the 'abuse' of "allowing a society in which a general lack of grit and energy prevails to dispose of the money of taxpayers in the home country."[15]

Even someone like Van Kol did not doubt that the population was lazy and lethargic. He blamed it, however, on the shortcomings of the Government. When the budget for 1914 came up for discussion he expressed the view that "if there were more development, more comfort also in Paramaribo, better homes, better drinking-water, etc., the people would have more needs and would have, and want, to work in order to satisfy them. Thus an inclination to work would be furthered. The slackness and lack of industry is part and parcel of their poor physical condition and in this matter the government has not fulfilled its task".[16]

The difference between the arguments used by the progressive Van Kol and those used by the conservative minister is clear, although both of them reached the conclusion that subsidizing was to be condemned. It also shows up the ambivalent attitude of Van Kol who "stood with one leg in the social-democratic and with the other leg in the liberal-democratic-ethical current."[17]

§ 2 THE GOVERNOR

The governmental regulations of 1865 (valid until 1936) decreed that Surinam would be allowed to run its own affairs. These were entrusted to its own legislative organ, namely the Governor together with the Colonial States. The Governor was the representative of the Crown.

The legislative task carried with it that the Governor and Colonial States could issue 'colonial ordinances'. The Dutch government reserved the right to pass laws and royal resolutions. For that matter, colonial ordinances had to be finally approved by the Dutch government, while (this was decreed in 1901) the legislative power could be further curtailed by the Government by means of ordinances issued from the mother country in the form of royal resolutions.

The Governor was assisted in his legislative task by the Colonial States and the Administrative Council, the latter acting only in an advisory capacity. The Colonial States possessed the right of initiative, petition and interpellation. For the rest the Governor was not responsible to the Colonial States but only to the Crown, also as regards his administrative function.

The Governor was further assisted in his task of administration by the Governor's Cabinet, headed by the Government Secretary, the governmental clerk, the various departments (analogous to ministries) and administrative departments.

The governmental regulations of 1865 also determined financial matters. Surinam was granted the right to draw up its own colonial budget, even though it had to be submitted 'for approval by His Majesty'. The Governor's salary and travelling allowance, as well as the expenses of the army and the navy, were not included in the domestic budget.

The Governor tabled the annual budget by presenting it to the Colonial States in the form of 'colonial ordinance' on the first Tuesday of March. The budget had to be finalized before the second Tuesday in May. In principle the Crown could then sanction the budgets (with amendments). In principle, for if the expenditure exceeded the colony's means, other rules were applied. And this was *always* the case. Invariably a contribution from the imperial treasury was required by way of supplement. As a result the Surinam budget was in the end settled legally by the Dutch government.

From the above it is clear that the position of a Governor in Surinam was no easy one. His function entailed a double loyalty: he represented the Dutch Colonial Rule and was at the same time responsible for the welfare of Surinam. While, on the one hand, he had to see that Surinam was financially as independent as possible of the mother country, he was obliged, on the other hand, to guard the land against financial ruin by constantly applying for new subsidies. Naturally the relationship between Governor and population was frequently strained. Many governors arrived in Surinam full of zest and with many plans; but after a while they were forced to admit that they could achieve very little with the means put at their disposal and most of them returned disappointed to the home country. "Each newly appointed Governor raised fresh hopes in the people's hearts which were bound to be disillusioned."[18]

A great deal also depended on the Governor's personality, especially in such a small community as this. His position as exponent of the colonial rule implied a certain paternalism, an adherence to hierarchical patterns, to power and prestige. The way in which he asserted his authority, the advisers with whom he surrounded himself, the policy of appointment which he adopted (higher officials were appointed by him) and, generally speaking, the measure of loyalty he displayed towards this territory entrusted to him were of great importance in gaining the people's goodwill and cooperation.

G.J. Staal, who was Governor from November 1916 to December 1920, had studied the problems of Surinam, also as Secretary General to the Minister of Colonies, and it was he who gave the impulse to the creation of the Surinam Study Syndicate. He was a follower of the 'ethical direction' and a kindred spirit of H. van Kol. He, too, went to Surinam 'full of plans' and 'eager for action', but he could not do much more than his predecessors. Moreover, as a result of the first world war the position was worse than ever. Although during his regime there were also conflicts between Colonial States and the colonial rule, he succeeded in preserving fairly good relations with the Surinam population. Staal regretted the fact that the advice of the Welfare Commission and of the Study Syndicate was ignored by the Dutch government and wrote after his return to the Netherlands: "Surinam is still waiting. Waiting for Dutch capital, knowledge, energy. Surinam is waiting for the Dutch *national action*. National: not on account of the investment of the Dutch guilder but on account of the investment of the Dutch heart in Dutch Guyana."[19]

Baron van Heemstra, Staal's successor (May 1921 - September 1928) was a completely different personality. He felt, more than Staal, frustrated in his administrative opportunities by the interference of the Dutch authorities and he did not hesitate to voice his annoyance. He protested that the independence which had, after all, been envisaged in the Governmental Regulations of 1865, was being 'strangled by the Supremacy of the Crown'[19] and that 'all efforts to advance' were being impeded. To prove that he was not alone in this view he declared that also ex-governors "have personally depicted the often untenable aspects of the above mentioned relationship"[20] in conversations with him.

Like Staal, Van Heemstra tried (while on leave in the Netherlands) to interest private persons in capital investment in Surinam. He also came to the conclusion that a greater interest was taken in the East than the West Indies and that "the prejudice against Surinam is still such that there is a general lack of courage to undertake anything new there."[21]

Governor van Heemstra was violently attacked on his policy of appointment during the final year of his administration, although he "had shown during the first years...a remarkable willingness to appoint residents of Surinam in responsible positions."[22] He was accused of 'nepotism' because he appointed someone to the much sought after post of District Commissioner who was regarded as incompetent, but who 'was married to someone from the Governor's close circle.'

§ 3 THE COLONIAL STATES

The institution of the Colonial States, a body representative of the people with certain legislative and administrative self-governing powers, reflected the spirit of the Governmental Regulations of 1865. After the abolition of slavery the aim was "to make the ex-slaves realize that they would in fact receive the same rights as their former masters. And the slaves of yesterday would become eligible tomorrow as representatives of the people if they complied with certain generally required property qualifications".[23]

In spite of these ambitious principles held by the drafters of the Governmental Regulations, in practice a good deal was lost of the envisaged rights of self-determination.

The Colonial States consisted of a minimum of thirteen members (one member to two hundred voters), four of whom were elected by the Governor himself up to 1901. The members served for six years, every second year one-third of them vacated office but were immediately re-eligible. Passive (and active) suffrage depended on requirements of citizenship, age (25 years) and a census of Fls. 40 in direct taxes.

The members, who exercised their administrative function without emolument, formed a mixed company of white and slightly coloured notables picked from the Surinam community. Among them were planters, jurists, teachers, doctors, journalists.

In their legislative capacity the Colonial States considered the colonial laws and ordinances submitted by the Governor. They could approve or reject these and they had the right of amendment and also of initiative, petition and interpellation.

An approved ordinance could be proclaimed by the Governor; if he had objections, he could defer its adoption. Moreover, 'the King' had to determine whether the ordinance was not contrary to the law or to a royal resolution.

According to the amendments introduced into the Governmental Resolutions in 1901, as has been mentioned, a law which could be proclaimed by colonial ordination could also be made by royal decree. It is obvious that this entailed a further regression of self-determination and that the threatened or actual interference by the mother country in the legislative activities of the Colonial States did not improve the relationship between the members and the administrators.

The definite drafting of the Surinam budget by the mother country entailed an intensive interest in the various items, in other words an endeavour to economize.

A "fine example of the economy drive was the removal from the 1915 budget of an item providing for a third porter in the detective department; however, this was found to be an exaggerated measure and the item was restored."[24]

In 1926 ex-Governor Staal wrote: "Undoubtedly the present condition which has been dragging on for so long is unsatisfactory and discouraging: every year Governor and States are earnestly occupied with a budget which they know will not balance and in the end will have to be tackled again and independently by the Minister and the States General. And since there is a general shortage it is all reduced to a paltry niggling, a wrangling about a few hundred guilders which one member wants to include and another to reject. This causes resentment and engenders ill-feeling."[26]

The way in which the Government constantly meddled with the budget drafted by the members of the Colonial States was a source of irritation and conflict: "a tussle... between the Representatives of Surinam and those of the Netherlands."[25]

There were continual complaints back and forth. The minutes of the Colonial States as well as the First and Second Chamber contain many examples of it, as has been mentioned under the previous section-heading, and the position of the Governor was complicated by it.

All the same, the colonial administrators who made a study of the work of the Colonial States were profuse in their praise. "Whoever has examined their achievements of the past quarter-of-a-century", H. van Kol declared, "will not dare to speak slightingly about their activities, which are often criticized most sharply by those Chamber Members who have the least or no knowledge whatsoever of it. The Minutes of the Colonial States are read (this is a generous estimate) by hardly three out of the hundred and fifty members of the States General! Ministers Rochussen and Van Goldstein... praised the excellent spirit in which their deliberations were conducted. The best governors of Surinam have no complaints at all about the quality and cooperation of the Colonial States."[26]

§ 4 RENEWED INTEREST IN THE BUSH NEGROES

The political policy of the 'ethical' period was aimed at the economic and social advancement of the colonial population. Education, development, was one of the means by which it was hoped to realize this aim; improvement of medical services, agricultural methods and the infrastructure (carrying out of public works) were others. It was in keeping with this policy that the entire population, including isolated groups of a colony should share in and contribute to the expected social and economic progress. In order to gain their cooperation these groups should be freed from isolation. With this in mind it was necessary to acquaint them with the society in whose service they were going to bring their man-power into action.

It is no wonder therefore that, in view of these ideas, attention in Surinam was focussed on the isolated group of Bush Negroes. They were regarded as a 'disturbing' element; as a group they were of no productive value for the colony, they lived according to their own political and religious views, paid no taxes, evaded administrative jurisdiction, in a word, one had no hold on them. All this should be changed, also for the sake of their own benefit.[27]

When the attempt of the Protestant Mission Church to educate and convert the Bush Negroes of the Tapanahoni came to an end in 1901, the Government's annual subsidy of Fls. 300 for each inland mission school was also discontinued. The Bush Negroes were given all the blame for the failure. When the Surinam budget for 1904 came up for discussion in the mother country, H. van Kol expressed the opinion that 'it was time they felt the bridle from time to time' and that 'their audacity should be checked'. He believed that the missionaries should double their efforts to convert – in other words subdue – the Bush Negroes. When the budget for 1908 was tabled, Van Kol voiced a different view: he believed that the Bush Negroes should be protected and that their state of health should be improved. In 1917 the question of the Bush Negroes was raised again: "the Colonial administration should do their best to draw them into closer relationship with the state. It would then also be able to restrain the abuse of strong drink by these people."[28]

This last-mentioned case did not bother the Surinam government overmuch. But one of the things it hoped to achieve was that the Bush Negroes would, thanks to their persuasion, no longer walk about 'naked' through the streets of the city.

In 1917 the colonial administration began to pay active attention to the problem of how the Bush Negroes (and Indians) could be educated to become 'useful members of the community'. The question was raised in the Colonial States by the Investigation Committee in the Preliminary Report drawn up for the draft budget for 1918.[29]

Under the heading 'Bush Negroes and Indians' the Committee stated that some of their members would like to know what measures were being taken by the Administration for the promotion of education and civilization among this group. They regretted the fact that the term 'Bush Negroes' should still be valid in Surinam while they believed that "in North America and the British West Indies the savage tribes had become civilized as a result of effective social enactments". (The Committee overlooked the fact that in British Guinea the Bush Negroes had been almost completely exterminated after a rising in 1763.)[30] They thought it was undesirable that the Dutch Authority had so little influence on the Bush Negro society and that one could speak of 'a state within a state'. Up till now the Government had distributed 'salaries and gifts' without the visible result of 'much actual social effect'.

A far better way of pointing out to the Bush Negroes and Indians that they formed part of the colony would be, they thought, to make them pay taxes. Especially the Bush Negroes, who earned a good deal with the transport of goods and passengers along the rivers, would be eligible for this.

Governor Staal declared in his Memorandum of Reply[31] that the education and civilization of the Bush Negroes had for many years been in the hands of the Catholic and Protestant missionaries. He, too, believed, however, that the Bush Negroes and Indians should be brought into closer contact with the social and administrative life of the colony, but was sure that this would demand much time. He did not respond to the suggestion of taxation, but agreed that the donation of allowances and gifts was not a good method of instilling a greater sense of responsibility into the above groups. There was already a considerable decrease in the number of gifts sent, but he did not think the time had come to stop them altogether.

During the following year, 1918-1919, Governor Staal was engaged in investigating the means of bringing stricter administrative supervision to bear on the Bush Negroes and Indians and of promoting their development. In those places where education had been taken in hand by mission endeavour an official could be placed with the group in question. In the case of the other groups he thought the best solution would be to appoint an administrative official with special instructions to give simple secular education as well as some agricultural guidance.

During the discussion of the budget for 1920 the Governor suggested in his Explanatory Memorandum[32] that such a plan should be carried out among one of the Bush Negro groups, the Djukas along the Tapanahoni. "The official's task was difficult to define clearly as yet" the Governor said in his speech. "As representative of the Administration he will have to establish and maintain the contact between Bush Negroes and Administration; he will have to awaken and encourage the realization that the Bush Negroes, just as much as the other inhabitants of the colony who do not live in such a peculiar state of isolation, form part of the community and will in the long run have to adapt themselves to it; he will also have to act in an educational capacity, to help them with word and deed. The postholder – this is the title the undersigned would like to give him – will thus in the first place be the local administrative official, but also the educator. Therefore it is also the intention of the undersigned that the postholder should provide the children with some – naturally very elementary – teaching."

The reason why he gave preference to non-Christian education was that both attempts made by the Moravian Brothers to establish a school among Djukas had failed. Besides, he had been informed by the Moravian Brothers as well as the Catholic Mission that they did not wish, for the time being, to occupy themselves with this region.

To this the Investigation Committee replied that a large majority of their members had expressed agreement and appreciation in regard to the plan. At the same time they wished to point out to the Administration "that the proposed work should be looked upon as an experiment and that after a while it would depend on the experience gained and the results achieved whether the necessary expense items on the budget would be continued."[33]

The objections to the plan raised by two members of the Committee were grounded on the consideration that the spreading of civilization and education could not be entrusted to anyone else rather than mission workers. Finally the plan was adopted unanimously, after the Governor had repeated the assurance in his Memorandum of Reply[34] that, for the time being, neither Protestant nor Catholic missions wished to embark on any enterprise in the Tapanahoni, and that he, too, agreed to consider the entire undertaking an experiment. He did, however, add that one should not expect practical results after only a short period.

In this memorandum he went into the matter of taxing Bush Negroes and Indians. He said that he had considered raising a levy on every boatload transported by the Bush Negroes. But he did not think it wise to combine such a measure with the appointment of a postholder, since it might spoil the relationship between him and the Bush Negroes.[35]

Now that the suggestion to create a postholdership had been unanimously adopted, the next step was to determine what this would cost. In the preliminary budget for 1920 the cost was estimated at:

Allowance for a postholder among the Aucaners along the Upper Marowijne	Fls. 3000
Supplementary full travelling allowance for idem	Fls. 1000
Allowance for building and furnishing a dwelling	Fls. 1000

A note was added to say that the postholder was intended to leave for the interior as early as 1919, and that the expenses attendant on this would be covered by money from the item 'Contingencies' for the year 1919.

Although the article was approved without a division, the member of States, P. W. Hering[36], availed himself of the opportunity to set forth once more in detail his objections, already raised in the communication of the Commission of Report. "Nowhere in the world has the civilization of heathen tribes been achieved otherwise than through Christian Mission endeavour". He had agreed to the establishment of the postholdership only because the Catholic and Protestant missions had declared that they were not going to concern themselves with it for the present, but as leader of civilizing enterprise a postholder was not the appropriate person. The most he could hope to attain was an improved relationship between balata and gold industrialists on one hand and the Bush Negroes on the other, and a lessening of the latter's distrust towards the Dutch authorities.

He feared that, as an experiment, it would become an expensive affair. "For the first year Fls. 5000 and after that Fls. 4000 per annum. Thus, if the experiment lasts for three or four years, it will cost Fls. 20,000."

Another Colonial States member, J. R. Thomson, who wished to add his reasons for voting in favour of the postholdership, expressed his view as follows: "It is the duty of the Administration to promote the work of civilizing the Bush Negroes, with whom there has hitherto been no contact whatsoever. This task should have been taken on half-a-century ago. And the efforts of the present authorities will help to make useful citizens of the people who are now living in isolation... And the time will come when the Bush Negroes will no longer go about half naked or entirely in nature's garb."[37]

The acting Government Secretary, A. T. Oliviera, defending the proposal on behalf of the Governor, replied to Mr. Hering's objections. Among other statements he made was the remark that there were, in fact, examples of civilizing work outside the scope of mission work and that "for instance, great success has been achieved in civilizing and pacifying the inhabitants in various parts of the East Indies by officials of the Inland Administration and by officers temporarily charged with administrative duties. Undoubtedly the most outstanding example is Atjeh, where, for the present, the fanatically Mahommedan attitude of the population rules out any chance of their being influenced by Christian mission work, but where latterly splendid results have been achieved by the efforts of Administration and Army. This was possible because officers and officials had a sense of calling for their work in Atjeh."[38] He concluded with an appeal to Hering to set his objections aside, for "if this item, which aims at redeeming the first installment on the long-standing debt of honour to the Indians and Bush Negroes is accepted without a division, it would be a fine page in the parlementary history of Surinam". This wish of the Governor was, in fact, fulfilled.

§ 5 NOTES ON THE DESIGN OF AN 'EXPERIMENT'

The measures that were taken to promote the 'civilization of the Djukas' may be divided into aspects which could have a favourable and others which could have an unfavourable influence on the aimed-at result.

a. Favourable aspects were:
1. The decision to adopt the plan was taken unanimously.
2. By viewing the plan as an 'experiment' the administration was not bound by rigid rules in regard to length of time, financial arrangements and policy of execution. Only once a year, when the budget was being drawn up, the plan and the provisions it demanded would be assessed anew.
3. As to the status of the executive: as postholder he occupied a fairly independent administrative position. He was responsible only to the Governor (via District Commissioner and Government Secretary). He had a certain margin of freedom to do as he saw fit since his activities, too, were scrutinized only once a year.[39] Adequate provision was made for his personal financial position, so that he was ensured of the official status owing to a person in authority. He had been chosen for his capacities: his long-standing acquaintance with the Bush Negroes and his knowledge of their language and customs had been the determining factors.

b. Alongside of these positive aspects one can, however, observe a number of negative aspects which might impede the smooth functioning of the plan:
1. Despite the final general approval by the members of the Colonial States a number of them maintained their objections to the fact that the enterprise would cost too much and that it was not being left to Protestant or Catholic mission churches. At each annual budget debate these dissenting voices could be heard and could influence the decisions taken.
2. The mission churches had, it is true, declared that for the time being they would refrain from activities in the area to be developed, but a period of time had not been agreed on, nor had a promise been made that missionaries would abstain from every form of contact.
3. The fact that the enterprise had been labelled an experiment also implied that its continuation depended on its success or failure measured during one year, a short period for a development project. This entailed a threat to the continuity of the work.
4. The fact that financial provision was made once a year and that decisions on important proposals had to be tabled during budget debates could prevent the taking of short-term decisions.
5. Communications between Paramaribo and the Tapanahoni were poor. This fact could hamper speedy deliberations between executive and employer, especially in urgent cases.

6. The administration had an inadequate knowledge of the inland situation. This could result in wrong instructions and ineffective advice being given.
7. The postholder-official had two kinds of instructions to carry out:
   1° he had to bring the Djukas within the scope of administrative jurisdiction;
   2° he had to promote the development of the Djukas . Thus he had a two-fold duty. If measures calculated to facilitate one task should be detrimental to the other, this could result in conflict situations.
8. The employer (the Governor) and the executor (the postholder) took a double responsibility upon themselves. On the one hand they had to obtain the cooperation of the people's representatives (the Colonial States). That was primarily the Governor's task. On the other hand the cooperation of the group whose development was envisaged had to be gained, which was mainly the task of the postholder. If this cooperation were suspended, there could be more conflicts: between Governor and the States, between Governor and the postholder, between postholder and the States and between postholder and the Djukas.[40]
9. The aim of the colonial administration: to obtain cheap labour and raw materials while eliminating the self-government of a community inside the colony lay at the root of the development plan. The fact that this policy was dictated by self-interest was not likely to escape the Djukas either, and it was natural that they should oppose it.

NOTES

[1] Surinam National Development Plan, 1965, p. 18.
[2] Plante Febure, 1918, p. 59.
[3] Minutes of Second Chamber, 14 Nov. 1900, p. 305.
[4] Van Kol, 1915, p. 15.
[5] Minutes Second Chamber, 23 Nov. 1908, p. 638.
[6] Minutes First Chamber, 20 March 1914, p. 489.
[7] Minutes First Chamber, 1916, p. 316.
[8] Plante Febure, 1918, p. 48.
[9] Plante Febure, 1918, p. 49.
[10] Furnivall, 1956, pp. 288-289: "Liberals looked to freedom as a key to economic progress, and regarded economic progress as a *cause* of native welfare, leading *automatically* to political independence. Modern colonial theory regards economic progress as a *condition* of native welfare, and native welfare as a *condition* of political advancement, but recognizes the need

of state intervention to further economic progress. Liberals thought to promote welfare through freedom; the modern tendency is to promote welfare, even at the expense of freedom.

[11] Wertheim, 1964, p. 211.
[12] Surinam National Development Plan, 1965, p. 17.
[13] Surinam Study Syndicate, 1919, p. 5.
[14] Surinam Study Syndicate, 1919, p. 196.
[15] Plante Febure, 1918, p. 47.
[16] Minutes First Chamber, 20 March 1914, p. 486.
[17] Tichelman, 1967, p. 690.
[18] R.A.J. van Lier, 1949, p. 319. A number of conflicts between various governors and the inhabitants of Surinam are discussed more fully in this book. The appointment policy played a major role in this connection. "Unfair and arbitrary appointments were often made in Surinam", Van Lier wrote (p. 320) "and the 'children of the soil' usually came off second best".
[19] Staal, 1926, p. 209.
[20] Explanatory Memorandum Budget, 1924.
[21] R.A.J. van Lier, 1949, p. 213.
[22] R.A.J. van Lier, 1949, p. 331.
[23] Staal, 1926, pp. 28, 29.
[24] Plante Febure, 1918, p. 18.
[25] Staal, 1926, p. 195.
[26] Van Kol, 1919, p. 13 et seq.
[27] These ideas were also held for a while during the nineteenth century: from 1845-1863 an (unsuccessful) attempt was made to integrate them into the colonial system (De Groot, 1963).
[29] Plante Febure, 1918, pp. 18, 19.
[28] Minutes and Appendices of the Colonial States, 1917-1918, p. 14.
[30] Kesler, 1940, p. 267.
[31] Minutes and Appendices of the Colonial States, 1917-1918, p. 15.
[32] Minutes and Appendices of the Colonial States, 1918-1919, p. 6 et seq.
[33] Minutes and Appendices of the Colonial States, 1918-1919, p. 9.
[34] Minutes and Appendices of the Colonial States, 1918-1919, p. 13.
[35] Bush Negroes and Indians had, in any case, been obliged since 1918 to pay a tax on all worked articles of wood not destined for their own use (Quintus Bosz, 1954, p. 335).
[36] Hering, a pharmacist by profession, was and remained an opponent of the whole plan.
[37] A fact which caused concern in administrative circles as early as 1856 (De Groot, 1963, p. 72).
[38] It is quite plausible that the Government Secretary was thinking here of the sketches published in 1913 in the *Soerabajaasch Handelsblad* by 'Abraham Exodus', pseudonym of M.H. De Croo. These sketches were subsequently collected and published by Leiter-Nypels, Maastricht, under the title "Het land van-bij-ons-buiten, Herinneringen van een officier-gezaghebber in de Indische Buitengewesten "("The land of in-our-countryside, Memories of a governing officer in the Indian outlying provinces").
[39] Goodenough, 1963, p. 386, also believes that there should be "overall objectives and general strategy, but only in broad terms", furthermore that "the agent must be free to develop his plan from to day".
[40] Goodenough, 1963, pp. 429-440, refers to the conflict possibilities indicated in 7 and 8 (§ 5b) as problems presenting themselves in administrative relations in general and in development projects in particular.

CHAPTER IV

DESIGN OF A DEVELOPMENT PLAN, 1918-1919

§ 1 ELECTION AND APPOINTMENT OF A POSTHOLDER

During the session of the Colonial States on 7 May 1918, when the budget for 1919 was brought up for discussion, the member H. R. van Ommeren spoke with reference to Article 12 on Bush Negroes and Indians. He wondered 'what the administration intended doing for the civilization of these people' and spoke of a series of articles that had appeared in the journal *Suriname* (of which he was editor-in-chief) on the Bush Negroes of the Upper Marowijne, written by W. F. van Lier. The acting Government Secreatry, A. T. Oliviera, answered that the case of the Bush Negroes enjoyed the administration's attention, and that he had read the articles with much pleasure and appreciation.

No doubt Governor Staal had also read these articles in which Van Lier gave proof of sound knowledge of the group in question and had, moreover, ideas about the way in which the work should be planned and carried out. Probably it was not a coincidence that the articles appeared at a time when interest was beginning to awaken in the development of the Bush Negroes (see Chapter III § 4). To what extent Van Lier was the motivating force behind these plans cannot be traced today. However, it was natural that the Government Secretary gave order requesting van Lier to draw up a detailed plan for the development of the Djukas. This plan was submitted by Van Lier on 20 June 1918. Among other suggestions he made was the proposal that an official should be appointed who would settle among the Bush Negroes, called a postholder (analogous to that function during the years 1761-1863, see Chapter I § 4), with special instructions to encourage their development.

Referring to the above and further additional notes, Governor Staal stated on 7 May 1919 in his Explanatory Memorandum for the 1920 budget that he thought he had discovered the most suitable person for the postholdership in Van Lier, who was willing to take on this task. The members of the Colonial States declared that they were 'in full agreement' with the Governor's choice, as Van Lier "had shown that he was thoroughly acquainted with the manners and customs of the Aucaner tribe".

On 12 May 1919 Governor Staal appointed Willem Frederik van Lier by Government Resolution No. 1584 as postholder in the Upper Marowijne at an annual salary of Fls. 3000. It was also stipulated that he would be subordinate to the Government Secretary and that his correspondence with the latter would be conducted via the District Commissioner of Marowijne, that he would keep a daily record of his activities and submit a monthly report to the Government Secretary.

§ 2 THE POSTHOLDER WILLEM FREDERIK VAN LIER

a Biographical data

Willem Frederik van Lier was born on 18 September 1877. His grandfather, Isaac van Lier, came from a Jewish family in Utrecht. He left as a young man for Surinam and married a Jewish girl from the wealthy Gomperts family. They lost their fortune and Isaac van Lier, who had started as a planter, was appointed to a high official post at the Court of Justice. His son, Jacob van Lier, educated in the Netherlands, also became an official. He ranked immediately below the Financial Administrator (Head of the Department) and was also chief banker-bookkeeper of the immigration service. Jacob got married outside the Jewish community to a light-coloured Creole girl (Josephine van 't Velde), an unusual step at the time.

Willem Frederik was the third son of a family of eight children. He completed the Hendrikschool[1] (a higher-grade elementary school) and then started training as a pharmacist. After a full two years he had to discontinue this course for financial reasons because of his father's death. Although the latter had held a high official post, the small pension was not enough to pay for Van Lier's study, especially as his mother, two sisters and a number of dependent relatives (as often happened in Surinam) still had to be supported. The responsibility for these persons fell on the shoulders of Willem, who now entered the plantation business. He became supervisor, then manager of the cacao plantation Leliendal on

Willem Frederik van Lier, born 1877, died 1957. Postholder among the Djukas 1918-1926. Photograph taken at his appointment as postholder, in the official uniform.   (photograph: Eugen Klein, Paramaribo, 1918)

the Surinam River. Unfavourable circumstances also brought this enterprise to a premature end. Leliendal was one of the plantations that was badly afflicted by the so-called 'curl', a disease which 'petrifies' the fruit, so that the production figure in 1903 for 278 bales of 100 kg each fell in 1904 to 26, in 1905 to 44, and in 1906 to 41.[2] In 1907 production began to rise again, but Van Lier was now working as a supervisor and prospector for such companies as the *Balata Compagnie Suriname* and the *Compagnie des Mines d'Or de la Guyane Hollandaise*. This entailed making trips through the interior with a number of labourers and marking out, with the help of surveyor's maps, an area to be investigated and worked within the borders of a concession.

For the *Balata Compagnie* he supervised the activities of the bleeders (the extractors of the rubber-like exudate of the balata tree, *Mimusops globosa*), for the *Compagnie des Mines d'Or* he determined, by analyzing soil samples, whether gold should be looked for in certain areas, and also supervised the work of the labourers.

These journeys into the interior lasted up to thirty weeks in the case of balata gathering. Gold prospecting required a trip of three to six months through the jungle.

In the course of this work Van Lier navigated most of the Surinam rivers and many of the creeks (tributaries) and remained in close contact with his labourers (urban Creole Negroes, sometimes Negroes from British Guyana), with Indians and with Bush Negroes. As a result of a number of circumstances he became acquainted with the religion and way of life of the Djukas along the Marowijne and Tapanahoni rivers.

For transport on these rivers Van Lier and his labourers depended on the Djukas, the only people who could steer the big, heavily laden boats across the many difficult rapids and who also claimed a monopoly in this field. So he had a great deal to do with them from about 1906 to 1918. He was an acute observer and recorded what he heard and saw in the diary he kept during his travels. He had an excellent knowledge of the Djuka language and put questions about everything he wanted to know. From the amount of information he gained from them it is clear that the Djukas were well-disposed towards him and that they were less distrustful of him than of the whites in general.

In 1918 he became co-editor of the newspaper *Suriname*, a liberal paper appearing on Mondays and Thursdays, with H. van Ommeren as editor-in-chief. Van Lier, as well as Van Ommeren, were members of the Social Democratic Society – political parties did not exist. (Van Ommeren died in 1923, after which P. A. May took over his duties.)

In this paper Van Lier began on 5 February 1918 to publish a number of articles on the Bush Negroes of the Upper Marowijne, which were to lead to his appointment as postholder. During and after his postholdership he regularly continued writing in this and other papers and gave lectures to various societies (see Bibliography). From his fortieth to this forty-sixth year W. F. van Lier was postholder. When he was honourably discharged on 1 January 1924 he was put on half-pay during a period of two-and-a-half years, despite the fact that he had been promised, when he was appointed, that he would be provided with an 'adequate' position if the postholdership were to be abolished. Since 1 August 1925 he had earned an annual salary of Fls. 4800. After being kept on half-pay for two-and-a-half years he was offered a pension of Fls. 842 per annum.

He had to keep his wife (to whom he was not legally married), his daughter, an invalid sister and an elderly aunt. He lived like a person of position and means, as he had been accustomed to do since childhood and in order to meet all these demands he tried to increase his earnings in all sorts of ways. He took a temporary job again with the *Balata Compagnie Suriname* and at the end of 1927 was taken into service by the publishing firm *Erven H. van Ommeren*. Eventually he was re-admitted into government service[3] (10 November 1930) as chief supervisor of the Health Service at an annual salary of Fls. 2700, a comedown after his position as postholder. He gave lectures and wrote articles on the Bush Negroes and the Urban Creoles (see Bibliography), summarized the contents of silent films for cinema programmes (e.g. Anna Karenina) and acted as interpreter and expert when difficulties arose between the administration and the Bush Negroes.

Van Lier was a member of the Dutch Reformed Church and of the Freemason Lodge 'Concordia'[4] and of several other societies, e.g. for social work and the protection of animals, of which he was the founder. He resigned from the Health Service and was honourably discharged on 16 July 1946 at the age of sixty-nine. In addition to his postholder's pension of Fls. 842 he received an annual sum of Fls. 684 by way of 'permanent public relief'.

He died on 3 September 1957 at the age of almost eighty.

b Van Lier and the Surinam community

In 1921 Paramaribo had at least 40,000 inhabitants (a good 38% of the population of Surinam). Thus it was a small, richly varied society in which, next to social and economic position, race and colour played an important role and helped to determine a person's place in the community. Since early times the white inhabitants of European descent had enjoyed the highest esteem and occupied the best positions. "The nearer one approached this group in colour, the more prestige one enjoyed."[5] This meant that the dark Creoles belonged to the lower and lowest ranks.

The white Jewish colonists had gained an influential position during the second half of the nineteenth century, expecially as many gentile colonists left after the emancipation of the slaves in 1863. Round about 1910 their influence began to wane and that of the (lightly coloured) Creoles increased, also owing to better intellectual development.[6] More and more frequently the Jews went to Europe for the sake of their education and often they did not return.

From the above it is clear that the Van Lier family, with its white Jewish and lightly coloured members, enjoyed an honourable status, added to (and because of) which father and grandfather belonged socially to the upper citizen class.

In this small, closed society with its few outside contacts (once a month a mailboat arrived from the Netherlands) the people were constantly thrown into each other's company. This had its positive aspects: close friendship, mutual aid and neighbourly affection, as well as its negative side: jealousy, rancour, dissension. Various factions formed round the core of religious (Protestant or Catholic) denominations, newspapers representing divergent views and personalities engaged in power rivalry.

W.F. van Lier belonged to the Protestant, progressive group (the paper *Suriname*) in which, among others, his friend H. van Ommeren was an important personality.

As regards Van Lier's social position: as prospector (before he became postholder) and also as chief supervisor of the medical services later on, he belonged to a lower stratum of middle class society than his father, but he moved in the upper circles. This, combined to his personality, caused reactions in these circles.

Van Lier was a self-made man. He read a great deal, also French and English, had wide intellectual interests and a sound brain. In addition, he had an acute insight into people and did not keep his opinions – positive or negative – to himself: by nature he was vehement and emotional and he found it difficult to adopt a neutral attitude. His progressiveness and his humanitarian ideals, his optimism and his religious bent explain his personal attitude as regards, for instance, the development of the Bush Negroes. His intellectual interest in people stimulated him to make a study of their society. He was an excellent raconteur, his tales of experiences in the jungle and of the Bush Negroes aroused much interest and his articles on the Djukas during 1918 brought his name into the limelight. In Paramaribo the fact that these Bush Negroes had an own history and culture, with complicated social manifestations, aroused amazement and often incredulity. The Bush Negroes were simply regarded as runaway slaves (with no claim to any form of culture) who led a most primitive existence in the jungle.

Thus Van Lier's accounts met with disbelief and he was often described as a visionary or even a liar. This reaction was based partly on a continued dread of the formerly dangerous Bush Negroes and of their supernatural knowledge, so that one preferred to keep out of their way as much as possible, and partly on Van Lier's method of recounting facts which were true on the whole but on which city-dwellers could not check up and which reflected his own violent and emotional reaction to those facts, his own interpretations and predictions. The enthusiasm and especially the optimism colouring his attitude to the development plan met with scepticism. Most of the members of the Colonial States were in favour of this development plan but it received very little support from the general public. They thought the money given to Surinam by the Netherlands should be used for the 'development of Surinam', which meant the coastal area of the colony. Since the Netherlands in any case skimped on the budget for this territory, it was regarded as inexpedient to spend money on this group of people who were, in their eyes, of no interest whatsoever. Moreover, the fact that Van Lier was offered the postholdership aroused envy: as regards salary he was placed between the District Commissioner and the District Secretary. It was customary for the inhabitants of Surinam (in contrast to Europeans sent out from the mother country) to start on the lowest rung of officialdom after having taken a course for the training of minor officials. The Government's argument that this difficult and demanding task should be well paid and that, for reasons of prestige, the postholder should enjoy a high official status did not carry much conviction. And, as will be shown (Chapter VII § 3) even the 'enlightened spirits' who had taken trouble to bring the plan to fruition dropped the whole matter for political reasons when there were no immediate results forthcoming: public opinion was against it.

The lack of immediate success was, however, largely due to active opposition by antagonists and the resultant decline of administrative support for the plan and its executives. Both Catholic and Protestant missions were opposed to it. The leading figures had, it is true, undertaken not to meddle in the matter, but the missionaries ignored this promise, as was demonstrated by the activities of Father Morssink (Chapter IX § 3). Christian members of the Colonial States also continued to voice their objections to a non-Christian development.

Then there was a significant group of traders who objected to the prospects of the Bush Negroes learning to read and write and thus becoming capable of promoting their own interests. Their influence was particularly noticeable in the environment of Albina.

The Catholic newspaper *De Surinamer* and the conservative paper *De West* interpreted the view of the opponents to the development plan and brought their criticism to the attention of the public.

Finally there were still a number of important personal opponents of Van Lier who held a position of power enabling them to bring him into disrepute and which they did not fail to make use of. The immediate cause for this was certain conflicts arising between them and Van Lier. Nor was Van Lier a person to attempt a tactful solution of these conflicts. He was extremely proud and not prepared to bow to superiors when he was convinced that he was in the right. As will appear from the case-history, the opposition worked in two ways: the town-dwellers became more and more prejudiced against Van Lier's development plan and the Djukas' habitual distrust steadily increased.

This resistance against the postholder and his work had become so strong by the time he returned to Paramaribo in 1926 that it may offer an explanation of the fact that Van Heemstra, the then Governor, did not find it necessary to provide him with the adequate position he had been promised in case the 'experiment' should fail.

No wonder Van Lier regarded his career as having been ruined.

c Van Lier as amateur ethnographer

Through his intense interest in the Bush Negroes, especially the Djukas with whom he came into close contact during his months of exploring the interior, as well as his gift of acute observation and his ability to get them to talk, Van Lier learnt a great deal about their way of life. Bush Negro tribes attracted increased attention in governmental circles in 1917, and Van Lier chronicled his experiences, probably encouraged to do so by Van Ommeren. The paper *Suriname* published his account in a series of articles during 1918. It was followed with interest (as appears, too, from remarks in the Colonial States) and praised by the critics. Since that time until the end of his life Van Lier enjoyed a reputation among most of his contemporaries as an expert in Bush Negro affairs. His aid was regularly called in when difficult issues arose between the administration and Djukas.

In a talk which was subsequently published,[7] he started by explaining that he made no claims to being an 'ethnologist'. "You must not expect any scientific argumentation or theoretically based comparisons from me; what I have to offer is a faithful account of what I observed during nine years' association with the Bush Negroes and noticed during my contact with several Indian tribes, the explanations I received from them personally concerning the why and wherefore of things."

This faithful account of his observations and of the explanations by the Bush Negroes is what lends importance to the work of this amateur ethnographer even in present times. As a preparatory study and as a touchstone for modern investigation among the Djukas a knowledge of the data gathered by Van Lier is indispensable.

Although a number of Van Lier's publications, especially his *Aantekeningen*[8] (Notes) did indeed contain an account of what he had observed and learnt during his contact with the Djuka society and nothing more, this series of talks and the brochure in which they were collected were actually intended to offer more. Van Lier, who had submitted his first memorandum containing his views on the 'civilization' of the Djukas, proposed to make clear that this community was worth regarding with serious attention and was ready to be 'developed' and that it was a moral obligation to right the wrongs done to them in the past. He hoped "to evoke sympathy for this tribe and by doing so to promote the cause of their civilization". By 'civilizing' them Van Lier meant in the first instance leading them out of the night of their heathen beliefs into the Christian way of life. He wanted to arouse the sympathy of his compatriots by telling them about "their religious and political concepts, their social relationships amongst each other, their training and education, their judicial procedure, their practice of medicine, their arts and science and, last but not least, their ethics and poetry". He wanted to show, too, that even the Djukas were amenable to more advanced development and that their antipathy to the Christian faith was not general. In order to prove the former he recounted in his article on *Onderwijs*[9] (Education) the story of earlier efforts at founding a school, the way in which, and the reasons why, these met with opposition. To illustrate the second statement he cited in his article on *Kerstening* (Christianization) the case of a number of Djukas who were not averse to Christianity. Moreover, the fact that the Djukas themselves were extremely religious by nature, so Van Lier reasoned, made them more accessible to other religions.

By depicting in his brochure of 1919 the Djuka talking, narrating, occupied with religious ritual or administrative affairs, he added a lively element which is absent from the rather dull enumeration of ethnographic data in *Aantekeningen*.

From the preface to the collected newspaper articles it appears that Van Lier intended writing in due course an extensive and illustrated work on the Bush Negroes. He wanted to add to it the knowledge he would gain in his capacity as postholder.

Nothing came of this plan. During his office as postholder he published a number of articles in the *West-Indische Gids* on his experiences. He also kept notes of whatever new facts he acquired. But when the – for him – catastrophic news of the abolition of the postholdership was announced, he burnt these notes in a fit of despair.

Although he still wrote an article on the Bonnis after his discharge and gave one lecture, it was not until 1930 and 1931 that an article on the Djukas appeared again from his pen. After that he was silent until 1938. In 1936-1937 De Goeje appealed to Van Lier during a visit to Surinam to take another look at such notes as he still possessed and to supplement them with further recollections. With constant prompting by De Goeje, who wrote to him regularly from the Netherlands for more and more detailed data, the "Notes on the mental and communal life of the Djukas" was completed, edited by De Goeje and published in 1940.[10] In the given circumstances it is amazing with what accuracy and completeness Van Lier was able to recollect and reproduce his knowledge after fifteen to twenty years. After the appearance of the 'Notes' van Lier started publishing regularly in newspapers and journals and giving lectures (also in order to earn some money). From these it was clear that he knew a good deal, not only of the Djuka society, but also of other Bush Negro groups and of the urban and rural Creoles.

d Appreciation and criticism by contemporaries

Van Lier's series of articles in *Suriname* during 1918 made a favourable impression on the Government and members of the Colonial States who were at the time considering taking a more active hand in the affairs of the Bush Negroes. As is shown in § 4a, Van Lier's knowledge was a reason for his appointment to the postholdership.

Father Morssink reacted to the brochure in which these articles were published[11] in the Catholic newspaper *De Surinamer* (22 December 1918). Father Morssink, as a result of his mission work among the Bush Negroes, his special interest in ethnography and familiarity with the Bush Negro communities, fully agreed with the weekly *Oost en West* (No. 33, 1918) which held "that these studies are the best ever written about the Bush Negroes". He looked forward to the publication of the book promised by Van Lier in the preface. Morssink knew the prominent Djukas described in Van Lier's articles and recognized 'their every detail'. "What has been so divertingly described is not founded, as, alas, many writings on foreign countries are, on subjective invention, but on objective fact" Morssink wrote. That he disagreed entirely with the conception and the execution of the postholdership, however, is shown in Chapter IX § 3.

When the collected articles on *Kandu, Kina, Mula* appeared in 1943, Morssink expressed his appreciation of Van Lier's description of the first two concepts but thought that he had said too little on *Mula* (*De Surinamer*, 17 August 1943). Van Lier responded by publishing a more comprehensive article on *Mula* in the same paper on 18 September 1943.

Dr. H.D. Benjamins, editor of the *Encyclopedie van Nederlandsch West-Indië*, Inspector of Schools in Surinam and editor of the *West-Indische Gids* wrote in this journal in 1920 (pp. 163-172) a long, appreciative review of Van Lier's brochure of 1919. He regarded the chapter on Religion (pp. 71-85) as of particular importance, but "at the same time that which will require the most painstaking further study when Mr. van Lier takes up his new post. For I suspect that in these observations he has not quite escaped the danger of *hineininterpretieren*". Benjamins does not explain what he means by this. Perhaps he felt rather sceptical about Van Lier's opinion that many Djukas, by force of their religious nature and their willingness to be amenable to Christianity, could, through tact, be brought to accept the 'true faith'. Benjamins specially recommends the last chapter on Training and Education (pp. 85-102) to the attention of ethnologists and educationalists.

The forester J. Junker, employed along the Suriname river and sometimes charged with special directions by the administration to clear up knotty matters concerning the Bush Negroes, made a study during the twenties of the society of the Saramaccaner Bush Negroes. Doubt has been thrown on the worth of his articles on this subject published in the *West-Indische Gids*. A thorough (modern) investigation among the Saramaccaners might be able to reveal in how far his facts are correct. Father Morssink, also well acquainted with this Bush

Negro group, disagreed completely with Junker's views on politico-religious and social problems and said so in the *West-Indische Gids*.[12]

Junker found much to criticize in Van Lier's brochure *On the Bush Negroes in the Upper Marowijne*. In 1923[13] he wrote: "Therefore I cannot subscribe to Mr. Van Lier's opinion that, in view of their further development, the Aucaners are descended from a people that had already attained a higher degree of civilization in Africa."

Junker starts his investigation of the Saramaccaner with reference to Van Lier's brochure of 1918 on the Djukas. In 1924[14] he mentions that it has become clear to him from the chapter on religion that "a good deal of fantasy has crept in and that elsewhere in this booklet his observations on religion also contain positive statements which, I have found on close scrutiny, do not tally with the facts." Junker still believed at the time (1922)[15] that there was very little difference between the Djukas and the Saramaccaners. Later on he changes his mind on this point; in 1925[16] he announces his intention to discuss the religious manifestations of the Bush Negroes under two headings: those they have in common, and those in which they differ from each other. And in 1932[17] he says that "conditions among the largest tribes, the Aucaners and the Saramaccaners, reveal wide disparity".

Junker also found fault with the way in which Van Lier carried out his duties as postholder and expressed this criticism in his articles.

The *Aantekeningen* which appeared at the beginning of the second world war elicited little reaction. In 1942 the agriculturist, Professor G. Stahel, wrote in *De West* of 11 February that this publication was of especial importance to the administrative officials and should be made available for consultation in the offices of district and departmental affairs and in libraries.

e Van Lier's attitude to the Djukas

1 His attitude as colonial official

The postholder was given a two-fold task. This placed him in a double position with regard to the Djukas. At first (up to 1924) Van Lier recognized the advantages of this, since he would be able to profit from the natural prestige attached to his official position for the furthering of his development plan.

Just like his employers, Van Lier set store by authority and prestige: a colonial official represented the colonial government and had the status to exercise authority and inspire awe. Van Lier felt he was, and called himself, the Governor's deputy among the Bush Negroes in the jungle. A uniform was a necessary outward insignia of his position. He also held that the Djukas should show proper respect for him as an official and should carry out his instructions, which virtually derived from the Governor. Although this was Van Lier's firm conviction, he was not a person to exact obedience in an authoritarian manner. In fact he was more inclined to maintain or strenghten his 'power' and 'prestige' through understanding, mutual deliberation and persuasion. This was one of the factors causing his opponents to believe that he *had* no authority. His official attitude was also 'ethical' in the sense that he regarded the Djukas as potentially worthy fellow-citizens and believed that his administrative task had an educational aspect too, namely the duty to teach the Djukas that they formed part of the Surinam (colonial) nation, with all concomitant privileges and obligations.

Van Lier's attitude as colonial official, compared to that of his employers, could be described as follows:

The colonial administration aimed at an increase in the prosperity of Surinam in general and of the Djukas in particular. The home government expected that this would lead to a conversion of the financial liabilities into profits. The government in Paramaribo hoped that it would help to persuade the Djukas to assist actively in heightening the level of prosperity in the colony. The postholder hoped to increase the prosperity of the Djuka community with the positive side-effect that they would then contribute to the general prosperity. It is clear that these differences in attitude and especially Van Lier's more pronounced loyalty towards the Djukas contained possibilities of conflict.

2 His attitude as 'educator'

Van Lier had no trouble in accepting the Djukas as equal human beings. His long acquaintance with them, his knowledge of their language and their society gave him deep sympathy with and appreciation of them. He praised their high moral standards, their well-ordered tribal system, their feeling for religion and many other qualities. This attitude of 'cultural empathy'[18] was indispensable for gaining their confidence and cooperation. He knew how to handle them and to establish human contact in a way that suited their way of life and social customs.

Van Lier's attitude to the Djukas was not, however, one of unmixed appreciation. He found their religious practices pernicious and saw in their conversion to Christianity the only means of ridding them of their deplorable and reprehensible 'heathen' condition. Besides, Van Lier regarded western civilization as being inextricably bound up with Christianity. Hence his conviction that if one could come to accept the former, the latter would follow by itself ('through a backdoor'). This ambivalent attitude did not escape the Djukas, for "an agent's failure to accept his clients (even if this is only partial) cannot be concealed. He may protest to the contrary, but his actions will belie him".[19]

Van Lier had personal preferences in his dealings with individuals. With some he stood on a friendly footing, others irritated him. He was apt to regard his friends as exceptional Djukas and to ascribe unfavourable Djuka characteristics to his opponents, like suspiciousness, slyness, laziness, avarice.

He did not suffer from the qualms of conscience that sometimes bother anthropologists because, in Foster's words, "they really do not like the people they studied as well as they thought they should".[20]

While he was framing his plans Van Lier became convinced that the cultural pattern of the adult Djukas as a whole could no longer be altered. Consequently he would only attempt to bring some improvement into existing habits with regard to hygiene and agriculture. But he hoped to educate the young from the start in an atmosphere of western thinking.

Van Lier saw no necessity to offer the Djukas a chance of voicing their view of the chief needs and problems of their community and of indicating which of these they regarded as the most urgent and how they would like to have them solved. He was sure that he himself was the best judge in the matter and that western civilization was the panacea. On the other hand he thought it important to keep the Djukas fully informed about his plans and to continue explaining to them how he intended carrying these plans out and what results and benefits were likely to result from them. This was not only a calculated way of gaining their confidence and cooperation but also a form of courtesy. He knew, moreover, that the Djukas set great store by these formalities and that their neglect might lead to unpleasantness. Since Van Lier regarded his work among the Djukas as a calling and wished to devote his life to it, he was able to face the fact that he would be cut off from his own world and be absorbed into an alien culture. He did not foresee the possible danger of 'emotional isolation',[21] but "No matter how mature emotionally a field agent may be, as a human he has needs that his emotional well-being requires to be met... If he is alone in a strange social and cultural world, his needs, which life at home has met so well, become increasingly acute... In time they may come to hate the place and its people...".[21]

Difficulties inherent to his development scheme, as well as this feeling of isolation, could be relieved by regular periods of leave, not of long enough duration to break the essential continuity of his work.

§ 3 THE DEVELOPMENT PLAN

Van Lier complied with the Governor's request to draw up a detailed plan for the development of the Djukas by submitting a 'note' on 20 June 1918. This was supplemented by further notes on 2 May 1919 and 31 May 1919 (after his appointment on 12 May) and rounded off by a 'plan of work' which he submitted on 24 September 1919.

a The notes

Van Lier drew up the note of 20 June 1918 "in reply to the question as to what could be done to civilize the Bush Negroes along the Tapanahoni so that they would regard themselves as citizens of the Surinam community and help to shoulder their share of the social burdens. Also to point out what immediate advantage could be expected to result from the expenses connected with the plan."

He mentioned the most important means of educating the Bush Negroes to become useful members of the Surinam community: in the first place by providing schooling – but not on a Christian basis – and in the second place by encouraging and instructing them to cultivate agricultural products of commercial value and higher nutritional value (the latter to combat the wide-spread and acute shortage of food). He thought it would also be possible to persuade them that they 'should contribute to the general cost of maintaining the community' by paying taxes.

The annual costs would not, he claimed, exceed the sum of Fls. 4000 and the 'creation' of the function 'of some sort of postholder and diplomatic agent of the Paramaribo Administration' would in the long run even prove to be 'profitable' for the colonial coffers if the Djukas could be persuaded to pay taxes.[22]

1 Education

The plan could only succeed, he said in the above-named note, if the teaching was of a neutral, i.e. secular, character. Moreover he believed that "in view of the suspicious nature of this tribe, added to the negative results previously obtained by a Christian school in their midst, it is of crucial importance that the management of a new school be entrusted to someone who is familiar with their manners and customs and who already enjoys their confidence, or of whom one may safely assume that he is capable of gaining that knowledge and confidence within a short while. This person, however, will not have to be only a teacher, I could almost say, in the first place a teacher, but a sort of postholder and diplomatic agent of the Paramaribo Administration. He will constantly have to encourage and develop the idea of solidarity with the urban and other inhabitants of the colony, an idea which has already taken root in the Djuka mind. He will have to try and remove the prejudices against the customs of the civilized world by explaining its advantages to them. Above all *he should earnestly endeavour* to rid them of the fear that the *Bakras*[23] will sooner or later reduce them to slavery again.

The tuition, which will have to be done through the medium of Negro English[24] at first, will begin with READING, WRITING and ARITHMETIC. The Dutch language will not be introduced as a subject until later on. (This method was used in Gansee.[25]) Where the primary object of education is to enlarge the pupils' thought-world and conceptual scope, it goes without saying that what already exists should be used as a basis for further development. Therefore it seems to me undesirable to start teaching in the Dutch language... The school will have to be established in Puketi,[26] so that *Opo* as well as *Bilo* Negroes can benefit from the education.

The undersigned has often heard *Bilo* Negroes (especially the chiefs) complain of discrimination because twenty years ago a school was built in Drietabbetje, so that only the *Opo* Negroes could profit from the teaching."

He thought it was particularly important to visit the villages along the rivers, for "the different *los* will have to be visited from time to time in order to establish regular contact with various members of the tribe and to exhort the parents to send their children to school", and "to make propaganda for the school as well as for the work of civilization in general".

In a supplementary note of 2 May 1919 Van Lier suggested that the postholder should be granted two months to prepare himself for his task. During this time he could attend "primary school lessons in order to familiarize himself with the way in which children are taught in the preparatory classes". The period for preparation was granted, and, since he did not leave till the end of October 1919, he had five months for this purpose.

2 Agriculture and cattle-breeding

Van Lier gave attention to agricultural guidance in his note: "It will have an immediately favourable effect, however, that the people will be taught to make their work productive. Much could be expected from the cultivation of food products if it is tackled systematically. Especially bitter cassava and the preparation of *kwak*[27] connected with it will expand enormously." He also attached much importance to the renewal and development of the groundnut cultivation which the Bush Negroes had previously practised. "It is a well-known fact" he wrote in the same note "that, while at present almost all the groundnuts used in the colony have to be imported, up to a couple of years ago the import of groundnuts was negligible,[28] and the local needs were met by own production, which was entirely in the hands of the Bush Negroes. In these days of shortage of fats and poor shipping facilities the disadvantage of the fact that groundnuts are no longer being produced is becoming painfully obvious. Needless to say, it would be extremely advantageous if one could persuade the Bush Negroes to take up this culture again at which they used to be so skilful and which they practised with success."

He proposed sending 'someone on behalf of the Administration' to the Granman in order to convince him and his Bush Negro chiefs, 'perhaps even by means of many *Gran-krutus*' of the value of the plan. "And once he has received the promise and given the assurance, for his part, that the producers will not be left stranded with their stock, the success will be ensured, that is to say the Bush Negroes will keep their word."

In a note of 2 May 1919 to the Government Secretary Van Lier entered into the details of his plan for agricultural enlightenment. In consultation with the Department of Agriculture he wanted to ascertain which foodstuffs could be profitably cultivated with the least trouble. He thought it was essential to persuade the Bush Negroes to exchange *bergpadi* (rice grown on upland ground without irrigation) for *sawahpadi* (rice grown on marshy or irrigated soil) since *bergpadi* is less productive, requires a longer growing-season, and is moreover dependent on weather conditions. No wonder crop failure frequently resulted. "This is the main reason, according to my investigation, of the almost chronic food shortage" Van Lier wrote.

As regards the carrying out of these plans, he thought that one of the first measures would be to lay out one or more experimental fields in the Tapanahoni and plant them with selected seed, supplied by the Agricultural Department, of maize, sweet potatoes, *sawah* rice and groundnuts. He thought that the postholder should be granted the necessary funds for this purpose.

One of the ways in which Van Lier prepared himself for his task was to consult the Department of Agriculture "about the crops that could be cultivated profitably with the least effort". (J. J. Leys, Director of the Agricultural Department, also principal of Agricultural Education, mentioned in his advice of 21 May 1919 on Van Lier's plans that Van Lier had for some time followed his course for overseers and managers of plantations, and said that he did not doubt "that he would benefit from the suggestions made by me"). Besides Leys, Van Lier also consulted Dr. G. Stahel, likewise connected with the Agricultural Department, who supplied him with selected coffee and cacao plants as well as other planting material. Furthermore he consulted Dr. Back of the same department, who analysed the leguminous plant *dolichos lablab* to ascertain its nutritional value, which turned out to be more or less equivalent to that of the brown bean. Van Lier had come across the plant as a weed on the provision grounds of the Djukas and was planning to cultivate it.

Leys recommended that the postholder should lay out a demonstration field on his own grounds so as to show the Bush Negroes in which way and with which crops they could achieve the best results. He would also have to persuade them to maintain the cultivation of a piece of land once it had been tilled, for instance with staple products (Leys mentioned coffee, cacao, limes, oranges, coconuts) and to plant soil that had been exhausted by the cultivation of annual crops with valuable kinds of timber such as cedar and rosewood.

On 25 June 1919 Leys, after a talk with Van Lier on this subject, submitted a written report to the Government Secretary in which he once more emphasized the importance of a demonstration field about two hectares in size. He thought the postholder should have a special labourer at his disposal for this purpose and gave the cost of the demonstration field 'at a moderate estimate' at Fls. 600 per annum.

Leys went on to observe that Van Lier did not mention cattle-breeding, but in his opinion it would be commendable to consider it "not merely with a view to getting a milk supply, for children and patients at any rate, but also in order to obtain manure".

The proposal to grant another Fls. 600 per annum for agricultural purposes was rejected by the members of the Colonial States.[29] The States member Hering feared that the request would not be restricted to this Fls. 600. He had expected the postholder to teach the Bush Negroes to improve their agricultural methods. Granting an extra sum of money would, according to him, amount to 'supporting the Bush Negroes financially'.

Another States member, Huizinga, thought that agriculture as practised by the Bush Negroes was quite satisfactory, that they had plenty of meat and game and that, for the rest, they earned enough money with their transport services. "Since money is so badly needed for bringing about improvements in that part of the colony where the civilized section of the community lives" he did not favour "spending it on the promotion of agriculture among the Bush Negroes".

In his defence of the item of Fls. 600, a 'small amount', the Government Secretary, Oliviera, said: "When the difficult task of civilizing the Bush Negroes was entrusted to Mr. van Lier, a preliminary discussion was held with him in the course of which it was decided to start with simple, practical measures, the dispensing of medicine and the promotion of agriculture and stock-farming, so as to endeavour to exert some influence on this recalcitrant, suspicious people. First and foremost their suspicions should be allayed and the Djukas be made to realize that the postholder's presence among them will bring them material benefit. Thus the way should be prepared for education and the other spiritual advantages of civilization. We have to do with a primitive people who, owing to a number of adventitious circumstances, has been excluded, not only from regular association with the rest of the population, but also from the true natural life of a natural people. The main source of their livelihood is not agriculture or cattle-breeding, hunting or fishing, but freight-carrying across the rapids, with which the Aucaners earn a lot of money that is mostly spent, however, in the Chinese shops of Albina to buy, as well as other things, various agricultural and animal products at exorbitant prices that they could have produced for themselves with a little more effort and practical sense. Stock-farming hardly exists among them; they do go in for agriculture, but in such an utterly primitive, injudicious manner that there can be no question of the tribe providing in their own requirements. Repeatedly there have been complaints about want, yes, about famine among the Aucaners. However this may be, it is a fact that, should there be a decline in the main source of their livelihood – the river transport – as a result, for instance, of a set-back in the timber industry, or of a further development of air transport, the Djukas would be in an extremely unfavourable position. The promotion of agriculture and cattle-breeding should be the postholder's main objective during the first years as a precautionary measure against such (possibly imminent) hardships and also as a first step on the way to a higher level of civilization for the tribe. In order to achieve something in this direction, Mr. van Lier naturally requires sufficient planting material for the laying-out of a demonstration field and some livestock to start breeding on a small scale."

The Director of Agriculture, Leys, and the States member, Thomson, also pleaded that money should be granted for the purpose of agricultural guidance, but the item was struck from the budget with six votes to four. They did, however, grant him a sum of Fls. 300 to buy a fishnet (Fls. 75), a fishing-boat (Fls. 50), a dug-out (Fls. 100), ingredients for salting meat (Fls. 25), agricultural implements (Fls. 25) and flags (!) (Fls. 25). The resolution stated that further necessities would have to be paid out of the grant of Fls. 500 for equipment expenses (for instance, a uniform of Fls. 200 and furniture).

3 Medical aid

The note of 2 May 1919 also contained the proposal to give the Djukas medical aid (as part of the development plan) as well as schooling and agricultural guidance. In the same note Van Lier suggests that the postholder should follow a course in first-aid. This was accepted by the Administration and Van Lier took the course.

On 31 May there followed a new note by Van Lier on the way in which, according to him, medicine etc. should be supplied to the 'Aucaner Bush Negroes in the Upper Tapanahoni".[30] The plans put forward in this note, as well as the supplementary advice by the Inspector of Health whose opinion was asked, were accepted by the Administration. Arrangements were made for Van Lier to receive medicine from the Military Hospital and regulations were drawn up to stipulate the way in which the medicine should be paid for. In the above note Van Lier wrote:

"Its is a generally known fact that the Bush Negroes are very fond of medicine. Anyone who has visited the villages will have noticed it. The confidence I enjoy among the Aucaners and the Bonni Negroes is largely due to the fact that they could always procure medicine from me and that I was able to do some doctoring for them (extracting teeth, dressing wounds, etc.).

Obviously, as I am now leaving for the Tapanahoni to settle there for good, I have to be prepared to provide them with medicine etc. on a larger scale than formerly, so as to gradually counteract their faith in the *winti* and *lukumans*[31] (people who are supposed to practise medicine under influence of invisible forces) and the use of *obias* (medicine made from herbs with hocus-pocus). I feel convinced that in the process of civilization the Bush Negroes should as far as possible be cured from the attitude of '*Lanti sa pai*' (the Government will pay). I shall always strive to eradicate this concept which is firmly rooted in their minds. For this reason I regard it as positively undesirable to give medicine free of charge except to the destitute.

As the Bush Negroes pay absolutely no taxes it seems reasonable to me that those of them who are well-to-do should at least pay for the medicine that is supplied to the needy. I believe the most practical way to achieve this would be for the Postholder to receive medicine charged to his account from the Military Hospital, just as the District Surgeon does. The Postholder then sells to those who can pay the medicine they need at a raised price and these profits cover the price of medicine which will be supplied free."

Dr. Schenk, Director of Medical Services, to whom the notes of 20 June 1918 and 31 May 1919 were sent for approval, also reacted positively although somewhat sceptically: "Quite apart from the question whether it will be to the Bush Negroes' advantage to have their faith in *winti-* and *lukumans* and the use of *obias* undermined, and merely mentioning in passing that the European, too, does nothing except work under influence of 'invisible forces' and also uses medicines from herbs, even if without Hocus Pocus (the latter is not altogether unknown in European medical practice either), I believe that, since European medicine will help to open a door which may give the administrative official access to the Bush Negro society and increase his chances of success in proportion to his deeper penetration into that society, Mr. van Lier should be provided with a stock of medicine."

Furthermore Dr. Schenk remarked that he thought it would be better if Van Lier's function fell within the scope of a 'branch of the civil service' so that the medicine he obtained from the Military Hospital would be charged to the colonial account and he would not be personally responsible for the cost. Money received for medicine not dispensed free could be put back in the treasury. This advice from Dr. Schenk was accepted on 21 June 1919 by Government Resolution (No. 3523). It was decided that the stock of medicines "will be sold at a profit – to be fixed by him – to the not impoverished Bush Negroes, while this profit will compensate for the loss on medicine supplied free of charge to the indigent Bush Negroes, which will likewise be conducted by the Postholder" and "that the money received by him would be put into the coffers of the District Commissioner in Marowijne, who would send him the required medicine".

b The plan of work

1 Education

Van Lier submitted a plan of work on 24 September 1919 which contained the scheme he intended to follow in his work among the Djukas. The establishment of a school and the actual teaching would have to be preceded by a number of preparatory measures. First of all a suitable terrain would have to be found for his settlement. While this terrain was being prepared for habitation, Van Lier would visit the various villages and explain to the inhabitants the advantages of his coming, set forth his plans and do his best to gain their cooperation. He wanted to "make propaganda for a closer congregation of the different *los*, so that school and church would have a better chance of functioning in future". He thought it would not be possible to start teaching immediately, but that his initial efforts should be concentrated on the promotion of the material and physical welfare of the Bush Negroes. By this Van Lier meant giving agricultural guidance, medical aid and advice that would lead to a general improvement in the standard of living.

He hoped in that way to win the confidence of chiefs and elders to such an extent that they would surrender their children to his care and entrust their education to him. The following plan was what he had in mind:

"At my headquarters a boarding-school for Djuka children, both boys and girls, will be started.[32] The physical care of these children will be put in the hands of such old people as will be glad to come and live with me... Suppose I were to start with some fifteen children between the ages of seven and twelve years and with two old women and the same number of men, then these children and old people can make a start with planting food crops for themselves and for those who follow their example. In this way the children will be getting training in practical agriculture. The increased yield of the plot and the products of a pig- and chicken-farm will cover the expenses of meat, fish and fats. If things go well, this enterprise will expand by itself...

As soon as a favourable moment arrives, a start will be made with teaching, which will take place through the medium of Dutch. In an earlier note I expressed the opinion that Negro English should be the medium, explaining my reasons for this. At the time (7 June 1918) I had, however, not yet thought of a boarding-school. Now that a boarding-school is being considered, it is naturally of utmost importance to start at once with Dutch." The reason for this was that he would have the children wholly and constantly under his guidance in a boarding-school and believed that their development would be served best if they were isolated as thoroughly as possible from their own milieu.

Van Lier hoped that he would succeed in "teaching the present generation to work somewhat more productively and live more hygienically" but, he wrote, "for the actual work of civilization I pin my hopes to the young ones. A change in the habits and customs of the Djuka can only come about when a generation has grown up under the influence of civilization."

He realized that his plan of work was easier to put on paper than to carry into effect, and that he would have to overcome many difficulties. "But on the other hand it is a fact" he wrote "that it contains nothing that cannot be achieved with energy and persistance" and that the difficulties could all be overcome with "tact and patience". The complete earnestness of his resolve appears from the following remark in this same piece of writing: "Therefore I hope to remain active in this post for at least twenty years, so as to be able to pick the fruit of the labour which I shall pursue with all my heart and all the strength at my disposal."

Although the plan for a boarding-school was thus already in existence, the earlier, modest scheme was all that was aimed at for the time being. In the official appointment of 12 May 1919 extra money was granted for the building of a dwelling-house; no mention was made of a school-building. At the postholder's official installation by the Governor in the presence of Granman Amakti all that was said was that the postholder would have to advise and help the Djukas and to start teaching the children something. Later on they would get schools.

2 Agriculture and cattle-breeding

In the plan of work Van Lier set forth more fully what he intended doing in the matter of agricultural guidance and cattle-breeding.

In the choice of his terrain it should be kept in mind that the place must be suitable for farming and cattle-breeding and large enough to contain dwelling-house, camp, school and provision ground as well as demonstration field, while there should also be room for peasant-farmers who might in due course come to settle there.

The clearing and laying-out would be done by Djukas under guidance of Van Lier and a labourer he would take along. Apart from the example set to them on the demonstration field, he hoped to give them advice on the tilling of their own provision grounds, to supply them with selected seed, to point out to them the advantage of growing staple products and persuade them to adopt better farming methods for their own benefit (and ultimately for the productive output of the whole country). He would do his best to get them to lay out a new provision ground next to the old one instead of anywhere they liked, and to grow cacao, coffee, and coconut on the old one with selected planting material which he would provide. He would try to get groundnut cultivation started again and to improve the cultivation of rice. All of it, thus, in complete agreement with the advice given by the Agricultural Department.

He would also pay attention to stock-farming: first he would show the Djukas the advantages of breeding pigs and poultry, keeping goats and, eventually, cattle. He would start a pig- and chicken-farm on his land, also for the sake of the school-children's needs. It would take time and money before this had developed sufficiently to produce the necessities for himself and his disciples. Therefore he hoped for a subsidy from the Governor 'in due course'.[33]

3 Medical aid

From his plans regarding medical care it was clear that he did not intend limiting himself to dispensing medicine and providing first aid, but wanted to educate the Djukas to practise better habits of hygiene in general. Thus he wrote: "I also hope to put an end soon to the eating of tainted meat by teaching them to preserve meat. By showing them how useful and easy it is to fish with the *tramaille* (the kind of fish-net used to catch herrings in Europe), I hope to be able in time to put a stop to the poisoning of fish with *Neku*,[34] which causes many intestinal troubles. I may add here that as soon as I am settled I shall make a request to His Excellency the Governor to send a doctor to the Tapanahoni for some weeks in order to give salversan injections to a large number of children suffering from yaws,[35] as well as the many adults who are afflicted with syphilitic sores.[36] Needless to say, if a large number of sufferers are cured at the same time in what must appear a miraculous manner to them, their faith in the good intentions of the Administration will be greatly increased.

Of the present generation I do not expect much more than that I may succeed in making their work slightly more productive and their way of living more hygienic, for instance by not leaving the corpses unburied for many days and by not eating decayed food."

§ 4 ASSESSMENT OF THE DEVELOPMENT PLAN

a Expected results

In view of the experimental character of the venture, the very scanty financial resources and the limited knowledge of circumstances in the colony's interior, the development plan as it was drawn up by Van Lier and eventually accepted by the Government was far too ambitious. According to the much more modest view of the prospect offered by the Governor when he tried to induce the States Members to give their consent, the design of the plan appears fairly well-balanced and not inordinately ambitious. It was thought that the aim of civilizing the Bush Negroes could be achieved by:

advancing their development through (simple) education;
improving their material situation by teaching better farming technique;
improving their physical condition by medical aid and hygiene;
general guidance.

The recommendation in Van Lier's note that the person who was to carry out the development plan should, above all, be familiar with the language, customs and habits of the people was not redundant. Its necessity was not generally recognized by his fellow-citizens and contemporaries. (The surmise that this statement has something of an *oratio pro domo* does not detract from its value.)

b The education plan

1. Van Lier assumed that the Djukas were 'pining'[37] for education. He based this conviction in the first place on the fact that the progressive Granman Oseisie (Amakti's predecessor) had asked for and received a school in 1896. This venture failed on account of the opposition of the conservative section of the Djukas who saw a danger in education – based on Christianity. In the second place his conviction was supported by statements of Bush Negroes with whom he had come into contact many years before his appointment as postholder. These were in the first place Bush Negroes who lived below stream, and Granman Oseisie's protégé, Kanapé. They had assured him that the Djukas were indeed interested in education on a non-Christian base. But Van Lier did not reckon sufficiently with the fact that Granman Amakti belonged to the conservative group and Kanapé to the opposition, while the below-stream Djukas had little influence on administrative decisions. In practice it would become clear that there was a fundamental difference between

the postholder's standpoint and that of a large and influential part of the Djukas, which was to have an unfavourable influence on the development work.[38]

2. Van Lier's view that only non-Christian education would have a chance of success was correct. The Djuka resistance to christianization lay at the root of the troubles which arose when the Moravian Brothers tried to establish a Christian school (with support of the authorities). The Government put an end to the attempt and blamed its failure on sabotage on the part of the Djukas, without recognizing the true cause.

However, Van Lier held his view only on account of tactical considerations: as a sincere Christian and in the firm belief that nothing but western civilization, combined with Christianity, could bring salvation, he hoped to introduce Christianity into their community, "even if this should take place through a backdoor".[39] A neutral school would be just the thing to lead them to the Christian faith, for the fact that Djuka society was firmly rooted in religious principles would, he thought, bring the Djukas at length – not until after many years, however – to turn 'naturally' to Christian doctrines, once they had reached an adequate level of development and had become thoroughly acquainted with the habits and customs of the Christian world. "Civilize the Djuka by educating him and his religious nature (for a Djuka is deeply religious) will by itself bring him to the Lord" he wrote at the end of his article on 'Christianization'.[40]

Even if Van Lier had kept strictly to his plan of giving neutral education, his personal sentiments and expectations would probably not be of such a nature as to abolish the Djukas' mistrust with regard to his intentions and make them surrender their prejudice against the 'customs of the civilized'. He proposed in his note of 20 June 1919 to continue building their education on that which was part and parcel of their store of concepts, and so thought it advisable to start teaching them in Negro English. In his working-plan of 24 September 1919 he gave up the idea of this method, which would have had the advantage of appealing more directly to them and winning their confidence more easily. He then thought that, in the event of a boarding-school being established, it would be better to introduce them from the start to western ideas and to teach them Dutch. In this way he set himself a harder pedagogic task which would, moreover, meet with greater resistance from the parents. That he himself was aware of this appears from his remark that "a revolution in customs and manners could only be attained after at least one whole generation had received a western education".

The intention of removing the children as far as possible from their own surroundings and isolating them had, in fact, a great deal in common with the viewpoint of a colonial administration who regarded this as the best way to put a stop to the 'barbarian and heathen' Djuka culture and to integrate them as quickly as possible into the rest of the community. Van Lier proposed to make propaganda for his plans among the parents and to undertake a tour of the villages for this purpose. The propaganda would consist in trying to convince them of the superior quality of western civilization. This met with strong resistance. He did not succeed in carrying out his intentions, for the Djukas and the Bush Negroes in general definitely do not regard their culture as inferior to that of the Christian world and are certainly not prepared to surrender it out of hand. An important factor, underestimated by Van Lier, was the indispensable cooperation of the women. "*Les femmes*," Hurault remarks (1961, p. 299) "*sont hostiles aux changements qui porteraient atteinte à leurs privilèges. Or, ce sont elles en fait qui ont en main l'éducation des enfants.*"

As to the site of the school, there were considerable advantages attached to his suggestion of having it on the border between the above- and below-stream Djukas: the accessibility of children of both groups, the neutral position between what might be described as rival sections. The possible disadvantages were not, however, fully realized. Neither of the two groups could, owing to the intermediate position, give him natural support if that should be needed. And he ran the risk of being used as a pawn in political and religious conflicts and of no longer having any hold on events which need not even be directly connected with his development plan but could still have an unfavourable effect on it.

In his plan of work Van Lier expressed the hope that he might be able to persuade the Djukas to re-group their *los*. By this he probably meant that the *los* spread over several villages should congregate in one or more villages situated close together. The practical implications of this: removal, re-division of provision grounds, to name only a few, far exceeded the financial and administrative resources of Van Lier's limited instructions.

Although it was impossible for Van Lier to have precognition of the many problems involved in the enterprise he was about to launch, he was not inclined to approach his new task lightheartedly. He realized that it would require time and energy and he thought that he would be able to cope with it. He even regarded it as a life-work (demanding at least twenty years) and optimistically assumed that the 'experiment' would in due course become a permanent project. He spent some months preparing himself for his task as teacher, also assuming that he would follow a western method of education, namely the 'Hoogeveen' method which was in vogue in the Netherlands as well as in the Dutch colonies. The difficulties likely to confront this emphasis on westernization of the Djukas have already been pointed out. His preparation for his teaching activities was necessarily brief, also on account of the many other things to be done before he left. Although it might have been sufficient for the very elementary teaching he expected to give, he was blamed for this lack of training when the hoped-for results did not accrue, or not within a short enough time.

c Agriculture, cattle-breeding and fisheries

The unstable food situation among the Djukas fully explains why the development plan contained proposals for its improvement. Van Lier's consultations with the Agricultural Department on this topic, his lessons in agriculture and his experience as plantation manager would, he thought, stand him in good stead during the execution of the plan. Van Lier suggested that the Djukas should receive full details of what was being contemplated and persuaded of the benefit it would bring them. A future market for their products should be guaranteed. This would be the first step towards breaking down the resistance of a society in a marginal situation. This very important step was not taken. Thus from the very start an opportunity for gaining cooperation was missed. The reason why Van Lier's suggestion was ignored cannot be deduced from the documents.

As for the improved farming method: in principle the substitution of irrigated rice-fields for dry rice might have been advisable. The problems which would arise in the course of the change-over were not taken into consideration. Of the various staple products whose output was to be increased, groundnuts stood the best chance. The Djukas were familiar with its cultivation and would realize the benefit of an increased production. In the case of citrus fruit and coconut the problem became more difficult. Leys's plan for encouraging the cultivation of coffee and cacao was not feasible in the given circumstances.

Strangely enough, no thought was given to the problem of transport although it was of crucial importance for the development of commerce. The rivers offer the only routes of communication and their navigability is much impeded by the many rapids, clusters of boulders and small islands. Even today the expansion of transport is hampered by these natural obstacles.

The suggestion that impoverished soil should be planted with valuable types of trees might prove useful in the long run, but the plan did not take into account the fact that the young plants would require care and add to the burden of labour. It was a project which would require a long period before it yielded any advantage. Another aspect of this plan, namely the intention to counteract the spreading out of provision grounds over a large area, did not reckon with the fact that provision grounds were not only divided according to a strict social pattern but that such factors as the impoverishment of the soil and the ant plague also played a determining role. It is remarkable that neither Van Lier nor his advisers ever mentioned this plague. It cannot be assumed that they had overlooked it. It was (and is) a widely-known problem. In the later reports on his agricultural projects, the ant plague is not mentioned either. It is possible that during the short period he spent on his newly developed land (on an island) it had not yet become a nuisance. His successors certainly complained of it (Chapter VIII).

The proposal to encourage pig-, poultry- and, later on, cattle-farming emanated from the Director of the Agricultural Department and was taken over by Van Lier. The Djukas themselves kept some poultry. Expanding the poultry stock should not, with the help of sound advice, meet many difficulties. Keeping pigs and cattle would be harder to introduce. For pig-farming special feed and sufficient vegetable refuse are required which were hard to come by in this society. For cattle-farming the cultivation of meadow-lands would be required, a difficult matter in the dense, tropical jungle. Van Lier himself might be able to keep pigs, goats and poultry profitably on his own land as a means of supplementing the food-supply for himself and his small entourage. His arable soil would benefit from manuring, but not unless it was tackled on a far larger scale than could be provided for by the plan.

Van Lier proposed to improve the fishing methods and, especially, to put a stop to fishing with poison. The latter was (and is) a harmful habit. Van Lier's argument that the poisoned fish caused intestinal trouble is unproven. It appears that the bowels are at most upset by the sudden eating of too much fish after a *ponsu*.[41] For the rest, the fishing methods of the Djukas were highly effective and the usefulness of a dragnet across the extremely rough river-bed would have to be proved.

Van Lier and Leys both believed that a demonstration plot, combined with a small stock of animals, which would illustrate the advantages of better planting methods with better materials than the kind used by the Bush Negroes, as well as the favourable results of keeping some livestock, would be of the greatest importance for the development plan. This was so. Before new methods are adopted there should be some convincing proof that they yield better results than the old ones.

While, if results were favourable, the plan would meet with general approval, failure could cause far-reaching repercussions. The entire prestige of western methods was at stake and a negative result would strengthen the resistance against a non-traditional way of doing things. Distrust, once it had been confirmed by failure of the venture, would be doubly difficult to overcome in future. To increase the chance of cultivating the demonstration field successfully with the help of sound methods and good materials and possibly to extend it in due course, Leys and Van Lier suggested appointing a special workman and allocating Fls. 600 per annum for the entire undertaking. The Colonial States voted this down, as has already been mentioned. This was the first clear instance of the influence that could be exerted by opponents of the whole development plan. The arguments against granting an extra loan showed lack of comprehension and financial pettiness. The plan now had to be put into effect on a much smaller scale. In actual fact it would mean that the arable land Van Lier cultivated to meet the demands of his small settlement would have to fulfil the additional function of a demonstration plot. Van Lier's labourer who assisted him in all the other work would also have to help with the care of cultivated land and animals. For the purchase of farm-animals, which Van Lier had to pay out of his own pocket, he received an advance. The task Van Lier took upon himself was so time-consuming and many-sided that the continuity needed for the smooth functioning of his little industry was impaired.

d Medical aid

Van Lier wanted to gain the confidence of the Djukas by supplying medical aid and medicines; his argument was that the Bush Negroes were extremely keen to have it. That was (and is) indeed the case. Western aid is always eagerly accepted. Not, however, without at the same time applying traditional methods. This attitude is better understood if one considers that in Djuka society itself "two or more specialists"[42] are employed. There is no objection to consulting outsiders. The often favourable results heightened the prestige of western medical practice. This attitude could, however, cause conflicts between the medicine-man and priests and their fellow-tribesmen. As he stated in the note, Van

Lier had been accustomed to supplying the Bush Negroes among whom he worked for months on end as balata prospector with medicine, treating injuries and even drawing teeth. This experience, added to what he had learnt as a young man during his two years' training as a pharmacist and the knowledge he had gleaned during the course he took in first aid before leaving for the Tapanahoni, convinced him that he was well enough equipped to play the role of doctor. He, as well as the Government, realized, however, that these activities were of secondary importance for the development work among the Djukas. The dispensing of medicine would create confidence in their kindly intentions and so pave the way for the main purpose: education, agricultural guidance, appreciation of and the desire to emulate western civilization in general. To give a fillip in the right direction, he asked for a doctor to be sent, who would achieve the rapid and dramatic results of which he, as civil servant, was naturally incapable, for instance by treating yaws and syphilis with salversan. "Certain changes have dramatic advantages and these tend to sell themselves" Ahrensberg and Niehoff remark (1965, p. 82) "The treatment of yaws, in which the disease is eliminated simply by injecting penicillin, is a case of this sort." This proposal was disregarded, so there was no spectacular medical début. Possibly an attendant drawback was avoided: that the Djukas would compare Van Lier's capacities with those of a doctor, to the postholder's disadvantage. Van Lier's suggestion to supply only the very poor with free medicine was intended to dissuade the Djukas from the idea which was indeed firmly fixed in their minds that they were entitled to everything the Government did for them and that it was unfair to expect them to pay for anything. Still, he was prepared for the fact that this endeavour would meet with opposition.

He hoped to teach them something about hygiene too. He does not state in what way he intended to teach them better methods of food preservation. For that matter, the Djukas had quite an effective method: meat and fish were barbecued (smoked and/or grilled). He thought he would be able to induce them not to leave the bodies of their deceased unburied for ten days or longer. A very difficult task since the burial rites connected with it are of utmost functional importance and intimately bound up with ancestor worship.[43]

§ 5 THE INSTALLATION OF THE POSTHOLDER

a Acceptance under coercion

Governor Staal wanted to install the postholder with ceremonial pomp at Paramaribo. In consultation with Van Lier he decided that this should take place in the presence of the foremost Djukas so as to impress upon them the importance the Government assigned to the occasion. "It is too well-known" Van Lier wrote in his note of 2 May 1919 "how fond the Bush Negroes are of a display of power and how ostentatious public events impress them for me to dwell on it". He indicated what he regarded as the best way to induce the Granman to come to Paramaribo with his followers without too much delay, in fact within six weeks. "It will be necessary, however, not to simply summon him in the ordinary manner by letter, but that someone, on behalf of the Governor, in the presence of the District Commissioner of Marowijne and Amakti's representative in Albina... should orally communicate to the messenger bearing the letter to Amakti (for a letter should be sent, preferably adorned with large seals)... that Amakti must come as soon as possible. Whether Amakti will arrive on time will depend entireley on the earnestness with which the messenger is given the injunctions which he, in his turn, will convey to the Granman... It is essential that the person instructing the messenger should be acquainted with Bush Negro customs and say the things that are guaranteed to prevent all quibbles. He will, for instance, have to send a special message to Kanapé (the High Priest) warning him to round off the various religious ceremonies which have to precede the Granman's departure on time, so as not to be responsible for Amakti's falling into disfavour with the Governor, etc."

Van Lier asked to be given this commission and thought of leaving for Albina on 28 April. Although the Governor did actually entrust the task to Van Lier, there are no letters connected with its execution to be found in the archives. The Granman and his retinue arrived, however – after having received a letter – on 7 July at Paramaribo. Van Lier and Staal gave a detailed account of the former's installation in the *West-Indische Gids*.[44]

From the start it was clear that Amakti had no intention of allowing a postholder to settle in the Tapanahoni. It cost the Governor many meetings and eventually an ultimatum threatening Amakti's position as Granman before the latter bowed to constraint by the Government and a section of his counsellors. On 22 July he gave in and on 26 July the installation took place. In his speech to Amakti and his followers the

Governor explained that, since 'our beloved Queen Wilhelmina' wished to care, for all her subjects like a mother, she also included the Djukas. Because of the comparative inaccessibility of their abode this could not be done directly by her representative, the Governor, and so the postholder would be sent. The Governor went on to say: "I want the Postholder to do everything that is to the benefit of you and your people. He will have to counsel and help you in all matters with which the Djuka is not yet familiar. He could start, for instance, by giving the children some tuition, until you have schools. You will always be able to go to him when you need advice and assistance. He will have to be like an elder brother who gladly helps his younger brother... I send Mr. van Lier to you because I know that he is fond of the Djukas." He solemnly assured the Djukas that the postholder would respect the Granman's rights; but the Granman must feel himself obliged to support the postholder in his endeavour.

Finally the Governor demanded that Amakti should give his oath to receive Van Lier cordially and give him whatever help he needed. The Granman refused, however, to add a new oath to the oath of allegiance he had sworn at the time of his appointment, and merely said: "Yes, let Mr. van Lier come." The ceremony was closed with a speech by the Governor to the chiefs and Van Lier, and one by Van Lier to the Granman and his followers in which he asked them to abandon their suspicions and put their trust in him. A week later Amakti left with his retinue to return to the Tapanahoni via Albina.

b The Governor's point of view

In order to carry out the resolve, once it had been taken, to appoint a postholder among the Djukas, Governor Staal had to enforce his authority. The vague rumours he had received about the way in which the Djukas had reacted to the changes expected to take place in their region, and the advice Van Lier had given him about the circumspection with which the Djukas should be treated, had prepared him for the fact that it would not be such a simple undertaking. He complied with Van Lier's request to humour the Granman's sense of personal pride and received him with appropriate ceremonial. He held a number of meetings with Amakti and his counsellors before issuing an ultimatum that Amakti's function of Paramount Chief, sanctioned (and paid) by the Government was in danger of being terminated on account of his refusal. Governor Staal was – in spite of himself – impressed by Amakti's attitude. "After the tales I had heard, my encounter with Amakti came as a surprise. He was delicate, frail, rather stiff and slow in his movements; his eyes seemed inclined to wander and search for something... Still, I found him an attentive and thoughtful listener who, headstrong in his objections, determined in his resistance, was able to formulate his views clearly and candidly.[45]"

Staal could appreciate the awkward position in which Amakti was placed: "Although I could give him positive assurance that he, and not the postholder, would be Granman of the Aucaners as hitherto – he knew very well that the latter's coming implied a change in the nature of his authority, the nature of the way in which he and his chiefs exercised control – he was convinced that surveillance would lead to fault-finding, admonition and finally coercion, a curtailment of free action."

Staal also saw through Amakti's "foolish disguise in ill-fitting, inappropriate dress, boots covering feet unused to being shod, gloves – oh! the cotton rags covering hands made to grip axe and oar! – choking collar, untidily sagging cuffs: it was a caricature of the bare-footed Amakti in loin-cloth and loose cotton jacket. The half-naked Amakti was the leader, invested with traditional authority, elected by the people, authorized to exercise justice and – who knows how much – injustice."[45] What the good-natured Staal did not take into account was the fact that his own administration had provided the Head of the Bush Negroes with this 'silly rig-out' consisting of cast-off military togs. It did not occur to him to have a uniform made to measure for this person in authority, and still less to let him appear in his own garb. He, too, seemed to think that Amakti should come accoutred like this as a tribute to the Government's power and prestige.

c The postholder's point of view

In his recommendation Van Lier supposed that Amakti and his followers would not be receiving enough recognition if only a special letter were delivered by an appropriately instructed messenger. It proved, in fact, an effective way of getting the Granman to come to Paramaribo in a reasonably short time. It did not, however, contribute noticeably to the solution or prevention of difficulties which Van Lier could foresee. He knew that the Djukas set great store by collective deliberation before a decision was taken and that it was regarded as a form of courtesy to give the Granman an opportunity, after consultation, of announcing the decision as though he had arrived at it by himself. With this in mind Van Lier recommended that he should go to the Tapanahoni personally to explain and extol the plan until, if need be after many meetings, it was generally accepted and submitted to the Governor as a request by the Granman. For the introduction of agricultural guidance he suggested something of the kind, but this was not carried out either. Perhaps it was true that a letter would be enough because a preparatory visit would cost a great deal of time and one could not be positive beforehand of its success. Furthermore: if the Djukas should refuse to accept the plan this would entail a serious loss of prestige for the colonial administration. The compulsive measures which would have to be taken in order to avoid that could lead to so much protest that the plan would probably fail anyhow. On the other hand, it might well be that the time spent on preparatory consultation would be amply compensated (if the plan were accepted) by the people's readier cooperation in its carrying out.[46] In that case, too, Van Lier would have been able to gather more information about the rumours that had been spread among the Djuka and the dissension aroused by them. Possibly he might have been able to lull their distrust by giving them a truthful presentation of the facts of the case. As things turned out, he did not realize why there had been such opposition to his appointment until a number of chiefs who were well-disposed towards him enlightened him more than a week after his arrival. He described this in his Journal and later on in his aforesaid article in the *West-Indische Gids* (1921, pp. 1-30).

d The Djuka point of view

Rumours of the Governor's decision to appoint an administrative official among the Djukas had reached the Tapanahoni even before the Governor announced it publicly. A section of the Djuka tribe, together with the Granman and the *Opo* Negroes, were opposed to it. No wonder: the rumours were disquieting: the administrative official was coming "to introduce taxation and govern the Djukas '*bakra*-wise'. He would supplant the Granman and the chief would have to carry out his orders." These reports were not entirely without foundation: the Colonial States as well as Van Lier at first insisted that the Djukas should pay taxes. Besides, the Colony found it most objectionable to have 'a state within a state'. They wished to consolidate the administrative power and put a stop to the insolent behaviour of a large evasive group in the interior. Governor Staal realized, however, that the introduction of taxation would call forth strong protest and make the postholder's task far too difficult. So the matter was dropped in Paramaribo.

Among the Djuka tribe the plan caused sharp conflicts, especially between the *Opo* and the *Bilo* Negroes. Van Lier described the reaction of the *Opo* Negroes as follows: "It was the *Bilo* Negroes who had long been clamouring for a school and church and who were well acquainted with Mr. van Lier through his former activities (balata exploitation in the Lower Lawa, where the *Bilo* Negroes have their provision grounds). They had had truck with Mr. van Lier and had instigated his coming to settle here. Van Lier, in compliance with the wishes of the *Bilo* Negroes, had managed to get the Governor to give him this commission. The *Opo* Negroes openly accused the *Bilo* Negroes in a *grankrutu* (big meeting) of this intrigue and they were held responsible for the consequences of their scheming".[47]

These reactions were not without foundation either: during his visits to the Upper Marowijne as balata prospector Van Lier did in fact come into contact mainly with the *Bilo* Negroes. In his newspaper articles in 1918 he regularly pointed out that it was the *Bilo* Negroes in the first place who wanted education for their people.

§ 6 THE ATTITUDE OF THE DJUKAS; RESISTANCE AGAINST WESTERNIZATION

The Djuka community did not appear amenable to western civilization in the sense that "an adequate number of them were prepared to allow, let alone actively promote, internal social reforms". Köbben (1964 and 1968a) mentions a complex of factors that influenced the resistance against westernization. He points out that it is possible to look at these factors separately but that, in fact, there is a marked interaction between them. They may be described as follows:

a Historically conditioned distrust

The Djukas were never completely cut off from contact with western civilization. This contact was partly accidental in the sense that it came about more or less by chance (during their journeys to the coast and in their work outside the community). Another part of it was, however, deliberately planned, for instance the attempt by the Government and by Catholic and Protestant Missions to coax the Djukas from their isolated position. The Government aimed at integrating them into the labour process and obtaining greater jurisdiction over them. Missionaries – naturally – wanted to persuade them to accept a different religion. The Government did not succeed in convincing the Djukas that they would benefit from integration. No adequate measures were taken to demonstrate the fact that their material position would improve, nor was any guarantee given that they would retain their independence. There was nothing in the nature of the situation to rid the Djukas of their deep-rooted 'historic trauma': their past as slaves and the long struggle they had to gain independence made (and still makes) them believe that their hard-earned liberty would be endangered if they yielded to the Government's proposals.

Their resistance to 'Christian civilization' as offered to them by the mission churches was based partly on the same distrust, partly on the fact that they wished to remain faithful to the gods and ancestors who had supported them in their struggle against the whites, and finally on the fact that there was no apparent 'directly favourable effect' (except perhaps the side-effect of medical aid).

b Contacts with western civilization

1 The Government

Nowhere, that is to say not in Surinam either, did the fact that western civilization was first encountered under colonial conditions facilitate its acceptance by the non-white population. Those who offered it were the conquerors, those who received it were the conquered. Mistrust of the motives of the dominant group has an inhibiting effect on every process of acculturation. The Djukas, too, harboured this mistrust in spite of their relatively independent position. They were very well aware of glaring inequalities in the balance of power as well as of the self-interest which motivated the overtures made by the rulers from the coastal region. Mistrust added to, and fed by, the 'historic trauma' strengthened their resistance. The knowledge that their independence was highly relative, especially in the material field, had a curious side-effect: the Djukas always believed that the Surinam government was morally obliged, because of its dominant position and far greater prosperity, to share its affluence freely with them, the 'underdogs'. This conviction gave rise to the attitude that it was permissible to ask the coast-dwellers for gifts (whereas begging from fellow-tribesmen was frowned upon) and that services received need not be returned. The current expression reflecting this attitude is: *'lanti sa pai'*: the Government must (will be sure to) pay for it. Although, as has been said, there was always some sort of contact between the Djukas and the 'civilized' coast-dwellers, the 'supply' of western civilization was always extremely superficial or short-lived. The postholders who had been detailed to work among the Djukas after the peace of 1761 were men of very slight cultural development; they lived among the Bush Negroes in practically the same primitive circumstances as their charges, it was their job to see that the regulations laid down in the peace treaty were carried out, and nothing came of the Government's vague instructions to win the Bush Negroes for western civilization by means of the example they set.[48]

2 Catholic and Protestant mission work

Both Catholic and Protestant missionaries made earnest attempts to convert the Djukas to Christianity. As a rule these were confined to the tour – lasting some weeks – made by one or more of them to the various Bush Negro villages. The only more prolonged and ambitious effort was that of the missionary Spalburg who tried to educate and convert the inhabitants of the Tapanahoni between 1898 and 1906. These few years also proved too short a period to achieve acceptance of a new cultural pattern. In other words: during these few years the resistance, especially against conversion to Christianity, proved insurmountable. The Djuka leaders declared that they did in fact want education for their people, but of a secular kind, not coupled to Christian indoctrination. Particularly the priests were opposed to it as they regarded the strange religion as a rival cult threatening to weaken their hold on the inhabitants who depended on them for religious support. While during the period under discussion mission work, combined with teaching, hardly got off the ground, it is tolerated nowadays, or at least in certain areas (along the Cottica and the Lower Tapanahoni). Christianity itself, although a number of Djukas have accepted it, has not "affected habits, institutions, religious concepts and values essentially".[49] It is not a substitute, but 'something additional'.[50]

3 Medical aid

At the beginning of the present century there was no question yet of organized medical care. Incidental visitors (among whom missionaries and, very rarely, a doctor) treated wounds, supplied medicine (quinine, laxatives and such-like) or extracted a tooth. The only hospital in the Marowijne area was in Albina. Van Lier made a first – primitive – effort to give regular medical aid. The Djukas had no objections whatsoever; they liked receiving medical treatment. That did not alter the fact that they also, and in the first place, turned to their priest and *obiaman* for help. For after all: sickness and death, according to the

Djukas, are "a sign that something is wrong with the social relations. One becomes ill as the result of jealousy, witchcraft, or from supernatural punishment for unsocial behaviour."[51] Only Djuka priests can reveal the cause and prescribe adequate purification rites. Here, too, there is no question of a substitute but of 'something additional'. It is clear that the priest and *obiaman* also suspect a rival in medical aid. Their power position, as well as their income, are jeopardized by it. Nowadays their opportunities for obtaining medical aid have been widely extended but the attitude of the Djuka has remained essentially unchanged (Chapter IX § 4).

4 Economic contacts with western civilization

From their early beginnings as an independent settlement, the Djukas were never completely isolated in their dwelling-place deep in the jungle. The large rivers, even though hard to navigate, offered them an opportunity of travelling fairly regularly to the coast. To some extent they had become acquainted with the western world through their shorter or longer stay on the plantations. Forced by circumstances, some of the Djukas regularly looked for work – of a temporary kind – in the coastal region.[52] They were always able to make some supplementary provision – however limited – to eke out a living. The job of freight-carrying, which many of them held, brought money into their pockets.

Another long-lasting form of contact is that between the Djukas and the Government in Paramaribo. Initially in the form of guerilla fighting, then, after 1761, of a more peaceful nature. A superficial form of administrative interference was accepted by them.

These types of contact which regularly forced them to compare the fairly prosperous condition of the coastal area with their own misery, made the Djukas aware of their social and economic inferiority.[53] They were – rightly – conscious of the fact their services (freight-carrying, timber-felling, etc.), were extremely ill-paid, just as the prices their forest products fetched were far too low. They had (and still have) keen appreciation of the technical accomplishments and knowledge of western civilisation and of the prestige these accomplishments confer on their owners. All the same, they definitely do not regard their own accomplishments as inferior. They believe that in many respects they surpass the white man, at any rate in their own environment.[54]

The Djukas' feelings about development can be deduced from their feelings about western civilization in general. This attitude has grown in the course of time from their contact with the outside world and is partly determined by factors that play a role *within* their community.

c Degree of social control

Strong social control is exercised in the Djuka community. In pursuit of an improved social position political manoeuvres certainly occur,[55] but they have to be kept within socially acceptable limits. A man may aspire to become chief of a given village, but only if he belongs to the *lo* which usually furnishes chiefs for that village. A Granman's protégé may, if he is a member of the required *lo* and, preferably, a son of the Granman's sister, hope to become his uncle's successor. The decision does not, however, rest with his patron and still less with himself. Manipulations carried out by priests at the funeral of a Granman can eliminate a candidate.

It is regarded as improper to try and better one's social position with outside help, that is, with the help of agents outside the Djuka community. To this kind of activity the term 'intriguing with the whites' is applied and it is closely related to treason.

The fact that the Granman is appointed by the Government and receives a salary is regarded, on the one hand, as an enhancement of his status, but, on the other hand, he is expected to use it only in order to improve the position of his people. If he makes concessions which could lead to greater interference by the Government, this would also be looked upon as 'scheming'. This attitude is another indication of the strong resistance which could be encountered by a liberal Granman, e.g. Oseisie.[56] The improvement of one's own position is literally regarded as an evil. The accumulation of possessions and a degree of prosperity surpassing the permissible deviation from normal wealth (or rather, from normal poverty) arouse suspicions which lead to the most serious accusation in this community, namely that of witchcraft. Wealth cannot be obtained by any other means except the aid of evil, supernatural forces. The fear of being suspected of witchcraft is a real deterrent to social ambition. If one has accumulated some possessions one would rather not display them. Another deterrent is the current fear that he who becomes rich arouses so much jealousy that witchcraft may be resorted to for the purpose of injuring him.

d Degree of social stratification

The balance of power in the Djuka community follows a clearly hierarchical structure with the Paramount Chief and the High Priest (functions occasionally combined in one man) as the supreme personification of power. All the same one cannot speak of an autocratic system of rulers.

They possess an 'incomplete ascendancy'.[57] The reason for this is that religious as well as civil administrative organizations have to exercise their power on a basis of dependence connections. That is to say: the administrative organizations have services and goods to offer (in the religious or the civil sphere) which the people require. The position of the offerors is weakened, however, by the fact that they have no monopoly of the things they offer. In order to satisfy certain needs one could also appeal to other authorities such as priests, medicine-men or oracles. The supreme authorities do not possess an apparatus of power to force a position of monopoly. Hence political manoeuvring to ensure the support of certain people, factions, sub-groups, becomes an important aid to the exercise of power.

In this situation one would expect that drawing the colonial administration (*mutatis mutandis* western civilization) into such manoeuvres would be looked upon as an aid. This is, however, not the case. The Djuka authorities have much to gain by keeping western influences at bay. Both administrative and religious functionaries are paid (and often well) for their services. Since they have no other income worth mentioning (except the Granman) it is essential for them to keep their clients. So the situation of dependence must be safeguarded. They know quite well that contact with western civilization is likely to endanger it.

NOTES

[1] The three upper classes corresponded more or less to the three lower classes of an H.B.S. (Dutch Secondary School).
[2] Encyclopedie van Nederlands West-Indië, p. 191.
[3] The Governor at the time was A.A. Rutgers (1928-1933).
[4] The Freemason Lodge 'Concordia' played an important part in the cultural development of many inhabitants of Surinam. Most of the prominent non-Catholics were members of the Lodge, a number of Europeans, amongst whom many Jews, were also admitted to it (R.A.J. van Lier, 1949, p. 282).
[5] R.A.J. van Lier, 1949, pp. 262, 263.
[6] R.A.J. van Lier, 1949, p. 259.
[7] Van Lier, 1919, p. 3.
[8] Van Lier, 1940.
[9] Van Lier, 1919.
[10] De Goeje (1879-1955) took part in a number of expeditions to the interior of Surinam, in 1903, 1904, 1907 and in 1937. The notes he made on the subject of the Djukas he incorporated in the *Aantekeningen*. In 1946 he was appointed professor extraordinarius in Leyden in the philology, geography and ethnography of Surinam and Curaçao.
[11] Van Lier, 1919.

[12] *West-Indische Gids*, 1935, pp. 91-105.
[13] *West-Indische Gids*, 1923, p. 311.
[14] *West-Indische Gids*, 1924, p. 74.
[15] *West-Indische Gids*, 1922, p. 454.
[16] *West-Indische Gids*, 1925, p. 82.
[17] *West-Indische Gids*, 1932, p. 332.
[18] Goodenough, 1963, p. 377.
[19] Goodenough, 1963, p. 379.
[20] Foster, 1962, p. 263.
[21] Goodenough, 1963, pp. 401-402.
[22] Both Van Lier and the Governor renounced this plan (Chapter III § 4).
[23] *Bakra*: Negro English for white man.
[24] Negro English or Surinam is a Creole language, with a vocabulary derived from West-African languages and from English, Portuguese and Dutch. It can be divided into:

1. Sranan, spoken in the coastal area, in which words of African, Dutch and English derivation preponderate.

2. Saramaccan, spoken by the Bush Negroes along the Surinam and Saramacca rivers, containing more words of Portuguese origin. There are fairly marked differences between Sranan and Saramaccan.

3. The Djuka spoken by the Bush Negroes along the Marowijne and along the Cottica and Commewijne rivers. Djuka differs less than Saramaccan from Sranan.

[25] Gansee, located on the Surinam river, approximately 125 km from Paramaribo, was a village that had been christianized by the Moravian Brothers since about 1850. In 1963 it disappeared, together with many other Bush Negro villages, under the waters of a barrage lake.

[26] Village on the Tapanahoni, 30 km downstream from Drietabbetje, where the Granman is stationed.

[27] *Manihot utilissima*, root-crop whose poisonous substance (Prussic acid) disappears when the roots are boiled or pressed out. *Kwak* is cassava-meal and is obtained by squeezing out the grated roots in long plaited cylinders to which a weight is attached. From this meal – which can be preserved a long time – cassava-bread is made: large flat grilled cakes. *Kwak* is also eaten raw (mixed with water into a gruel) or stewed with fish or meat.

[28] The *Encyclopedie van Nederlandsch West-Indie* mentions, however (pp. 25-26) that: Groundnuts are used in large quantities by the population, for, apart from local production, there is a considerable import from various countries such as Curaçao, the Netherlands, French Guyana. In 1910, 122,000 kg, worth Fls. 18,000, was imported.

[29] Minutes and Appendices of the Colonial States, 1919-1920, p. 16.
[30] Secretarial Agenda No. 227.
[31] The term *lukuman* is not employed by the Djukas; they say *obiaman*. *Lukuman* is a word used in the city.
[32] This is the first time Van Lier mentions his plan for a boarding-school in writing.
[33] As a matter of fact, he received this afterwards.
[34] See Chapter II § 3.
[35] Framboesia tropica.
[36] This request was not granted.
[37] Van Lier, 1919, p. 23.
[38] Batten, 1964, p. 21: "There is often a wide gulf between what the agency thinks the community needs, and what the community actually wants."

[39] Van Lier, 1919, p. 35.
[40] Van Lier, 1919, p. 26.
[41] This information was given orally by Dr. L. Doornbos who worked for years in the hospital on Stoelman's Island at the mouth of the Tapanahoni.
[42] Thoden van Velzen, 1966, p. 24.
[43] Even today the legal prescriptions are generally disregarded. The Bush Negroes know that it is practically impossible to keep a check on their burial practice in the Tapanahoni.
[44] Van Lier, 1921, pp. 1-30; Staal, 1921, pp. 630-636.
[45] Staal, 1921, pp. 631-636.
[46] Batten, 1964, pp. 21-23, mentions four "general principles underlying all good community work". Two of them are as follows: "The agency must reach agreement with the people on what the change should be" and "The agency must demonstrate that a suggested change is safe".
[47] Van Lier, 1922, pp. 1-30.
[48] De Groot, 1963.
[49] Köbben, 1968a, p. 71.
[50] Köbben, 1968a, p. 72.
[51] Köbben, 1968a, p. 76.
[52] De Groot, 1964.
[53] Thoden van Velzen, 1966, pp. 27-28.
[54] Thoden van Velzen, 1966, pp. 27-28.
[55] Thoden van Velzen, 1966, p. 252 et seq.; p. 267 et seq.
[56] Van Lier, 1918, p. 17 et seq.
[57] Thoden van Velzen, 1966, p. 318 et seq.

CHAPTER V

PERIOD 1919-1921

§ 1 FIRST STAY IN THE TAPANAHONI, 11 DECEMBER 1919 – 26 JUNE 1920

a Reception and installation among the Djukas

On 28 October 1919 Van Lier left Paramaribo. From Albina, situated at the mouth of the Marowijne and seat of the District Commissioner, he despatched a message to Granman Amakti to come and fetch him. He waited until 1 December before the boats, sent by Amakti and manned by Bush Negroes, turned up at last and on 11 December, accompanied by the District Commissioner, De Sanders, he arrived in Puketi where he was to be installed. During his voyage up the river from Albina, Van Lier saw signs already of the unrest which was rife in the Tapanahoni on account of his arrival. When he reached the second *Bilo* Negro village where he was to spend the night, the chief, Jenta of the Compagnie-*lo*, an old acquaintance of Van Lier, sent word that he did not wish to receive him until he had presented himself to the Granman. Later on Jenta came to apologize and explained that he, as a *Bilo* Negro, wanted to show that he was not the first to welcome the postholder with open arms.

From what followed it became apparent, however, that the Granman and his supporters were not only somewhat reassured and had resigned themselves to Van Lier's presence, but that, moreover, they regretted their decision to palm the postholder off on the *Bilo* Negroes. On 13 December, only two days after Van Lier's arrival, a *gran-krutu* was convened at Puketi, to which *Opo* as well as *Bilo* Negroes were summoned. Through 'a misunderstanding' the *Bilo* people thought the *krutu* was to be held the following day, and the gathering consisted entirely of *Opo* Negroes. After Van Lier's inaugural address two *Bilo* chiefs did in fact arrive on the scene, but when it became evident that the Granman was not prepared to repeat his exposition of matters already dealt with according to Djuka custom, and simply invited them to attend a *krutu* at Drietabbetje the next day, they left the meeting in high dudgeon.

With this undisguised affront the Granman achieved a double effect: in the first place it was now made clear that Van Lier's installation was an *Opo* concern from which *Bilo* was excluded, and secondly the *Bilo* Negroes were given to understand that they were not forgiven for having brought about Van Lier's coming.

Van Lier stated in his address to the Djuka chiefs that it was the desire of the Queen and the Governor to aid them in every way, by word and by deed, and to establish a school, declaring: "It is necessary for the Djukas to learn to read and write, for this is indispensible for the achievement of happiness and prosperity. For the children who want to learn I shall start a school. I shall force no one to send his child to school for I am convinced that everybody will know where his interest lies." To this he added: "Within the limits of my knowledge I shall provide those who are ill with medicine; those who are needy will receive it free of charge."[1] After this speech and the interlude with the *Bilo* chiefs the solemn inauguration of the postholder took place. *Da*[2] Tamuka, the oldest chief present and spokesman for the others, and Van Lier vowed an oath that the Djukas and the postholder would maintain faith and friendship towards one another, and that Van Lier would do everything in his power to promote the interests of the Djukas. The oath was affirmed, Djuka-wise, by the drinking of rum and its libation at the ancestral sacrificial site.[3] The District Commissioner, De Sanders, who was not acquainted with the background of the whole affair and thus could not see through Amakti's strategic game, wrote in his report on the rapidly planned installation: "I believe this change-over from anxiety and fear to reassurance was too much for Amakti. He was in such a transport of delight that he forgot that all the chieftains were not present and at once proceeded to install Van Lier. Mr. Van Lier did in fact speak remarkably well. Granman and Van Lier embraced each other, a toast was drunk to Van Lier, there was even a sacrifice offered. I, too, felt for a moment as though it were all a dream; just a short while ago Mr. Van Lier was the bogey-man, and now the *Opo* and *Bilo* neighbours were vying for his favour. The *Opo* Negroes now wanted him as near possible to, even at, Drietabbetje."[4]

b The choice of a dwelling-place

The most important point, namely the place where Van Lier was to settle, had not yet been discussed. He hoped to deal with it at the *krutu* to be held on 13 December at the Granman's residence in Drietabbetje. However, Van Lier declared from the start that he wished to settle among the *Bilo* Negroes. He was convinced that this was the best policy to get the Djukas to attend a school in large numbers. The advantages were that this section of the Djukas would surely side with the postholder, while the *Opo* Negroes would attend school of their own accord because they begrudged the *Bilo* Negroes the start in development. If the school were founded in Drietabbetje among the *Opo* Negroes, as had happened previously, the chances were that the *Bilo* Negroes would be excluded. Besides, the *Opo* resistance could prove to be far more effective in their own territory. At the outset the *Opo* Negroes came to the same conclusion as Van Lier, but on entirely different grounds, that the school should be started among the *Bilo* Negroes: at the *krutu* held by Amakti after his return from Paramaribo it was decided "that the Postholder would settle among the *Bilo* Negroes so that they would shoulder the hardship of his presence in the Tapanahoni." But now they formed a different opinion. If there were advantages attached to Van Lier's stay, they wished to claim the largest share of these for themselves. The arguments on which Van Lier had based his decision to go and live among the *Bilo* Negroes were precisely the reason why the *Opos* wanted him in their own neighbourhood: they would be able to turn away the *Bilo* children and to keep a closer watch on Van Lier, and, if necessary, oppose him.

The *krutu* to decide on the place of settlement was postponed and Van Lier now received regular visits from *Opo* chiefs who tried to persuade him to alter his plans. The old *Bilo* chief, Jenta of Powie, offered him his own view on the political relations between the *Bilo* and *Opo* Negroes, and Van Lier wrote in his Journal[5] on 22 December: "In spite of the cautious manner in which this veteran expresses his opinion, I am convinced that a school here (*Bilo*) will have a fair chance. The resistance of the conservative *Opo* Negroes will definitely be overcome in time."

When Van Lier, grown impatient, had sent a message to Amakti in which he insisted on a meeting being called and pointed out to the Granman that the choice of a site should, according to the decision of the Government Secretary, be left entirely to the Postholder, the *krutu* eventually took place on the 30th December. On this occasion he was asked once more to come and live among the *Opo* Negroes. Van Lier refused and gave as reason that he had not been able to find a suitable site anywhere except adjoining the *Bilo* village of Powie. He stated that he wished to favour neither *Bilo* nor *Opo* Negroes and he hoped to start a boarding-school so as to solve the problem of the long distance the *Opo* children would have to travel. Finally it was decided that Chief Jenta of Powie would provide a temporary home until Van Lier was able to occupy his site adjoining that village. Jenta asked him to remain at Puketi until he, Jenta, had returned from a religious gathering in the village of Benanu.

The High Priest Kanapé, of whose support Van Lier had high hopes, still kept himself in the background. He was not present at the inauguration ceremony at Puketi. During Van Lier's first visit to Drietabbetje on 14 December he did, however, come to greet him in a friendly manner. "He was pleased to see me again. He expects considerable benefit for his people from my coming to the Tapanahoni. I was to count on his wholehearted support and aid. For his part, he hopes to continue enjoying my friendship as in the past." But at the large meeting of 30 December there was not a word from him.

On January the 22nd he visited Drietabbetje again, had a long, intimate talk with Kanapé "and learned from him in great detail how Amakti was planning to supplant him (Kanapé)" (Journal, 22 January). Kanapé warned him against a number of scheming chiefs, with whom, as a matter of fact, he was to have dealings later on, namely Adikontu, *Opo* chieftain and Popo, *Bilo* chieftain (both of whom had been corpse-bearers of Granman Oseisie when Amakti was appointed successor instead of Kanapé) and Gagu, vice-chieftain at Drietabbetje, who had tried unlawfully to claim the title of *Granfiskari* (grand fiscal, i.e. deputy Granman, for the exercise of secular, especially legal, authority.)

On the 29th of January Van Lier was at last able to settle at Powie, where Chief Jenta received him with great friendliness, 'even with cordiality' (Journal, 29 January 1920).

Granman Amakti, passing through Powie on his way to Drietabbetje, held a *krutu* at Van Lier's request in the course of which he declared that Van Lier was free to select a site (adjoining Powie) and urged the Djukas to give Van Lier all the help he might require from them (always against payment).

The temporary accommodation Van Lier obtained from Jenka left much to be desired. First he was allotted a sort of shed, in which he and his servant could hardly move among the luggage, then the ground floor of Jenta's own home, in which he could not stand up straight, and which involved many other inconveniences. In the room above him slept Jenta's granddaughters from whom he "occasionally got a wetting at night".[6] He did not have a moment's peace as he was constantly visited by Djukas who came out of curiosity, or to ask for medical aid, or to beg for food, rum and tobacco. In desperation he moved to the mortuary[7] which was naturally also a temporary, hardly attractive solution.

On 5 February 1920 Van Lier, together with his temporary host, choose a site adjoining the village which satisfied his requirements. But he had trouble in finding labourers to start clearing the ground: the rainy season had set in and "under no circumstances will a Djuka work in the rain" (Journal, 8 February). However, on 14 February four Djukas and Van Lier began to fell the trees. Van Lier started buying materials in the vicinity for the erection of his camp dwelling. On 17 May he mentioned that the shelter had been completed and on 18 May: "Amid a salvo of guns the flag was solemnly hoisted this morning at 6 o'clock at Granman Staalkondré."[8] The name was officially accepted in the Government Resolution of 27 October 1931. On the 27th of May he took up his abode there and the next day he started at once to plant all available ground with maize, sweet cassava and sugar-cane. In his Journal (28 May) he wrote: "I managed to persuade four young women and two youths to watch how I selected and planted the maize seed. For their help with the planting each one received fr. 3 as well as free meals".

It took a long time before the camp was 'comfortably habitable' (Journal, 4 June). Especially for the preparation of the soil he was dependent, apart from his diligent assistant, on the very irregular assistance of Djukas.

c Medical aid

On January 4th Van Lier wrote for the first time about his medical activities, and after that almost daily. During such periods as he was not able to continue teaching, these were his chief occupation after the building of his camps and the maintenance of his provision grounds. When visiting other villages his advice was also sought, he was even called to other villages by worried relatives to attend to the sick. On 4 January he wrote: "A number of Djukas, both men and women, come to ask me for medicine for a number of complaints. The news that I have received medicine has got abroad. Since my arrival here, however, not a single day has passed without some person or other coming to ask for *dresie* (medicine)."

On 10 January 1920, still in the village of Puketi as no decision had been taken yet about where he would take up abode, and moreover hampered by heavy rains, he wrote: "Life is very sombre here, especially when one has not seen the sun for days. I spend my time, apart from treating the sick, in reading and studying (First Aid, Hoogeveen's Reading Method, etc.)".

The following entries in his diaries indicate the way in which Van Lier fulfilled his task of 'playing doctor':

January 17: "I extract a molar for Abon of Puketi. Today I had to attend to no fewer than fourteen patients."

January 27: "Tamuka, the man who 'drank' the oath with me on 13 December[9] visits me to 'request' medicine for himself and his family. He receives ointment for rash, castor oil, potash, quinine, etc."

On the 29th of January Van Lier left Puketi for Powie. The day after his arrival a girl was stung by a *spari* (sting-ray, *potamotrygon reticulatus Gthr.*). Van Lier did not treat her, but noted in his journal: "The sting of the *spari* is extremely dangerous and almost always causes terrible wounds, which heal with difficulty and very slowly. The old Jenta vaccinated the girl with *sparikoti* and had her carried to the spot on the river bank where the accident happened. The girl had to immerse the vaccinated foot into the water and was then carried back to the camp. Jenta predicted that the *spari*, attracted by the *koti*, would return to the place within half an hour and would then be killed. He posted a boy, armed with bow and arrow, there. Within quarter of an hour after the incident a *spari* was killed on the spot. I immediately bought some of this vaccine and sent it to the Military Hospital to be analyzed.[10] The day after the incident the girl was walking about as though nothing had happened."

Koti is a remedy used by Bush Negroes as well as Indians and Creoles not only against ray stings, but also against bites or stings of poisonous snakes, scorpions, spiders, etc.. Although the word is often thought to be derived from the English word *cut* (*koti* is applied by rubbing the medicine into an incision made in the skin), it is probably of African origin. Powders and potions for other illnesses are often called *koti*, too, if they have a preventive effect. The name as well as the method of preparation occur in West-Africa.[11]

Faith in the salutary action of a *koti* was, and still is, widespread in Surinam. Many articles have been devoted to it, especially to the *sneki* or *snetji* (snake) *koti*[12] but scientists attach no importance to it.

Van Lier's account, offered without comment, closely resembles many other miracle tales about the effects of various *kotis*. In this case Van Lier's information gives no certainty as to whether the girl was actually stung by a ray, and, if she was, whether the wound was serious and whether poisoning had resulted.

The composition of a *koti* is as a rule kept secret by its manufacturers. All the same, a number of investigators got to know about it or managed to obtain a sample of it. Laboratory experiment, however, yielded negative results. Usually poisonous and other parts of the animal in question are boiled, dried and ground into a powder with herbs and other ingedients. This powder is rubbed into incisions made close to the wounds and administered internally. The action is supposed to be prophylactic as well as curative.

On the 31st January 1920 Van Lier wrote in a letter to the Government Secretary about medicine sent to him for the sum of Fls. 356.36. He complained that the dispensary of the Military Hospital added another 40%, i.e. Fls. 142.65, for 'costs of preparation and distribution'. This extra 40% related particularly to the most frequently used medicines (tirol, potassium iodide, iodoform) and Van Lier requested its discontinuance in the case of these three preparations. An argument he put forward was that the dispensing of medicine and the treatment and dressing of wounds was the most important means of propaganda at his disposal and the most effective method of eventually gaining the full confidence of the Djukas. Therefore he thought it was important to provide medicine free of cost as far as possible for the time being, until they "had learnt through experience to give preference to *bakradresie* (the white man's medicine) above their *obias*". In the same letter he asked for an apothecary's balance for the preparation of medicines.

This letter was forwarded to the Director of the Military Medical Service, L.C. Aletrino, who replied to the Government Secretary that the 40% addition could not be cancelled "as that would be to the detriment of the State" and that there was no balance to be had, that furthermore it seemed inadvisable "to allow an unqualified person to prepare compounds (prescribed by himself) since he must be regarded as being ignorant of the action as well as the composition of medicines."

Government Secretary Eekhout informed Van Lier that the price of medicine could not be reduced, that nevertheless he had no objection to its being supplied free of charge for the time being, but that this would have to be changed eventually. Evidently he did not object to letting Van Lier, with his (brief) training as medical dispenser, practical experience and course in first aid, have a balance, for it was despatched at the same time as this letter of 6 March.

On February the 1st Van Lier treated a man who had been ill for six months. Van Lier found that he had "eight scrofulous tumours in the region of the head and neck. I am treating him with Goulard water and administering Bromnatria for sleeplessness and hydrochloric acid for constant vomiting. I also explain to him and his family that he must not drink lukewarm water when he is thirsty, but plain cold water (as soon as a Djuka falls ill he anxiously avoids the use of cold water)".

The next day he was again called to the patient's bedside. Van Lier had to change the bandages himself; the patient would not benefit from his family's help "because the *ogri sani* (evil force) causing his illness fears no one except a *bakra*. The patient had improved so much after only one visit, so would I kindly come along. I do so in order to please these people."

Occasionally Van Lier complains about the large number of sick and suffering who pester him daily. But he neither could nor would shirk his duty as a bringer of relief, especially when he considered that it would facilitate the task for which he felt a genuine calling: that of educating the people. "The numerous tales of all the complaints from which they suffer are most tedious. There is not one among them who has not been 'bewitched'. No Djuka is ever taken ill as a result of a natural cause. Usually it is a case of *Wisi* (i.e. of being poisoned or having a spell cast on them by others)" (Chapter II).

On February the 3rd a boy was brought to him from a village above Drietabbetje with "an enormous occipital abscess. His head looks so bad that at first I decided against operating... The night brought council. My pity for the lad, who had lain groaning all night long, exceeded my caution. After assuring myself that he had no fever, I cut the tumour. Judging from the amount of pus discharged, I do not believe the operation should have been put off a day longer." He kept the boy with him and even took him along on his journeys so as to be able to dress the wound himself. On February 29 Clay went home, fully recovered.

On the 7th February Van Lier "was startled from his sleep by a young man who came to ask him to visit his father, Batrafutu, who was dying. "Batrafutu" he wrote "who has been ailing for a long while, has suddenly had an attack of acute breathlessness. The old man (roughly 75) seems to be suffering from an acute heart condition. By the application of a few drops of anisated ammonia his breathing was restored to normal. Consequently I am regarded as a miracle-worker. Chief Jenta asks me to undertake the treatment of Batrafutu who is his cousin and *Blakadjakti* (Chapter II). I explain to Jenta that Batrafutu is, in my opinion, a heart patient. That he is an old man already and that only a quiet life and nourishing diet can help him to some extent, but that my medicine would not be of much use."

On 14 February Van Lier wrote: "Batrafutu's condition is getting steadily worse. From *Opo* and *Bilo Wintimans* come to practise their 'medical science' to the accompaniment of an infernal racket. It is disstressing to see how a seriously ill person is being tortured in all sorts of ways. Still, those who do it mean well. Their 'medical science' is responsible for all this physical misery the patient has to undergo.[13] He tells me that he knows he is going to die in spite of everything that is being done to promote his recovery. He asks me to take over his treatment so as to bring an end to the tortures he has to suffer at the hands of his Bush Negro physicians. I reply that I cannot do it, so as to avoid giving offence to the *Wintimans* (*obiaman*, medicine-man)".

Van Lier was consulted in all sorts of matters besides illness; thus, on 23 February, a number of visitors came to demand "why the *bakras* had behaved so irresponsibly as to let the year 1920 start on a Thursday again. Experience had surely proved that a year beginning on a Thursday always brought disaster...".

Van Lier tried to accustom the people gradually to the idea that medicine could not always be provided free. On 26 February a Djuka brought his brother, who had a long, deep gash in his hand. Van Lier expressed his willingness to treat him but wanted payment for the dressings and the medicine. The injured man's escort protested vehemently: "His father is Gran-chief and the medicine was given to me by Wilhelmina (omitting the Queen's title of Missie – Madame), just as I get paid by her. He could not understand, therefore, that I dared ask money for medicine destined for the son of such an eminent chief. He is quite capable of understanding that others have to pay. Because the man spoke in such a pig-headed manner, I gave him a sound rating and emphasized the fact that there would never be any question of the Queen providing such powerful men as him and his brother with free medicine... Like all Djukas against whom one takes a firm stand, Edna accepted it very meekly. It was the incorrigible Djukas, forever given to the art of lying, who had played him this trick. They had told him that I distribute medicine free of charge (*prati dresie fu soso*). In any case, at the moment they had no money, so would I treat Maronti and wait until he had recovered, then he would find work on a cargo boat in order to pay me. I agreed, even though I know for a fact that I shall never receive a cent from him."

On the 27th he visited the man he had treated for scrofulous tumours. "He is practically cured. I had given him medicine for fr. 38 in all, but charged him only fr. 15 because the man had been ill for a long time and was evidently short of money."[14]

On February the 28th he mentioned that Maronti's hand had improved to such an extent that he could go back to his village for a couple of days. Another Djuka who had been cured came to thank him and to wish him a long stay among the Djukas. "If I am pleased" Van Lier wrote "that the patient is so grateful, I am even more pleased that Atuli occupies an influential positon among the Missiedjans".[15]

On the 1st of March the old Chief Jenta of Powie, also a loyal supporter of Van Lier's plans for a school, complained in the presence of two obstinate opponents of this project, Chief Aganga, an *Opo* Djuka, and Chief Popo from *Bilo*, of the fact that payment was exacted for medicine and treatment. Once more Van Lier explained that this was the wish of the Government and that he had no intention of "providing medicine free to people who could pay for it. That, in accordance to my oath, I would do everything in my power for the Djukas and that nobody would have to exhort me to give free help to the needy".

This time Aganga agreed with him and declared that the Djukas should be grateful that Van Lier helped them so efficiently and not grow too demanding. Popo did not offer any comment.

Amakti, the Granman at Drietabbetje, where he went visiting the next day, also broached the topic. "He thought", Van Lier wrote on 4 March "that he should take me to task for selling medicine. He could not countenance that. Medicine should be supplied free of charge. '*Lanti sa pai*' (the government is sure to pay). I gave the same reply as on 1 March at Powie, and added that, as soon as I begin to find the distribution of medicine too much of a bother, I would stop doing it. Amakti, too, was taken aback and cried out: '*Ho, ho, masra Van Lier, so ju fa tan?* (so that's what you're like?) I did not say that you must not sell the medicine, but that you must not charge for the treatment. You must not stop it, for I am always hearing of many Djukas cured by you."

As far as that was concerned, Van Lier did not charge for treatment but, when at last his camp had to be got ready, he did ask those who were able to help him with chopping wood, building and clearing operations and such-like.

When Van Lier returned to Powie on 10 March, it appeared that the old man Batrafutu (see 7 February) had died on the 8th. "It strikes me" Van Lier wrote "that the corpse has not begun to reek yet. I enquire when the funeral is to be held and learn that nobody can tell. I decide to go to Pulugudu and return 'home' once the corpse has been buried. While I am busy packing, I am overwhelmed by an appalling stench. The men who conduct funerals wanted to have a drink and the coffin was now opened to allow the *jorka* (the spirit of the deceased) to join them in the pleasure. I flee head over heels to the boat, leaving behind many things I need on the journey."

During his trip to Pulugudu Van Lier touched at a number of villages where he helped the sick and injured as much as he could. Naturally his knowledge was often not adequate to the task, as in the case of a boy of the village Malobbi who was suffering from 'swelling sickness' (nephritis?). "The lad was considerably swollen. I say that I have no medicine with me to reduce swelling and advise them to bring Politie (that was the boy's name) to Albina as soon as possible."

A *krutu* was called in the same village to thank Van Lier for all he had done for the sick and injured, sacrifices were made to the *jorkas* and "masra Van Lier is commended to their protection".

Batrafutu was buried on 18 March, his corpse had thus remained above ground for ten days. Van Lier had not yet begun with his plan of persuading the Djukas to bury their dead within three days.

On his return to Powie he found many visitors there who had come to attend the mourning ceremonies for Batrafutu and who availed themselves of the opportunity to consult Van Lier about their ailments. The bustle and noise of the *broko-dé* (mourning feast) prevented Van Lier from getting any rest for days on end. "At four o'clock in the morning there is already an uproar in the village as though all hell had broken loose. Some forty men are busy *fu fon tjifunga*, that is, driving evil spirits from the village by beating on empty tins and boxes, firing off guns and especially by shrieking in a chorus as though possessed... At six in the afternoon the feast starts with a salvo of at least a hundred gun shots." A day later, on March 31st, he wrote: "Last night I had hardly a wink of sleep on account of the hellish noise right in front of my house."

On April 6 the ceremony to determine what the cause of Batrafutu's death had been took place. It appeared that it had been the *jorka* of a deceased relative who wished to punish Batrafutu for the fact that he had 'made it up' with a woman from whom he had been separated.

On April the 7th event occurred which at regular intervals caused unrest in the Tapanahoni: "News is spreading that another *lanti siki* (epidemic) is on the way; this time it is an intestinal disease which has already claimed a number of victims in the city. The Djukas are greatly alarmed and at Drietabbetje measures are being considered to stop the carrying trade." Van Lier was able to circumvent this by sending a report to Drietabbetje that the illness rife in the city was not of a serious nature and that a timely warning would be issued if there was danger of its spreading. The only cautionary measures to be taken now consisted of forbidding everyone to go into the forest, on the river or into the provision fields during the first four days. In the village of Krekuna, situated above Drietabbetje, a religious ceremony was to be held to drive an evil forest-spirit out of the region, who during his flight towards the sea was likely to molest everybody along his path.

The boy Politie, who suffered from 'swelling disease' and whose parents had been repeatedly advised by Van Lier to take him to Albina, died on 14 April, and for this child, too, *broko-dé* was held.

At Granman Staalkondré large numbers of people also came regularly to appeal for his help, so that Van Lier became overwrought at times. On 6 June he complained: "Much to my regret the weather was fine today, so that the Sunday visitors came in large numbers and I did not have a moment to myself from early morning till afternoon." Nonetheless he did not turn them away without helping them, for in spite of everything he was far too deeply interested in the 'doctoring game' and concerned about the suffering of those who were sick or injured.

Thus he got a patient for treatment from a village above Drietabbetje, about whom he wrote: "Yesterday the wound had a peculiar appearance: the wound, about 10 cm across, which I was treating with Pritsnietz dressing, suddenly showed a large number of suppurating pimples and the patient complained of severe itch. I remembered that I had an ointment of Dr. Heus for parasitic rash with me and applied it. It acted like a magic cure: Asapasa was practically healed overnight. The astonishment felt by him and his wife and the other patients at this 'miracle' can hardly be described."

He was likewise interested in Djuka remedies, as appeared when he sent *spari-koti* to be analyzed. On 7 June the man who was his 'sworn brother', the old Tamuka, came to visit him with a friend "who is suffering from a large syphilitic ulcer. He is treated and given medicine (on credit) to take away.[16] Tamuka also needs various kinds of medicine which he receives (free, of course, for it would not do for a *bakra* to demand payment from his sworn brother. The opposite is perfectly permissible, however). Besides medicine, Tamuka also receives salt, meat, bacon, sugar and flour. All this so as to win his favour. Tamuka knows many medicinal herbs and it is worth trying to find out about them from him."

On 10 June Chief Jenta of Powie came to fetch him; a child had suddenly been taken ill and was dying. "I go along at once and discover that the child is suffering from an attack of worms. After administering castor oil and worm mixture the little fellow got rid of eighteen worms and was much better. The old Akodi (the child's grandfather) is delighted at the recovery of Swietiesiri (Sweetmeats), as the boy is called.

That afternoon a sacrifice is offered to the *Granjorkas*[17] and '*masra* Van

Lier' commended for the umpteenth time to their care and favour." The happy grandfather, Akodi, brought Van Lier a cutting of a coconut palm as a token of thanks, the first to be planted at Granman Staalkondré.

Van Lier, who had decided to go to Paramaribo to consult the Administration, left on 13 June for Drietabbetje to take leave of the Granman and other worthies. On the way back to Granman Staalkondré he paid another visit to his 'sworn brother', Tamuka, who, as Van Lier had been told, knew the bark of the tree from which the Indians made worm mixture. "I begged Tamuka to show it to me. No Bush Negro likes to reveal forest secrets to an outsider. I reminded my sworn brother that we had promised faith to one another and that treachery was thus out of the question between us; that I had already cured so many in the Tapanahoni and that the more kinds of medicine I knew, the better it would be for the Djukas. After pondering the matter for a little while, the old man agreed to show me the tree and explain how the medicine is prepared. I went with him into the forest and at last became acquainted with the tree for which I had searched for at least six years already. (I had witnessed the beneficial effects of this remedy along the river Lawa.) When we were back in the village, I asked Tamuka to confirm his secret by giving me *Mula*. *Mula* is a ceremony conducted on such occasions and which serves as proof that someone who learns about a remedy from another has in no way been deceived. Without hesitation my sworn brother gave *Mula*. There are many specimens of the tree in question round about my post. When I leave, I shall take some bark and leaves along to be examined at the Military Hospital. Seed and flowers cannot be obtained until February, when the tree comes into flower."

On June the 15th he was fetched to come and have a look at Akodi's grandson, Swietiesiri, whom he had rid of worms a few days earlier. "When I arrived at Powie I saw the boy running around, so I asked what was wrong. And now I was to hear that Swietiesiri refused to eat, so his grandfather had sent for me to pull faces at him (*meki sani gi him*) to induce him to eat. 'Last time it had helped so well'. Annoyance would not have restored my lost time, so I pulled faces at Swietiesiri, with the result that he ate, laughing away, to his grandfather's deep satisfaction." He was duly rewarded for this virtuous deed. *Da* Akodi was reputed to know various *kotis*, but so far Van Lier, despite many attempts, had not managed to coax the secret from him. But now Akodi declared that Van Lier had won his confidence and that he did not object to teaching him the remedies against snake bites and ray stings. "As he happens to be ill, he can give me only one prescription (*sneki-*

koti). But I may rest assured that, unless he dies before my return, he will then tell everything he knows. He cannot do so now, for according to tribal custom, he is not permitted to mention the names of the various herbs unless he has gathered them personally for me. For him to teach me about the *basi* (master) *koti* (a *basi koti* is a renowned and tested *koti* against snake-bite and sting-ray), it is moreover necessary that I submit to certain punishments meted out by his hand. We agree to postpone these matters until I am back, and the old man asks me to offer a Christian prayer for his recovery. With this I complied. It is incredible with what tenacity every Bush Negro clings to life".

Van Lier makes no further mention of *Da* Akodi telling him about the promised secret remedies. Probably the old man thought better of it after all, in spite of the fact that he was restored to health.

d Education

In the meantime Van Lier was pleading the cause of education. This seemed to meet with success for, as soon as he had settled at Powie, he was able to start "half in fun to give lessons to seven children (Hoogeveen method). At first success seemed certain; the children were greatly taken up with the coloured reading-boards and displayed great ambition. Within two weeks the number of regular 'school attendants' rose from seven to fifteen."[18]

Van Lier was pleasantly surprised at his success. He had expected that it would take a long time to win the Djukas' confidence and accomplish what he regarded as his chief goal: the establishment of a school.

Soon, however, it became apparent that the matter was not quite so simple. After a fortnight, on 25 February, the children stayed away and did not return. The good Chief Jenta had forbidden them to continue with their schooling. The explanation for Jenta's sudden decision was that Amakti and the *Opo* Negroes did not want Van Lier to teach only the *Bilo* Negroes. Chief Jenta himself declared, according to Van Lier's journal, that he had issued the ban for the following reasons: when he noticed that other children, as well as his own, came to school, he felt that he should put a stop to it. He had been accused of bringing Van Lier there; by now allowing him to teach in his home, without the Granman's permission, he would make this accusation true. That was why he was asking Van Lier to go with him to Drietabbetje. He wanted to discuss the school with the Granman in front of Van Lier. If Amakti kept on refusing permission for the school, then he, Jenta, would on his own responsibility get Van Lier to teach his children (Journal, 29 February.)

Jenta's plan to send his own children and grandchildren to school without the Granman's permission also proved to have been too audacious. When Amakti declared that Van Lier had come unlawfully to establish a school, and uttered veiled threats against everyone who sent their children to school, Jenta, too, did not dare oppose the Granman.

On the 4th of March Van Lier left again for Drietabbetje, where he had a discussion with Kanapé. The latter reiterated his promise to give him all possible support in the matter of the school, but predicted that he would run into serious trouble over it with Amakti. Van Lier now realized that Kanapé was hardly in a position to exercise much real influence and concluded "that the only way to obtain speedy results of my work would be to invest Kanapé with some official power" (Journal, 4 March). He spoke to him about it, and Kanapé himself "would welcome this, as long as there was not too much delay, which might create the impression that he had begged for the uniform". To this Van Lier added: "The awe and keen appreciation with which the Djuka looks upon a uniform border on the ridiculous" (Journal, 4 March).

An interview with Amakti took place on 7 March, when it was decided to convene a *gran krutu* at Puketi some time later. This took place on 27th April. On this occasion Amakti at last publicly aired his view about the school, although by mouth of Aganga. He stated that the Governor had assured him expressly that Van Lier would not come to start a school. But, according to that day's entry in Van Lier's journal, he informed the meeting "that he would leave everyone free to send their children to school if they wished to do so, that he himself had no children to send, that he was not in favour of the school because of the distressing experience his predecessor, Granman Oseisie, had had in that connection. Oseisie had not been in favour of education for the Djukas, yet a school had been foisted on him. He (Amakti) had obtained the Governor's assurance that I would never establish a school there. That he was now leaving it to the chiefs to decide for themselves whether or no they would accept a school was just to oblige me. Before the Granman had given these directions to Aganga, he had declared in his presence that he had a very high opinion of Van Lier because of his 'pleasant manners' and willingness to help the Djukas. For that reason he would obtain everything he asked for from him, providing he did not keep insisting that a school should be started. Amakti's statement that he was opposed to a school but would leave the matter to the discretion of the chiefs, was, in their view, tantamount to a prohibition, and to disregard it would bring on disgrace. So the chiefs, after going into committee to discuss it, declared that, to their deep regret, they had no children to send to school – all of them had died of influenza".

Now it was Kanapé's turn to speak. He declared that he had come to regard the school affair as a personal matter and would in due course have more to say about it. He warned those present not to abuse Granman Oseisie's name in this connection. Thus Kanapé took a stand openly, and the fact that Van Lier had promised to procure him an official administrative post no doubt had something to do with it.

Van Lier expressed "his sympathy at the loss of all the Djuka children who had died of influenza" and promised to make a tour of the villages as soon as his camp was in order "so as to explain to each of the chiefs and other leaders in turn what I plan to accomplish with the school".

e The Governor refuses to appoint Kanapé as Head Chief

In the meantime Van Lier had written a letter on 28th March 1920[19] in which he requested that Kanapé should be appointed salaried Head Chief. The arguments he advanced were Amakti's disobliging attitude in the school matter, and the fact that Kanapé would be able, in an official capacity, to back the educational project. Van Lier thought that Amakti, who had many opponents among the Djukas, would suffer marked loss of prestige if he had to put up with a strong figure like Kanapé at his side. As long as he had virtually absolute power the chiefs, and certainly the people, would not dare to oppose him openly. The Government Secretary was in favour of the plan, the deputy Governor Rietveld could not be persuaded to support it. He took the matter into careful consideration and saw more disadvantages than advantages in an official appointment of Kanapé. By deviating from the rule laid down in the peace treaty of 1836 (Art. 13) that the Paramount Chief and the chieftains were to be elected by the Djukas themselves, after which the Government would – as a rule – endorse the appointment, the Government would in this case be guilty of a hostile act toward Amakti. To his mind, this would aggravate rather than improve matters in the Tapanahoni and encourage Amakti's opposition. The Government Secretary asked Van Lier on behalf of the Governor to set out his viewpoint and plans once more and in greater detail, but also told him that the Governor could not agree to it for the above-mentioned reasons and thought, moreover, that the postholder should not meddle in Djuka party politics. He wrote further, with

The Granholle Falls in the Tapanahoni, between Puketi and Drietabbetje, the largest of the rapids between these villages. The – empty – boats are dragged with ropes over the rocks, the load is carried across, the crew manning the boat walk across the rocks to the opposite side. The man with the barge-pole, *kulaman*, instructs the driver (if the boat has an outboard motor, otherwise the helmsman) how to keep clear of the rocks and currents, and steers with his pole. A second man manoeuvres with a pedal (lying on top of the load in the photograph).

(photograph by the author)

reference to Van Lier's fear that no results could be expected in the near future without active help of Kanapé's party, that the Governor did in fact not expect any results, either, in the *near* future from his activities. "Much patience will have to be exercised; by means of persuasion much distrust will have to be overcome."[20]

A letter to Amakti, who had submitted a request for an increase of salary,[21] stated that the Governor had been informed that he had refused his aid in the matter of starting a school, and that, unless he quickly changed his attitude, his salary would be lowered rather than raised and that he would even risk losing his post if he continued to oppose the postholder openly or covertly, thus betraying the promises he had made at Van Lier's installation.

f Van Lier decides to go on leave

The letter in which his plan was turned down reached Van Lier on 5 June and as a result of it he decided to take leave and go to Paramaribo. On June 13th he went to Drietabbetje to take leave of Amakti and his entourage, who begged him urgently not to stay away too long as the Djukas did not wish to be deprived of the many benefits they owed Van Lier. Amakti and his *Opo* followers, as well as Van Lier's *Bilo* opponents, requested him not to discuss his grievances about the school matter in the city, but rather to call a *krutu* on his return.

It was obvious that the conservative group also wished to convey their appreciation of Van Lier's presence in the Tapanahoni, especially on account of the medical aid he rendered. Moreover, they did not want to fall into disrepute with the Government that, as had become evident, was already threatening to reduce Amakti's salary and was capable of adopting even severer measures. By making Van Lier promise not to lodge a complaint with the Government during his leave and not to broach the school matter till after his return, they hoped to keep the decisions concerning it, and possibly a renewed passive resistance, under their own control.

When Van Lier thanked Amakti for his hospitality and for the trouble he had taken to provide accommodation until the camp at Granman Staalkondré was ready, "the Granman expressed his appreciation. However, he could not accept my thanks. It was from Paramaribo that gratitude was due to him, so he definitely counted on my reporting to the Governor how well I had been treated in the Tapanahoni. While the Granman was speaking, I pretended not to listen (a trick I had learnt from him). If I had been obliged to reply, a discussion would no doubt have followed and I know nothing more futile than arguing with Amakti.

Also, it would not do to raise distasteful matters on the eve of my departure" (Journal, 13 June 1920).

Two days later Aganga arrived at Granman Staalkondré to fetch medicine. Just as Amakti had done, he, too, begged Van Lier to return soon. *"Djuka no pooi tan sondro joe moro"* (the tribe can no longer do without you) he declared, according to Van Lier (Journal, 15 June 1920), who went on: "Then he reminds me of the fact that I had drunk the oath with him (*dringi sweri*) and so, even if anything rather unpleasant had befallen me during the first part of my stay here, I was not to complain of it in Paramaribo, but should wait till I get back and then discuss these matters in a *krutu*." Van Lier, who realized that Aganga was referring to the school affair, promised to keep his mouth shut. Even Chief Popo, Van Lier's outspoken opponent in spite of the fact that he belonged to the *Bilo* Negroes, gave him to understand in a very special manner that he wanted Van Lier to return. When Van Lier touched at Popo's village, Benanu, the day after his departure, he found him with *Gado na hede* ('God in his head', i.e. his *Winti* had taken possession of him) (Chapter II). Van Lier described the scene as follows: "Popo approached me immediately, but it was not Popo, it was the *Winti*. Popo was only the instrument. Djibri (as Popo's *Winti* is called) had heard so much good about me and could also confirm that from the spirit-world. On behalf of the Djuka mortals Djibri asked me not to stay away too long in the city. He gave me his blessing by singing a Djuka religious song in Kromantin,[22] which greatly delighted the bystanders... That evening Chief Popo paid me a visit. He had been absent all day since his *Gado (Winti)* was witnessing. The *Winti* had only just left him and he heard that I had come to Benanu. The request that I should not stay away too long was now repeated by the man Popo" (Journal 19 June).

Van Lier arrived in Paramaribo on 26 June 1920 and stayed there until 14 September. He held discussions with the Governor and the Government Secretary on whether or not Kanapé should be made Chief, on the agricultural prospects, on Amakti's authoritative position, on the continuation of the agricultural demonstration plan, and on the building of a permanent home for the postholder.

As for Amakti and Kanapé, it was decided to write the letter of thanks Amakti wanted, in which the Governor said that he had been gratified to learn that Van Lier had been well received by him and his people.

Concerning the boycott of the school, the Governor simply wrote: "I hope to hear soon that Mr. Van Lier has started to teach the Djuka children: I do not doubt that in this matter, too, you will give him the powerful support you promised when you were in Paramaribo." To this letter, however, another was added, addressed to the postholder, who had to convey its contents to Amakti. The Governor stated in this letter that he had been pleased to hear that Kanapé, just like Amakti, desired above all the betterment of their people. "Consequently I do not understand" the letter ran "why the Granman does not suggest that Kanapé, from whom he receives so much support, be nominated Head Chief. I have decided, therefore, to inform you that, if Amakti wishes to make such a suggestion, I shall consider it favourably."[23]

Amakti did not respond to this effort at persuading him by means of diplomatic wile to take the initiative in the matter of Kanapé's nomination. Not until he was driven into a corner as a result of the strike he had instigated among the Bush Negroes in the carrying-trade on the Marowijne, did he actually ask that Kanapé should be appointed joint Head Chief along with himself.

Concerning his agricultural plans Van Lier wrote a letter to the Governor on August 5, in which he asked for a loan of Fls. 1000, free of interest, with which to develop – at his own cost – his provision ground demonstration fields. He pointed out that he was totally dependent on his own provision grounds for his prime necessities; that a Bush Negro could be persuaded to work on the provision ground only if he was given food as well as payment; that a provision ground demonstration field would be the only way to teach the Djukas improved agricultural methods, and that, if this attempt should succeed, it would be a powerful means of making propaganda for his work.

The Director of the Agricultural Department, J.J. Leys, supported Van Lier's petition. "Since it is the postholder's task to civilize the Aucaners, surely he should be supplied with the means of performing that task" he wrote, and further: "Since the Colonial States were unwilling to provide him with those means, it should be keenly appreciated that Mr. Van Lier now says: "Then I shall do it at my own expense". He was granted the credit in Resolution 2930 of 30 August, 1920.

He also requested permission to build a permanent home for the sum of Fls. 2000, as he was planning 'to get married to a cultured lady' who would help him in his work and whom he would have to provide with a decent home. Despite the objection of several members of the Colonial States who found the amount too large, it was put on the supplementary budget. However, Van Lier's marriage did not take place and the house was never built.

§ 2 SECOND STAY IN THE TAPANAHONI, 29 OCTOBER 1920 – 22 MAY 1921

a Medical aid

On 14 September Van Lier left again for Albina, where he waited a month for the members of an expedition he was to accompany to a placer of the *Compagnie des Mines d'Or* on the Lawa. One of the members was the military surgeon, Hille Lambers, from whom Van Lier learnt as much as possible. When they arrived at Pulugudu on the way back, he even sent for *Da* Akodi from Powie to be examined by the doctor. The latter had left by the time Akodi arrived, but the old gentleman was grateful all the same, "for he could see in what high esteem I held him since I sent for him to be examined by a *gran datra* (fully qualified doctor)."

On his return to Granman Staalkondré on 29 October it appeared that one of his assistants had sold medicine for the amount of 456 francs during 4½ months. Referring to this, Van Lier remarks that he himself had sold medicine for 280 francs from January to the middle of June, and concludes "that the free distribution of medicine is decreasing here, while gradually faith in *bakra-dresie* is growing. As far as the treatment of ulcers is concerned, it can already be said without doubt that the Djukas prefer *bakra-dresie* to the *Obiaman*."

This conclusion was only true as regards the increased faith. The Djuka definitely did not give preference to the white man's medicine, but also, and probably in the first place, consulted their *obiaman*. As for the larger income from the sale of medicine: Van Lier's assistant may have been somewhat stricter in the matter of exacting payment.

On 11 November Van Lier wrote in his diary that he would henceforth mention only exceptional cases in his journal. As a matter of fact his notes now give less attention to his medical activities.

On 24 November, however, he was called to visit a sick woman at Powie. "Her whole body was badly swollen. As it happens, a young woman in the village of Cottica in the Lawa suffered from exactly the same symptoms when I was there with Dr. Hille Lambers. The doctor examined the patient at my request and diagnosed kidney disease. He gave instructions as to the treatment she was to have and what diet she was to follow. To ascertain whether this patient is suffering from the same complaint I test her urine and find that it contains much albumen. Ordered her to be treated the same way Dr. Lambers had prescribed in Cottica."

On the 30th November a boy of three was brought to him "suffering from severe bouts of fever recurring every second day at the same hour.

The spleen is much enlarged and his bowels are obstructed. I give him quinine-and-rhubarb-powder and *Lactis-ferromi*(?). Since I possess a vademecum of Dr. Eerntman I am able to determine the dosage."

On 2 December he was called to the bedside of a woman who, "as is evident even to a layman, was in the last stages of kidney disease". The woman and her family beg him to do something about it, and he advises her to drink large quantities of weak tea before he puts her on to medicine. He was anxious to help her, also for the incidental reason that the woman had been accused of *wisi*. She had been to Drietabbetje to undergo trial by poison so as to prove her innocence. Her illness was now interpreted as proof of her guilt (Chapter II).

At the end of December Van Lier mentions the death of two women, whose corpses were carried around and questioned about the cause of their death. The first gave as cause the fact "that, when she was a little girl, she had warned her father more than once that her mother was unfaithful to him and received a lover while he was away". Her father had twice given the scoundrel a good flogging. The lover died about twelve years ago and only now did the *jorka* come back to break Amujere's (the woman's name) neck (*kon broko en nekki*) to punish her for tale-bearing (Chapter II). The other woman, Donia, (see 2 December) appears, during the interrogation, to have died as a result of the *sweri* (trial by poison) and was consequently pronounced to be a *wisiman*. Therefore her corpse was not to be buried, but to be cast into the forest (Chapter II). However, the announcement of her death, as well as the result of the inquest, had to be sent to the Granman, as usual. Donia's corpse had declared "that she could not fix the day on which to be thrown away as she had not yet settled her affairs". (Every corpse, except a witch, 'fixes' the day on which it is to be buried.) The Granman, however, sent back a message to say "that she must leave his realm immediately; her affairs will be settled by Grantata (Chapter II). Donia 'states' that she will obey him and fixes the hour on which she is to be thrown away the following day at noon". Van Lier describes the sequence of events as follows: "During the time that the corpse is not being carried about, it is wrapped in a sheet and laid on the bare floor of the mortuary, to be cursed and mocked by the villagers and those who have come specially for that purpose from other parts. Nobody, not even her children, may mourn for a *wisiman*. Today, on December 30th, a lugubrious feast is being celebrated at Gran-Powie. Donia's corpse is being taken away. There is laughter and merriment because a wicked person has left the earth. At about noon all the villagers and visitors gather at the landing-stage to be able presently to pursue the spirit with their jeers. The uncoffined corpse, carried on the heads of two men, is deposited in a large boat. Four oarsmen take their places. When they push off, there is a loud and general outcry: '*Héru ooo, mi gi ju héru,*[24] *héru, héru, héru ooo!!!*', which amounts to: 'I wash my hand of you'. This repeated at every village along the way." Van Lier was deeply moved by this happening, and added: "I have witnessed much that was tragic in the course of my life, but I do not remember having ever been so deeply moved by anything."

The next day, however, he mentioned a comical aftermath: a woman came to him complaining of a sore throat. It appeared that she had shouted *héru* till she was completely hoarse. He gave her an alum solution to gargle with.

b Agriculture

Having received an interest-free loan for the development of his agricultural scheme, Van Lier started working with a will as soon as he got back. In the meantime his servant had already, with the help of some hired Djukas, cleared another ¼ hectare of land, so that the whole piece was now 1¼ hectares in size. But Van Lier wanted 2 hectares for his agricultural demonstration fields and set out again to look for Djuka labourers, without much success. He himself worked hard along with the others. In his Journal of 5 November 1920 he wrote: "Besides attending to the sick, I am busy every day with the clearing and tidying of the many trunks and branches of the trees that have been chopped down here. The forest was very dense here and many a giant had to be laid low. These factors do not make the development of this settlement any cheaper. Especially now that I have to consign many costly types of wood like Walaba, Kabes, Barklak, etc. to the flames because I have not yet been authorized to start preparing building materials for the house that is to be erected here. The few trunks I could leave lying for possible later use have not been removed, of course." On 6 November his assistant went on leave, for an indefinite period, to Paramaribo. Van Lier went on working without interruption. "As there is still a great deal to be tidied up before the rainy season starts, I am busy every day from early morning till evening. Fortunately my health is good and manual labour has no ill effects on me. Because I cannot find any Djukas yet for regular employment, I avail myself of the opportunity when people come to ask for medicine or something else to set them some task, however small (to be paid for, of course, what Djuka ever does anything for nothing?).

So the work does show some progress, although slow." On 9 November two sons of *Da* Akodi came to work for him and refused to accept the remuneration he offered, saying they only wished to show their gratitude for all that Van Lier had done for their father. But this kind of gesture was always an exception.

In the meantime he tried to persuade the Djukas to treat young planting material according to his method: on 20 November (Journal) he mentioned: "The planting material like coconut-palm and fruit trees I had obtained from the nursery but had not been able to plant yet on account of the weather, receives daily care from two Powie girls. The many Djukas who come here do not understand why I do not follow the cheaper course of setting the plants in a shallow part of the river near the landing-stage instead of spending money to have them watered. I explain to them that if I set the plants in the river they would get too much water, while, if they are sprayed, the leaves are moistened too. They are also much struck by the many holes for planting I have dug to receive the fruit trees, etc. as soon as the rains start. I explain to them, of course, what the object is." By 29 November it had in fact rained enough to set out the plants, and Van Lier once more explained the aim of his method to the Djukas who were watching him with interest. For the rest, he still had the greatest trouble in hiring Djukas for the clearing and cultivation of the soil. As a rule he could not find more than two or three at a time, and then they would usually not work for more than a day. Moreover, only one camp was ready in which Van Lier, albeit in a separate room, housed together with his assistants, and where Djukas staying over for the night had to be accommodated too. On 4 December he could report that the provision ground had at any rate reached a stage where "the rains can no longer prevent me from thoroughly clearing both the agricultural plot and the grounds around the house" (Journal, 4 December 1920). On 17 December he made a trip to the Lawa to buy planting material – bananas and root-crops – from the small agricultural plots situated on the French bank. "Typical of the agricultural conditions among the Bush Negroes" he noted here, "is surely the fact that (as a result of inbreeding) there is always a shortage of planting material."

Under the given circumstances it was not possible to persuade the Djukas to practise forest exploitation. They did not realize the (especially long-term) advantages of the extra work it entailed. Added to this was the fact that women were responsible for the cultivation of the soil and that the introduction of male workers would mean a drastic change in the traditional division of labour. A plan for making the Djukas collect forest products was basically not a bad idea. But here, too, the results were not evident to the Djukas: A guarantee of sufficient demand, attractive prices and transport facilities was not given.

c Education

In the meantime Van Lier kept on making propaganda for the establishment of a school by regularly expounding his educational plans and emphasizing the fact that he did not intend teaching the Christian religion. He spent a week at Drietabbetje and cheerfully reported on 25 February that he "had succeeded in making considerable headway towards solving the school question". Amakti sent word that "now that he had got to know me he was willing to give the school a try-out. Only, I would have to be prepared to give the assurance that no religious instruction would be included". Aganga, too, allowed himself to be persuaded and solemnly declared that Van Lier might count on his support at the forthcoming *krutu*. Finally, Kanapé advised him to "have everything ready for the opening of the school and then return to Drietabbetje where the matter would be settled by means of a *krutu*."

However, Van Lier received no pupils and his activities remained limited to general enlightenment. Amakti's statement that he was now willing to give the school a chance was probably bound up with the plans he was forging for a strike: he wanted to keep the atmosphere as favourable as possible before starting his revolt. Van Lier, acquainted with the plans for a strike, does not seem to have noticed the connection. The results of the strike were of great consequence to Van Lier's development scheme.

d The strike

In the same week that Van Lier wrote the above-mentioned optimistic letter, a strike was called among the Bush Negroes of the Marowijne carrying-trade, who were now refusing in Albina to take freight up the river.

Freight transport on the Marowijne, the Lawa and the Tapanahoni was carried out by the Djukas and, to a lesser degree, by the Bonnis, especially on behalf of the balata extractors and gold seekers who explored the interior in order to meet the demands of the French and the Dutch trade. All transport of passengers, material and food was largely dependent on Bush Negroes for traversing the many falls along the rivers. So there was a great hullabaloo on account of a strike instigated by Amakti, Paramount Chief of the Djukas, abetted by Awensai, Paramount Chief of the Bonnis. While there was ample cause for dissatisfaction among the freight carriers, both Paramount Chiefs also had personal reasons for provoking the action. For three years Awensai had received no salary from the French government and therefore wanted to put pressure on the administration by means of a strike. Amakti

Photograph taken in 1921, after a strike, as a result of which High Priest Kanapé (right) was appointed Paramount Chief together with Granman Amakti, and granted equal administrative authority. The *Granfiskari* (Grand Fiscal) Gagu (left) represented the Granman on certain occasions. (photograph reprinted from *De West-Indische Gids*, 1922/1923, p.209)

probably thought that his prestige among his own people would benefit if he took a firm line for once. Possibly the Governor's refusal to raise his salary also entered into the matter.

At first neither District Commisioner De Sanders nor Van Lier succeeded in suppressing the strike. On 22 May Van Lier left for Albina where he eventually managed to induce the freight carriers to resume work. The Administration intervened and adopted certain measures. Amakti was commanded, together with his followers, among which the High Priest Kanapé, to come to the city to answer for their conduct. Van Lier was also summoned to Paramaribo. A commission was appointed to investigate the underlying causes of the strike. This 'Albina commission'[25] found that the strikers' demands were justified. After the world war prices had risen so much on account of the depreciation of the French franc that the Bush Negroes had every reason to complain. They used to receive payment in francs and do part of their purchases in St. Laurent. The rest was done in Albina. But there, too, prices had risen. Besides, when they changed their francs into Dutch money they felt (often rightly) that they had been cheated. The measures taken to improve this situation had been insufficient, according to the commission. The blame lay with the present District Commissioner, De Sanders, and his predecessor. They had failed in the proper application of the efficient system of pass-books, adopted in 1909, for the freight-carriers and consignors, and had not consulted with the officials, traders and companies on the French side so as to rectify the position. But the commission also believed that the demands of the strikers should not, at the moment, be conceded, because the strike had been called without a preliminary consultation with administrative officials. Amakti was severely blamed for this, for it was contrary to the declaration which each newly appointed Granman made under oath to the Government.[26]

The fact that postholder Van Lier, who knew about Amakti's plans for a strike, did not intervene locally (in the Tapanahoni) was regarded as quite acceptable on account of the explanation he offered. He had regularly informed, warned and advised the District Commissioner. If the postholder had personally called Amakti to task, the latter would undoubtedly have denied everything, and Van Lier would have learnt nothing more from his talkative informants. The District Commissioner had not responded to Van Lier's letters and for this he was also blamed. The Government dismissed the District Commissioner from his post and one of the injunctions given to his successor was to maintain the pass system.

After he had acknowledged his guilt and begged forgiveness, Amakti was allowed to keep his position as Granman, but with (at his request) Kanapé at his side as Head Chief. Henceforth Kanapé would be held co-responsible for all the Granman's actions.

At Kanapé's request Chief Gagu, who was to receive the title of Granfiskari, also joined him in order to help with the maintenance of order and discipline among the Djukas.

In the *West-Indische Gids*[27] Van Lier gave a detailed report of the strike and of the meetings during Amakti's stay in the city. In the same annual issue of this periodical the agreement made with the Djukas is set forth,[28] with a supplementary piece about the causes of the strike, by Governor G.J. Staal. The stipulations in this agreement that bear on the postholder's position are as follows: (3) The present or future postholder among the Aucaner Bush Negroes must be consulted in all matters pertaining to the whites. Orders given by him in the name of the Governor must be obeyed. (8) The postholder is to start as soon as possible with the education of the Djuka children; the Bush Negro chiefs in this area undertake to encourage school attendance as far as possible and to quell the opposition raised by others against the school.

The penalty attached to non-compliance with these stipulations was (10) that self-government among the Djukas would be abolished, and officials, police and militia would be sent to the Tapanahoni to govern that territory in the same manner as the other districts.

When this point was under discussion, Kanapé asked that education should also be made compulsory for the Djuka children, but this was not acceded to[29]. Kanapé wanted a more binding assurance that a boarding-school would be established and asked the Governor in a private interview to promise this personally. "The Governor made this promise", Van Lier wrote in a report on the year 1923 and the first quarter of 1924 which also contained a recapitulation of this affair "but pointed out that the approval of the Colonial States and the Dutch Government, as well as the sanction of Her Majesty the Queen would have to be obtained before the school could be started".

At the end of September the meeting broke up and the members parted in a fairly satisfied spirit. The administration had been able to demonstrate and re-establish its authority.

The band of Djuka worthies returned to their tribe, relieved at the turn of events, pleased with the resolutions that had been passed and deeply impressed by the display of power by *lanti* (the Government). At all events, Amakti repeatedly declared in public that he would rather resign as Granman than to have to appear again before the 'hundred uniforms'. By this he meant the meeting at the Government House where Amakti, in the presence of a large number of bigwigs, e.g. the Officers of the Garrison and the Artillery, had been reprimanded by the Governor in person and told in no uncertain terms that he would have to toe the line in future.

Van Lier, too, was pleased with the turn of events. His role in the matter of the strike had won the approval of both Government and Djukas, no mean achievement in the delicate position in which he was placed. Two points which were important to him had now been settled officially: Kanapé was appointed Head Chief and the Djuka leaders had sworn to give their support to the project of education.

e Request for financial aid to start a boarding-school; plan for extension of forestry

Under these circumstances Van Lier thought the moment had come to ask for money for the building and equipping of a boarding-school, such as he had envisaged in his working-plan of 24 September 1919. This plan had taken shape during talks with the Governor and the Government Secretary; the members of the Colonial States had not been officially informed of it. In October 1921 he submitted a note in which he set forth, just as in his working-plan, why he found it necessary to take a number, provisionally about twenty, of Djuka children completely under his care and provide them with board and lodging so as to obtain the best educational results. The amount he asked for (Fls. 3000) he regarded as essential to start the institution. He expected to reduce the annual expenses by teaching the children tillage and stock-farming and persuading the parents to give contributions. He was convinced that after two to three years the boarding-school would be self-sufficient.

In the meantime Van Lier had made use of his stay in Paramaribo to work out a plan for stepping up the exploitation of forests along the Tapanahoni. In this connection he consulted the Official Forest Conservator, J.W. Gonggrijp, who recommended the scheme in a report accompanying the memorandum Van Lier wrote to the Government Secretary on 18 August 1921.

In this document Van Lier asked for a forest-keeper to be placed at his disposal, who would search for valuable kinds of timber in the vicinity of his post, encourage the Bush Negroes to cultivate these on their abandoned provision grounds and teach them to dress the wood (rosewood, mahogany, cedarwood, etc.) for sale. In his report Gonggrijp remarked that it might also be profitable to collect gums, resin, balata, chicle and teak resin.

Besides, Van Lier hoped to gain much from the presence of another assistant to the postholder's office. The keeper he had in mind, H.W. Bakboord, would, together with his young wife, be able to fill his place when he, Van Lier, was absent on duty. This was all the more important as the school would now soon be started at Granman Staalkondré and should be kept going without interruption. Bakboord's wife, especially, would be of great service to him in this respect. Gonggrijp set the condition that the forest-keeper to be appointed would be placed under supervision of a superior who could be held responsible for the activities of his subordinate. So he found that the best solution would be to appoint Van Lier superintendent of Forestry. The suggestion was approved by the Government and as from 15 October 1921 Van Lier was appointed superintendent, while on 1 January 1922 Bakboord was appointed deputy forest-keeper and assigned to Van Lier, together with a labourer, J. Tol.

NOTES

[1] Van Lier, 1922, p. 9 et seq.
[2] Form of address.
[3] Van Lier, 1922, pp. 24-25.
[4] Government Resolution, No. 862, 1919.
[5] Extract from the Postholder's Register of Daily Notes among the Aucaner Bush Negroes in the Upper Marowijne (henceforth referred to as Journal).
[6] Van Lier, 1922, p. 206.
[7] In each village there is such a place: *kre-oso* (cry house). Here every corpse lies in state until it is buried (sometimes after a considerable lapse of time).
[8] Governor Staal Town.
[9] That is, on the occasion of Van Lier's installation.
[10] I have not come across the results of this analysis (De Groot).
[11] Lichtveld, 1930, pp. 50-52.
[12] Benjamins, 1929, 1931.
[13] Van Lier, 1944, writes that every desire expressed by a sick person is inspired by an evil spirit, and may not be acceded to; the opposite should rather be done for the benefit of the patient. Thus the thirsty Batrafutu kept begging for water but was not given a drop.
[14] The Djukas liked to pay in the French francs they earned in the river carrying-trade in French Guyana.
[15] The second most important Djuka-*lo*.
[16] Van Lier specifies neither the treatment nor the medicine.
[17] The spirits of important (great) ancestors.

[18] Van Lier, 1922, p. 209.
[19] Government Resolution, No. 16, 28 March 1920, Confidential.
[20] Government Resolution No. 1, 25 May 1920, Confidential.
[21] Government Resolution, No. 192, 25 May 1920.
[22] Kromantin, Negro English *Kromanti*, sacred language, containing words from the Akan language.
[23] Government Resolution, No. 3139, 14 September 1920.
[24] Literally: I give you *héru*, I hold you alone responsible.
[25] Appointed by Government Resolution of 11/14 June, 1921, Highly Confidential.
[26] In this declaration, made by Amakti in 1916, he had promised: (7) Differences which might develop between his tribe and other tribes or persons would be submitted to the Governor or to the authorities appointed by him and: (13) If he should suffer injustice at the hands of an inhabitant or someone else not belonging to his tribe, he would lodge his complaints with the Government Secretary, entrusted with the care of Bush Negroes and Indians, and immediately report those who had wronged him to the competent authorities. (Agreement with the Aucaner Bush Negroes, W.I.G. 1922, pp. 48-49).
[27] Van Lier, 1922, pp. 213-230.
[28] Agreement with the Aucaner Bush Negroes, W.I.G. 1922, pp. 48-52.
[29] Compulsory education for children from seven to twelve years existed in Surinam since 1876, twenty-four years before it was introduced in the Netherlands.

CHAPTER VI

PERIOD 1921-1924

§ 1 THIRD STAY ON THE TAPANAHONI, 21 NOVEMBER 1921 – 22 JUNE 1922

Van Lier, having settled his affairs in Paramaribo and submitted his new suggestions, left again for the Tapanahoni, where he arrived on 21 November 1921.

a Agriculture, cattle-breeding and forestry

His long absence had had disastrous consequences for the small agricultural plot he had got going so laboriously, and particularly for the rice harvest. His assistant, who had stayed behind, had not managed to procure the help of any Djukas with the harvesting. Not only had the crops failed, which meant a loss of Fls. 700-800, but because of his absence the new planting season had not been turned to account. His poultry-farming had also been neglected. "As a result of all this I have to face the sad truth" he complains in a letter on 29 November "that the hope of being able to produce the elementary necessities of life for myself and my servant here cannot be fulfilled for the time being. Consequently I shall have to continue getting my commodities from Paramaribo and Albina." The budding interest among the Djukas for his methods had petered out and had to be reawakened. After a primary failure this was twice as difficult to achieve.

The newly appointed forest-keeper, Bakboord, his wife and the labourer Tol arrived at Granman Staalkondré on 29 January 1922, accompanied by a letter from Gonggrijp requesting Van Lier to allow Bakboord the opportunity of building a camp for himself, to cultivate a plot, to search for rosewood and gather as much of its seed as possible, as well as the seed of the bamba-tree (*Oreo Daphne*). After that Bakboord should start getting the Bush Negroes to plant valuable timber like Woccacapoua (*Americana*), letterwood and rosewood on their plots. He asked, too, whether coconut-trees could be planted on the arable fields near the villages. Van Lier replied on 31 January, writing that he would try "to carry out the instructions contained in it as soon as possible". According to the Bush Negroes there was plenty of bamba-wood in the vicinity, coconut-trees had already been planted on the demonstration field and some of the trees were about six feet high already.

Neither Van Lier nor Bakboord had enough knowledge for putting these rather ambitious plans into operation. Especially Van Lier did not have time to devote to it. But also Gonggrijp, the forest conservator, had underestimated the difficulties. A number of problems, e.g. the transport of timber across the many falls in the river (practically impossible) and the chances of disposing of timber and of forest- and other products in the coastal area had not been considered. As a result the expectations of the optimistic beginners were disappointed. Gonggrijp put all the blame on Van Lier.

During the rainy season in January and February Van Lier could do little about replanting his neglected fields. Bakboord and Tol came to settle with him and informed him that, as soon as the provisions they had brought along were finished, they counted on receiving supplies from him. They would start tilling and planting, but it would take at least three months before anything was produced. Although they had provisions for three months, they had to get fish and meat by hunting for it. No steps had been taken to meet the needs of the Djukas who were to help Bakboord in prospecting the forest, and Van Lier anticipated – what actually happened – that he would have to supply the Djukas with food.

The food problems were not insolvable. Gonggrijp had some more supplies sent along and Bakboord, who had connections with the Bush Negroes and French along the Lawa, was able to buy provisions from time to time. Van Lier had, moreover, received an advance of Fls. 600 for 1922 for agricultural purposes, which he used, as well as acquiring new plantings, for the purchase and care of a number of pigs, goats and chickens.

The question of how and from whom Bakboord, his wife, the labourer Tol and the Djukas they were to hire would receive food supplies led to a violent dispute by letter between Van Lier and Gonggrijp. This culminated in a rupture, the recall of Bakboord and Tol, and the end of Van Lier's position as supervisor in the forestry department.

b Meeting at Drietabbetje

A month after Van Lier's return to Granman Staalkondré a large *krutu* was held on 23 December 1921 in Drietabbetje.[1]

At this meeting, where practically all the chiefs were present, the events in Paramaribo were recapitulated and many matters concerning the Djuka tribe were discussed. On this occasion Van Lier played the main role. He did not fail to emphasize how concerned he was for the welfare of the Djukas, with whom he had sworn the oath of loyalty, and the pains he had taken to defend their interests. He elaborated at great length (according to Djuka custom) the course of events in Paramaribo, to which – according to Van Lier – the reaction of the shocked Djuka leaders was: "No Djuka would tell all these things in public; as usual they would again hear with what marks of honour the Granman had been received and treated. How fortunate that at last someone has come along who is not a toady, but speaks the truth, etc."

He told the meeting that Amakti had finally admitted to the administration that he no longer enjoyed any authority in the Tapanahoni, that all his friends were fair-weather friends and that he realized he needed Kanapé at his side in order to restore his prestige. This roused indignant reactions at the *krutu*: Amakti as well as Gagu had declared that the Government had made the appointment without their knowledge or approval.

Van Lier availed himself of this mood to present the part he had played in Kanapé's appointment in a light which was more favourable both to himself and Kanapé: "Since my return I have been told" he said "that the slanderous rumour is being spread that Kanapé used cunning methods to persuade me to procure his appointment. I warn you not to persist in this. If you do, you will create fresh difficulties for the Granman. Moreover, it is a disgrace to slander a person here who has done as much as Kanapé has done in the city, for the tribe as well as for Amakti personally." He told them how Kanapé had time and again tried to intercede on behalf of the Granman with the Government Secretary as well as with other senior officials, and that, having gained a private hearing with the Governor, he had seized the opporunity to beg His Excellency personally to forgive and forget all that had happened."

This statement also had its effect on them, so that one of Kanapé's chief opponents from the Missiedjan-*lo* exclaimed with relief: "I thank God that Mr. Van Lier has come to put an end to the Djuka scheming. Before Granman Oseisie's death everyone knew that Kanapé would become Granman; well, this has happened today. Amakti himself has

The house in which Granman Amakti lay ill while Van Lier was explaining the events connected with the strike in 1921. In the background a Djuka hut in modern style. The wood carving has been replaced by colourful paintings. In both media the motives have symbolical as well as decorative significance. (photograph by the author)

appointed him." The humiliated Amakti, lying in his own hut with influenza, replied to Van Lier's question: "Granman, you're in your house, but all the same you can hear everything that's being said here. Haven't I told everything exactly as it happened?" "Yes, it happened like that."

When the matter of education was brought forward, the meeting expressed disappointment because there was to be only one school, at Granman Staalkondré, but Van Lier explained that he would offer lodging to the children who lived too far away. If the first school proved a success, more would no doubt be started in future. Van Lier also used this opportunity to repeat a number of 'commands' which, although not put down in writing, had to be imparted by instruction of the Governor. He, Van Lier, would have to see that these commands (which, in fact, he himself had suggested to the Governor) were carried out. He had made sure beforehand that Kanapé would support him, which the latter did at the *krutu*. The commands entailed that:

1. All forms of corporal punishment were to be abolished immediately.
2. No corpse was to remain unburied for more than three days.
3. The corpses of *wisimans* were not be thrown away any more, but must henceforth be buried.

The Djukas declared unanimously that they agreed to these measures. Chief Popo, the strongest opponent of reform in general and of Kanapé and Van Lier in particular, even found that "this day is a blessing of God, now that an end has come to so much that oppressed the Djukas and which would never have been changed without help from the *Bakras*, since it was a matter of ancestral usage".

The meeting closed with Van Lier's statement that he accepted the gratitude offered for all he had done for the Djukas, but that he took it simply as a polite gesture. "For it is a fact which I now repeat that I regard myself completely as a Djuka. What I did, I did for myself, and nobody may claim gratitude for what he does for himself."

The Djukas wondered when the school that had been announced would now be started. A number of chiefs came to ask Van Lier to take their sons under his care and Kanapé declared, according to Van Lier's journal entry of 18 May 1922, "that if presently a letter should come to ask why the school had not yet been opened, I shall have to find some answer; it is no longer the Djukas who do not want a school".

Van Lier blamed the delay on his urgent activities: he was busy taking a census of the Bush Negro population for which purpose he had to visit all the villages one by one; his accommodation at Granman

Staalkondré was not yet such that he could take in children. As a matter of fact he was, while waiting to hear from Paramaribo whether or not money would be granted for his boarding-school, in a state of nervous tension ("highly neurasthenic" as he wrote in his diary. Van Lier kept small notebooks in which he jotted down in pencil the description of events he later on copied into his official journal. Now and then he mentions his mood in these jottings.).

c Notes on the meeting

The above report on the meeting indicates how Van Lier viewed the state of affairs. Naturally he did not mention that the Djukas' exclamations of praise and approbation could not be taken at their face value. Many of their statements were utterly insincere, others had to be taken with a liberal pinch of salt. This was the traditional reaction, part of the Djuka technique displayed at meetings. But Van Lier transgressed against a number of widely accepted codes with his demagogic tactics. The danger to his educational scheme seems obvious. Van Lier sinned against "two aspects of culturally determined behaviour or propriety particularly resistant to change: personal dignity and modesty... if he (the individual) must act in a way that lowers his esteem in the eyes of his fellows, he is likely to resist the innovation."[2]

He thought – and to my mind correctly – that in the given circumstances he was justified in running these risks.

1. The Granman enjoys the general adulation of his subjects, which is out of proportion to the scope of his power. He is surrounded by pomp and ceremony. He "may suffer no loss of face: his tribesmen see to this... If he has misbehaved in the eyes of priests or influential persons of standing, he will never be reprimanded or penalized in public."[3]

Van Lier, too, was aware of this.[4]

In spite of the obeisance done to the Granman, his decisions are in no wise carried out slavishly. In a less direct but nonetheless effective manner an opponent or group of opponents can prevent him from doing certain deeds or force him to do others. Opponents (or renegade followers) can in fact turn an incidental or permanent loss of prestige on the part of the Granman to their advantage. Van Lier used this type of manoeuvre in his attempt to stabilize his position.

2. The Djukas considered that good relations between the Granman and Government were essential for the proper distribution of power in the Tapanahoni.[5] It was clear to all the Djukas, in spite of the touched

up representation which Amakti himself gave of his interview with the Government, that the Granman had suffered great loss of prestige. He had been obliged to confess his guilt and make fresh promises.

3. A proof of Amakti's diminished authority was the fact that Kanapé was invested – in the eyes of the Government – with just as much power as the Granman. Kanapé's opponents also realized that in future they would have to take him definitely into account.

4. It is doubtful whether Van Lier's positive statement that he and Kanapé had not 'manipulated' the latter's appointment was believed, but the Djukas realized that under the circumstances it was at all events better to pretend credulity.

d The population census and the survey of health conditions among the Djukas

During March, April and May 1922 Van Lier made a tour of the villages above and below Drietabbetje, in order to estimate, on instructions of the Government, the number of Djukas living in the Tapanahoni. His report on the census was handed in on the 8th of August to the Government Secretary, rather late considering that the 'General Director' for the drawing up of the civil registry, N.E. Hendriquez, expected the data not later than the beginning of March. Van Lier estimated the number of Djukas present in the surveyed area at 3482. This included the villages from Pulugudu up to Godo-oro (above Drietabbetje).[6] The Djukas along the Marowijne and Lawa, Upper Commewijne and Cottica were counted by other surveyors.

In the memorandum he affixed to the register of the census survey of the Tapanahoni (12 June 1922) Van Lier described the method he applied as follows:[7] "In order to make the survey, I visited twenty-six villages in the Tapanahoni personally. There are in fact *twenty-eight* villages in the Tapanahoni, not counting the settlement at the agricultural development plots. Acoté and Akrékuna, situated respectively between Pulugudu and Tabbetje (*Bilo*) and Upper Godo Oro (*Opo*) were however, not mentioned because the former is peopled by inhabitants of the three villages known as Godo Oro. Their numbers are included in the figures assigned to the respective villages.

I may mention here at once that the sum total stated in this register includes the Bush Negroes living in the settlements of the Lower Lawa, between the Apoma and Pulugudu falls. These settlements are only camps attached to the agricultural plots. (They were surveyed, so I was informed, by the supervisor of forestry, Warning.)

I was only able to make an accurate survey of the inhabitants of Powie, opposite Granman Staalkondré.

On the basis of the results of this survey I estimated the numbers in the other villages. The results were obtained from the survey of a *certain number* of huts in each village and further information gleaned from the inhabitants themselves.

Estimating the number of Bush Negroes in a village according to the total number of huts it contains is not to be recommended. This method would yield an erroneous result for in every village there are some huts, the so-called *massangas*, which are not inhabited but used by the owners only for storing valuable possessions. Moreover, one person often has one or more huts in two or three villages, and it is the general rule for one man to have two, but often three and sometimes four wives, and he builds a hut for each of these wives in the village where she belongs.

Thus the most important thing for me, in making the survey, was to know as near as possible how many huts belonged to the same person.

In order to ascertain this fairly correctly I had to set to work with the utmost caution so as not to arouse the inhabitants' suspicion.

After I had established, in the case of Powi, how many huts should be taken into consideration for the estimate, and the number of men and women had been surveyed, I calculated the average number of persons per hut (divided according to sex) and multiplied this average with the number of huts in the other villages to be considered for the purpose of the survey."

Van Lier was convinced that the Bush Negroes in general and the Djukas in particular were doomed to extinction. In his report, which he also submitted to the health inspector, Dr. Wolff, in August, he wrote: "The death rate in the Tapanahoni is exceptionally high and seems to have been like that for the past hundred years. At any rate, all the historians who have written about the Aucaners state that this group is becoming extinct. The remark has been made that, if this is true, the process is a very slow one. Objectively speaking this may be the case and, as such, due to the great fertility of the Negro race, yet I can state here with the *utmost conviction* that the end is now in sight. Anyone who makes a quick visit to the Tapanahoni will, if he pays attention to the matter, be persuaded of the truth of this assertion. Apart from the many villages that have ceased to exist (new ones have not been built since) because their inhabitants, with a few exceptions, have died, one can notice in almost all existing villages numbers of ramshackle or tumble-down huts whose former inhabitants have departed this life. One need not stay long among the Aucaners to observe how high their death rate is and how many young men and women are carried off in the prime of life. The infant mortality rate, especially among young babies, has now become so common among the Bush Negroes that it hardly attracts any attention." In the same report he described the most common illnesses and remarked: "Like among other primitive people who have no conception of hygiene, almost all illnesses assuming epidemic proportions are prevalent among the Djukas." In the first case he mentions syphilis "in all its varieties and so widespread that its victims can even be recognized by the layman."

All Djuka children suffered from yaws (*framboesia tropica*), and most Djukas from *anchylostomiasis* and other worm ailments. Tuberculosis abounded everywhere, but was, according to Van Lier, more prevalent in the Lower than the Upper Tapanahoni. Leprosy was comparatively rare, but more frequent in the upper than the lower areas. He had formed the impression (because of the total lack of isolation) that the disease could not be contagious. Malaria was very common and especially a killer of young children, while the old were more prone to succumb to the endemic influenza. *Filariasis* (*elephantiasis arabum*), a disease which was very common in Paramaribo, occurred much less frequently in the Tapanahoni.

Van Lier concluded his report with the remark: "I attribute the fact that the Djukas are still so robust and strong, in spite of the circumstances described above, to the natural selection which exists. Since from before birth, so to speak, they already have to cope with so much in the way of disease and physical misery, those who do not succumb are indeed resistant."

Van Lier's sombre view of the chances of the Djukas' survival is contradicted by the statistical figures, scanty and inexact though they be.

The number of Djukas in the Tapanahoni he estimated in 1921 at about 3500. Thoden van Velzen (1966, p. 12) estimated their number at 6000 in 1961.

The total number of Djukas was estimated in 1922/23 at 5643, in 1964 at 15,000 (according to unpublished official data).

While the number of Djukas was thus doubled, the total number of Bush Negroes was more than trebled.

(The total number of Bush Negroes were estimated
in 1863 at 8000
in 1923 at 18454
in 1946 at 22000
in 1964 at 27678 (or 8.5% of the entire Surinam population.)

This increase was undoubtedly the result of improved medical care. A far larger number of Bush Negroes can now resort to polyclinics and hospitals because a number of these have been built in the backwoods and because of augmented transport facilities (outboard motorboats and – in emergencies – airplanes). Improved medical techniques have lowered the death rate further.

e The Colonial States refuse a grant for a boarding-school

When the supplementary budget for 1922 came up for discussion, Van Lier's request for a grant to build a boarding-school was laid before the Colonial States. The Governor, A.J.A.A. Baron van Heemstra, in office since 23 May 1921, supported the plan in his Memorandum of Advice, and at the meeting of 28 February 1922 the members of the Colonial States discussed the article: "Grant for feeding and care of Bush Negro children attending the school at Granman Staalkondré... Fls. 3000."

The debate on this topic revealed that a number of members, never optimistic about the educational scheme in its original form and strengthened in their views because of the scanty results obtained so far, had not changed their attitude in the least. The idea of now starting a boarding-school seemed to them over-ambitious. Moreover, it did not conform to the original agreement, and finally they believed that the whole undertaking was going to cost far too much money. The experiment had up till then cost Fls. 25000 already. Nor did they believe that the expenses related to the boarding-school would decrease annually, as Van Lier predicted. They thought, too, that accommodation for twenty children would not be enough. The objection was raised once more that the teaching would be done by a lay person and not by a Catholic or Protestant mission society. It was stated explicitly that they had nothing against Van Lier and greatly admired his idealism and his perseverance, but that they held that so far nothing had been achieved and that it would be unwarranted to vote more money for the purpose.

The arguments put forward by the Government Secretary Eekhout, who maintained that the postholder should be given a 'fair chance' as long as the experiment lasted; that the Governor – and thus the Administration – had pledged himself by a promise to the Bush Negroes; and that the situation in the Tapanahoni after the strike, now that Kanapé had been invested with authority, seemed favourable enough to start the teaching, failed to convince the members and the motion was rejected by five votes to three.

On 4 May 1922 the matter was again brought forward in the Colonial States meeting on the draft budget. The motion now read: "Grant for feeding and care of Bush Negro children attending the schools at Granman Staalkondré and near Albina... Fls. 3000." The addition, intended to let the mission school at Albina share in the proposed grant, was made because several members had raised the question during the meeting on 28 February as to why mission schools received such a small subsidy. Also in this form the motion was rejected with five votes to three, on more or less the same grounds.

f Van Lier leaves for Paramaribo

Van Lier received notice in March that the grant for the boarding-school had been refused and in May an official notification from the Government Secretary that a second attempt had failed. "Needless to say," the official wrote "the Governor is distressed at this turn of events and His Excellency deeply regrets that the promise made by the Administration – even though pending approval by the Colonial States – cannot be fulfilled. On behalf of His Excellency I have the honour of requesting you to explain to the Head Chief Kanapé and the other Chieftains the state of affairs and that there is no money available for the school and the boarding-school."[8]

Van Lier was deeply disappointed. So much so that he decided to go to Paramaribo to argue the case personally once more. He regarded the establishment of a school, with the necessary addition of boarding facilities, as a *conditio sine qua non* for his civilizing mission among the Djukas. Without that boarding-school the postholdership among the Djukas would have forfeited its chief justification. He did not abandon all hope, however, and did not carry out the administration's instruction to inform the Djukas of their decision. In a letter dated 8 June to the Government Secretary he wrote: "In the interest of the prestige of the authorities I would like to request His Excellency the Governor respectfully to grant me an interview before I impart the sad news regarding the school to the Bush Negroes. In this connection I hope, availing myself of the fact that leave is due to me, to arrive at Paramaribo by mailboat on the 27th inst."

Before leaving he attended a *krutu* at Drietabbetje on 14 June. In order to elicit a clear statement from the Djuka leaders Amakti, Kanapé and Gagu, he declared that he would ask the Governor to transfer him to another post. He gave as reason the fact that he "could not count on sufficient co-operation from the leaders and the people". He continued: "Abuses are still rife in the Tapanahoni and I see very little chance of order and discipline being established... I might still be able to accept all this, but I could not tolerate the contempt with which Popo treated me" (Journal, 14 June 1922). (Chief Popo of Benanu had given orders to refuse Van Lier, who was on a census-taking tour, the right to enter his village during his absence.) The astonished Djukas had no difficulty in pointing out to Van Lier the inconsistency of his motives and in making him promise – as he had intended them to do – to return to the Tapanahoni. Kanapé said: "You want to leave, what will happen to the school then? Will the Djuka children again get no education after the matter has been settled with the *bakras*? You may not desert us. You are going on leave now, and if you do not return soon, I shall come and fetch you back." Steps would be taken against Popo, but it would not do to deprive the Djuka children of education because of one man's offensive behaviour. Finally Amakti said: "*Masra* Van Lier, I have listened to your decision, but I ask you one favour. Promise me you'll come back and stay here until you have buried me, that won't be long now. But don't leave the Tapanahoni as long as I'm still alive, come back to start the school so that you may write on my behalf to the Secretary that I've kept my word. I promised him faithfully that the school would be started. If you stay away and another *bakra* comes here, the Aucaners might not feel like entrusting their children to him and probably I shall be blamed for it again. So do come back."

"There was nothing else for me to do now" Van Lier added, "and I promised to come back."

To find out how they would react to the possibility that the school might not materialize, he told Kanapé that he had not yet heard whether money would be granted for the school and asked him whether it had ever occurred to him that it might be refused. But Kanapé had no doubt on that score: if the Governor asked for money for a school for the Djuka children, he would be sure to get it, and since it was, moreover, the wish of Her Majesty the Queen "that all her subjects should learn to read and write, nobody could refuse the money needed for it, especially not now, since the new treaty contains a stipulation relating to the school" (Journal, 18 June 1922).

With these utterances by the Djukas recorded in his daily jottings, Van Lier left on 22 June 1922 for Paramaribo, hoping that he had enough arguments to persuade the Colonial States to retract their decision. Although he had intended staying in Paramaribo for only some twelve days, fourteen months elapsed before he arrived back at Granman Staalkondré on 26 August 1923.

g The loan is granted

When Van Lier arrived in Paramaribo he drew up a report on the school question. This report, accompanied by a missive from the Governor,[9] was submitted to the Colonial States for consideration. The missive, Van Lier's report and an excerpt from his daily notes describing the *krutu* of 14 June, were discussed in the Colonial States meeting on 16 August.

In his report Van Lier once again briefly recapitulates the attempts at educating the Djukas, his plans for a boarding-school as set forth in his note of 24 September 1919, the trust which the Djukas placed in him, and their wish to get the school that had been promised by the Government actually started. "I hope to have shown to Your Excellency's satisfaction, by means of the above facts, that it is hardly possible to go back on the promise given to the Bush Negroes regarding the school, without seriously damaging the prestige of the authorities and dealing a severe blow to their faith in the word pledged by the *Bakras*, not to mention the fact that Kanapé and his followers regard this matter as having been settled by treaty." His opinion was: "If the school is not founded, the postholder cannot be maintained in his position. After all, the object of the postholdership was to make a forceful effort at civilizing the Aucaners and, to my mind, it goes without saying that civilization is unthinkable without schooling."

Besides education, which Van Lier regarded as of central importance, he attached so much weight to other aspects of the civilizing process, especially training in forestry, that he thought the Djukas would be doomed to extinction if the postholdership were abolished. The transport business, with which the Djukas earned their money, would soon be greatly reduced as a result of the falling off of gold and balata production in their area. The culture of superior types of timber as well as the coconut culture would provide new ways of maintaining themselves through trade with the coastal districts.

Lack of medical instruction could also have disastrous effects: their ignorance of hygienic principles would lead to their downfall. The advances which had been made in this field: burial of the dead after three days instead of at least eight, and interment of witches instead of throwing their corpses away, would be lost again. (This was a white lie.)

As a result of his census-taking in the Tapanahoni he believed that "in the not so distant future this tribe would be extinct".

He concluded his report with the request: "Your Excellency, on behalf of the 3644 surviving Aucaners in the Tapanahoni, I humbly beseech you to do all in your Excellency's power to allow the work in the Tapanahoni to be carried on."

In a missive seconding the report the Governor expressed his disappointment at the fact "that the Colonial States were not willing to help maintain the prestige of the administration, which should be based upon the trust the Bush Negroes place in their promises".

Once again there were lengthy debates on the school, boarding-school and postholdership. The arguments for and against differed very little from those advanced at the meetings of 28 February and 4 May.

The promise made by Governor Staal and his successor, Baron Van Heemstra, with regard to the establishment of a school among the Djukas, and acknowledgement of the fact that Van Lier's suggestion to have a boarding establishment attached to it had been made as early as September 1919, carried more weight this time.[10] It was also pointed out that a grant of Fls. 3000 for the first year amounted to just 25 cent per day per child. The argument advanced by some opponents that it was bad educational policy not to let the parents themselves provide housing for their children, while it should rather be brought home to them that they ought to pay taxes, was refuted by the remark: "Taxes are paid as a contribution to the maintenance of a society of which one enjoys the privileges and benefits. What benefits do the Aucaners receive from our state? None whatever."[11]

The proposal to place a grant of Fls. 3000 on the budget for the boarding-school at Granman Staalkondré and for a school at Albina was finally adopted with seven votes to one and submitted to the Budget Commission in the Netherlands.

In an extensive 'confidential' and 'highly confidential' correspondence between Governor Van Heemstra and the Minister of Colonial Affairs, De Graaff, and particularly in a letter of 28 February 1923 (No. 17, highly confidential) Van Heemstra set forth the reasons why he supported this proposal: When he was appointed, he accepted arrangements that had already been made. A promise given should, for political reasons, be fulfilled. French influence among the Djukas was increasing.

A Government-subsidized boarding-school was necessary, because children coming from distant villages, especially those of the Granman and Chieftains of Drietabbetje should be given the opportunity of attending school. The large falls and rapids between the Lower and Upper Tapanahoni (corresponding to the *Bilo* and *Opo* Negroes) were, in particular, hindrances that made travelling back and forth impossible.

This geographic obstacle also prevented the postholder from living in the main village, Drietabbetje, as the falls were sometimes impassible for weeks on end during the rainy season.

To fill the school exclusively with *Bilo* Negro children would not succeed: "If you are familiar with the Aucaner mentality, you know that no member of a lower caste will dare accept anything if the Granman and his entourage cannot share in it."

The idea of feeding the children sprang from the fact that the Bush Negroes had never paid for anything the Government supplied to them and certainly would not want to do so now, either. It would serve as 'counter-propaganda' for the school if payment were demanded.

Van Heemstra stated clearly in his letter that Van Lier had not acted 'on his own' but had, as early as September 1919, proposed in his plan of action that a grant should be assigned for a boarding-school, and that this had been approved of by Governor Staal.

The intention was to use the grant for getting the boarding-school started. After three or four years it would have to be self-supporting since the cultivation of foodstuffs and some stockbreeding were regarded as part of the children's education.

Finally Van Heemstra remarked that he had told the Head Chief, Kanapé, that he would do his best to carry out his predecessor's promise. He had explained to Kanapé that for this the co-operation of the Colonial States, of the First and Second Chambers and "even of *Missie*[12] Wilhelmina would, however, be indispensable." This explanation, he added, "was evidently beyond the grasp of this child of nature since he kept on repeating, in spite of all my efforts at making it clear: "What the Granman[13] wishes, can be done."

Considering Kanapé's intelligence and his proficiency at the political game, it seems likely that he understood perfectly that the Governor did not wish to commit himself and that his remark was, in effect, intended ironically.

On 1 March 1923 the grant for the boarding-school was made for a period of four years. The Minister cancelled the memorandum which stated that part of the money was to be employed for a (Roman Catholic) boarding-school in Albina that was being contemplated.

In the meeting of 2 May 1923, at which Fls. 1750 was made available for the boarding-school for the rest of that year, the members of the Colonial States still grumbled a bit, but eventually they agreed to this amount without taking a poll.

According to Government Resolution No. 1461 of 23 April 1923 Van

Lier was instructed to return to his post and to open the school and the boarding establishment attached to it on 1 July. Meanwhile a sum of Fls. 1000 was put at his disposal for the period from July till December (inclusive).

Van Lier had not gone back to his post while the Governor and the Minister were negotiating, because it was feared that the prestige of the administration would suffer if he arrived back without bringing a definite decision to announce. For the time being he was employed by the Government Secretary and charged with "Bush Negro Affairs".

h Notes on the matter of the grant

In the notes relating to the design of the 'experiment' (Chapter III § 5) factors were pointed out which might have a negative effect on the smooth execution of the educational project. A number of these factors came to the fore when the grant for the boarding-school was discussed.

1. The opponents of the experiment also opposed the boarding-school. Their arguments were partly the same: it would cost too much money, education should be based on Christian principles.
2. The fact that they found the results disappointing also influenced the decision. There was no appreciation of the viewpoint (of the Governor) that it should be regarded as a long-term project.
3. The Governor who, bound by a promise to the Djukas, favoured the boarding-school, was obliged to agree to the decision of the Colonial States.
4. Van Lier had submitted his request in November 1921; during February and May 1922 it came up for discussion and at the end of May the definite report that it had been turned down reached him. Now the consequences were felt of the fact that decisions could be taken only once a year and of the great distance between Paramaribo and the Tapanahoni.

Van Lier now made the matter a question of confidence: without a boarding-school the postholdership could not be maintained. The shirking of a promise that had been made harmed the authority and prestige of the Government. This argument was accepted by the Governor.

The approval of the motion necessitated the sanctioning of a change in the budget by the Dutch authorities. This, too, cost much time.

Fear of loss of 'power and prestige' was once more the argument put forward for postponing Van Lier's return to the Tapanahoni until after the definite approval had been granted. Against this argument the fact was not weighed that a speedy return to his post and the start of a day-school for the time being, pending the decision, could have a favourable effect on the continuity of the educational work and also on the co-operation and goodwill of the Djukas.

§ 2 FOURTH STAY IN THE TAPANAHONI, 29 AUGUST 1923 – 15 MARCH 1924

a Fresh difficulties

On 23 May, a month after receiving his official notification, Van Lier left for Albina to sail from there to Granman Staalkondré. On request by Van Lier, Kanapé sent his brother-in-law Jangaman and his son-in-law Péson with two boats to fetch him. Owing to a series of set-backs he did not actually arrive at Granman Staalkondré until 26 August.

On account of the high water-level the boats could not leave until 13 June. "On the very first day after we left", Van Lier wrote[14] "Péson had to turn back, because of an attack of influenza, with the boat-load of planks and planting material I was taking along. Two days later it was Jangaman, in whose boat I was travelling, who was taken seriously ill and had to be taken to Albina... Back in Albina, I myself had a bout of influenza complicated by pneumonia and the hiccoughs." He was taken to hospital and stayed there for thirteen days. In the meantime Jangaman and Péson returned to the Tapanahoni, but Jangaman died on the way and Péson remained in a sickly condition for months. A number of the animals Van Lier had taken along also died.

"After my recovery it became clear", Van Lier wrote in the abovementioned report "that not a single Djuka was willing to take me up the river. All efforts made by me, as well as by the acting District Commissioner, Dr. Fernandes, to get hold of a boat came up against the Bush Negroes' passive resistance. They even went so far as to refuse to take a letter from the District Commissioner to Amakti asking the Granman to send a boat to fetch me."

Unable to break this passive resistance, Van Lier left again for Paramaribo on the 9th of August to discuss the situation. By order of the acting Governor Rietveld he drew up a report of what, in his view, had prompted the Djukas' behaviour.[15]

In the first place: The system of pass-books had not yet been properly enforced, despite the fact that its necessity was obvious after the strike of 1921. Since this control measure was lacking, it was not possible to exercise authority over the Bush Negro freight carriers.

In the second place: the ill-luck which had dogged Van Lier's footsteps since his arrival at Albina, the illness of his attendants and the death of one of them must have had a supernatural cause according to Djuka superstition: there was *wisi* involved.

He advised, above all, that the pass-system should be strictly enforced so as to strengthen the authority, and moreover that a Djuka chief should be appointed in Albina.

Ignoring the proposal of the acting District Commissioner of the Marowijne area (who felt that his authority was being disregarded) that Van Lier, accompanied by a military patrol, should be sent to the Tapanahoni, the Governor accepted Van Lier's suggestion that he should try Creole carriers from Albina.

On August 13 Van Lier set out once more from Paramaribo to Albina and on the 22nd he managed to find two Creoles who were willing to take him to Granman Staalkondré, where he arrived on the 26th, satisfied with the performance of his carriers who had proved that they were not less skilled as boatsmen than the Djukas. Directly after his arrival at his post Van Lier started planning and equipping a small school. He made an investigation of the events during his absence and of the causes of the difficulties between him and the Djukas. This revealed that during Van Lier's absence regular reports from various sources in Paramaribo and Albina had reached the Tapanahoni, warning the Djukas of Van Lier's evil intentions towards them. These plans were supposed to include, among others, Christian education and the practice of black magic against the inhabitants. The slander campaign which, according to the leaders of the Djukas, was conducted by whites as well as by Chinese, met with success, especially when Van Lier suffered all sorts of adversity in Albina and the Bush Negroes sent by Kanapé fell ill, one of them even dying.

Van Lier's assumption (in his letter of 12 August, written in Paramaribo) that Amakti and Kanapé were unaware of the situation in Albina and had not received Van Lier's request to send some boats again to fetch him, proved on investigation to be incorrect. Although the Bush Negroes refused to carry letters from Albina to Drietabbetje, all news reports were delivered. Kanapé declared in private, as well as at the *krutu* which was called to discuss the matter, that after what had befallen Jangaman and Péson he could not send anyone to fetch Van Lier because he was being accused of having their misfortune on his conscience and of being in league with the *wisiman* Van Lier. Amakti declared that he had no one to send because 'everybody was ill'. At the *krutus* held on 3, 5 and 7 September to discuss Van Lier's position they declared, according to him, that they still had full confidence in him and that all the accidents were due to an unfortunate coincidence, namely that the *lanti-siki* (influenza) happened to break out just at his return. The blame for all that had happened, Kanapé averred, was to be found in the slander campaign in the coastal area. At a final *krutu* held in the village of Powie the 'reconciliation', as Van Lier called it, took place and all the chiefs present promised to trust him again as they had done in the past. Later on many leaders came to repeat this personally to him.

Van Lier, satisfied with this result and somewhat mollified, no longer reproached Amakti and Kanapé about their failure to send boats, nor did he offer any comment on the letter Kanapé made him write to the Governor on behalf of Amakti and himself, in which no mention was made of the role played by the two chiefs in the matter.

"Your Excellency", they wrote in this letter of 21 September 1923,[16] "we can testify that everything that prevented Mr. Van Lier from getting a boat to return to us has been the work of Mr. Van Lier's enemies in Albina, as well as in the city, for since he left here till he came back there was not a boat that arrived from Albina or the Cottica that did not carry warning against Mr. Van Lier... It is the Chinese, especially, who are against us; they do not want us to have a school, for as soon as the Djuka children have learnt enough, they will not be able to continue robbing us as they are doing now." With regard to the school they made positive statements and promises: "The fact that the school had not yet got properly under way is due to Mr. Van Lier's long stay in the city. Now that he is back again, and everything has been cleared up, the school will soon be started. And with God's help it will not close again... The children of the two of us, Kanapé's Atrondee and Amakti's Koninkje, will be the first to be enrolled. And soon, God willing, Your Excellency will learn that there is no more room for all the children presenting themselves. Governor, the Aucaners really long to have their children educated, and the chiefs will see to it that the promise made to the Administration to support the school is kept. Our yea will remain yea." They added the earnest request to the Governor to see that the Djukas would no longer be incited against Van Lier by malicious gossip and to take steps to have the passbook system strictly enforced in Albina so as to keep the Djukas in order. Finally, after a plea to be pardoned for all that had happened recently, the letter concluded with: "Your Excellency, we pray that God may help you and the *Bakras* who are assisting you to govern the country and that under your guidance there may at last come a permanent improvement in the life of the Aucaners."

The Governor, too, was pleased with the statements of the two Djuka leaders, as appears from his letter of the 13th October which he ends as follows: "I accept your apologies and also your good wishes for my Administration, but keep in mind that this Administration has many cares and problems so that all the inhabitants of Surinam, including the Djukas, should help to relieve our task by means of their obedience."

It was, however, not only the 'slanderous gossip' of the whites and Chinese that shook the Djukas' confidence in Van Lier. This gossip played a minor role, which Kanapé, especially, was only too eager to represent as a major one. Both whites, in whose estimation Van Lier's enterprise was sinking, and Chinese, who may actually have seen their profitable commerce endangered if the Djukas learnt to read and cipher, did in fact give negative accounts about Van Lier to the Djukas visiting them. Another factor was Van Lier's long absence, which had the effect of lending creditability to all sorts of rumours. These circumstances were not enough to make the distrust so great and widespread: the cause of this was an internal Djuka problem.

b The controversy between High Priest Kanapé and Chief Popo

High Priest Kanapé and Chief Popo of Benanu were engaged in a contest of power which was bound up with historical events and now reached explosion point.

Although Kanapé belonged to the *Opo* group and Popo to the *Bilos*, that was not the immediate reason for the conflict between these two powerful personalities. The cause was a religious issue which had existed for years but only now, in 1922-1923, came to a head. Another factor was the point that, partly through Popo's mediation, Kanapé was not appointed Granman at the death of Paramount Chief Oseisie.

Oseisie had educated Kanapé (his mother's sister's son) in the abilities his successor should possess. Oseisie, as well as his cousin, had progressive ideas about the development of their people, which were naturally repudiated by the conservative opposition. When Oseisie died in 1915 this conservative faction was strong enough to prevent Kanapé's succession. After the death of a Granman, his body is placed on a plank which two men carry around on their heads. The priest questions the corpse, whose answers are given by the two bearers nodding and shaking their heads to say 'yes' and 'no'. In this way, they believe, the spirit of the deceased conveys his wishes. Van Lier wrote the following about the interrogation of Oseisie:

"A granman's corpse may never be carried in any other way than by two chiefs, an *Opo* and a *Bilo*. And now the remarkable fact was that the meeting ordered Oseisie's corpse to be carried around by two of Kanapé's strongest opponents, namely Popo, chief of Abenanu (*Bilo*) and Adikontu, chief of Godo-oro (*Opo*). The questions were put by Aganga, another opponent. After many days of questioning Oseisie at last 'agreed' that Kanapé should not succeed him. The deceased was now asked who should be the successor, and like an arrow shot from the bow Popo and Adikontu, with poor Oseisie (who would surely have been raised from the dead, had he been aware of it) on their heads, walked straight toward Amakti, son of another aunt of Oseisie's. The die was cast. The schemers had won the day."[17] Amakti was chosen, and during the solemn inauguration Kanapé burst into tears. "Oh, this man is jealous of the granmanship" his opponents exclaimed.[18]

So Amakti became Granman but, since he had no training for the priesthood, Kanapé became High Priest. Although everybody accepted the will of the ancestral spirits, many believed that this will had been forced upon the spirit of Oseisie by the interrogating priest and the bearers.

The early history of the religious struggle between these two ambitious Djukas, Kanapé and Popo, was also known to Van Lier. He described it in his daily notes on 4 June 1922. Two of the chief Djuka gods are Gwangwella (Grantata) whose abode is at Drietabbetje, and Gedeunsu of Tabbetje. The latter belongs to the *Bilo* Djukas, and is also served by *Bilo* priestesses (and priests). Popo had great influence on the Gedeunsu priests, in spite of the fact that he belonged neither to the Pedi-*lo*, from whose ranks the priests were recruited (he belonged to the Dika-*lo*), nor lived in Tabbetje.

Now, in 1922, Kanapé wished to install a new deity who would have to be recognized as such by the god Gwangwella and his priests, as well as by Gedeunsu and his servitors.

This new god, Akrekuna, had manifested himself in various persons during the past hundred and fifty years, without a single influential priest paying serious attention to it. But in 1922 the situation changed. Van Lier described the course of events as follows (Journal, 14 June 1922):

"At last the *Opo* Negroes began to have faith in this Gado (God) and Kanapé was asked to help promote his recognition. At first Kanapé would have nothing to do with it, but in January the oracle (Grantata) gave a verdict in favour of Akrekuna-Gado, as a result of which Kanapé gave his assent to the recognition. Among the items on the 'agenda' of the *krutu* that was to be held at Drietabbetje today, was also the discussion of this recognition. But Popo knew how to manipulate it that 'Gedeunsu' 'forbade' the *Bilo* Negroes to accept Akrekuna-Gado. Contrary to the general custom that gave only the Granman the right to convene a *krutu* about such matters, he called the *Bilo* chiefs together at Tabbetje and made Gedeunsu utter the above-mentioned ban in their presence."

It was indeed a humiliating business for the ambitious Kanapé who had doubtlessly intended to strengthen his authority over *Opo* as well as *Bilo* Negroes by appointing a new god under his priestly office. No wonder he declared to Van Lier, when he spoke to him about Popo's power, that "he would watch Popo carefully and wait for the day when he would be able to get square with him".

That day did come, in fact, and with it came Van Lier's involvement in the controversy. On 1 May 1922 Van Lier intended visiting the village of Benanu, of which Popo was the chief, in order to take he census there. Popo, who heard of this plan, came to tell that the would be absent and asked him to come another time. When Van Lier declared that he could manage without Popo's presence, the latter forbade him to visit his village on that day. Van Lier "listened to him calmly" and simply replied that he would "re-open the matter later on" (Journal, May-June 1922).

He complained of Popo's attitude to Kanapé, who expressed great indignation and believed that the hour had come for settling accounts with the recalcitrant chief. On 4 June a big *krutu* was to be held at Drietabbetje and on this occasion the rebuke was to be administered. The meeting did not take place since the *Bilo* chiefs, egged on by Popo, refused to respond to the call.

At the next meeting of 14 June the *Bilo* chiefs were not present either. Now Van Lier publicly stated his complaint about Popo's conduct. Kanapé informed the *krutu* that he had heard that Popo did not like the idea of Van Lier visiting all the villages to take a survey of the population. That was why he objected to his village being visited. Since Popo was not present, Kanapé declared that he would go to *Bilo* himself to deal with Popo.

This eventually happened at a *krutu* in Powi on 19 June (a village opposite Granman Staalkondré). Popo attended this meeting together with sixty-five other chiefs. Van Lier's report in his journal reads as follows:

"After the numerous Djuka ceremonies had been enacted, the meeting was opened. Kanapé began by telling Popo that he had sailed to Powi specially on his account. He pointed out to the *krutu* that he had never so much as mentioned the fact that he had been rejected as Granman while he was the true successor to Oseisie. He had not been upset by this, nor meddled in 'administrative matters' in the Tapanahoni, even though he had noticed how things were being bungled. The *Bakras*, however, could not accept the fact that the chaotic condition was getting worse, and the 'treachery' (*fufuru feti*) of the strike was the last straw, as a result of which he, Kanapé, was summoned to the city, where the Governor conferred the legal authority over the Aucaners on him.

When he was accepted as Head Chief at the *krutu* in which the tribe confirmed the new agreement with the *Bakras*, he had stated 'that he had not aspired after that position, but now that it had been conferred on him, he would do his duty even if it cost him his head."

He thought the time had now come for him to show that these were no idle words. The fact that there were still so many abuses to be found here, that scheming and wire-pulling were rampant, was due to one person only, Popo, whose arrogance had now driven him to insult the *Bakra* who was the Governor's representative here.

He, Kanapé, had come here today, not to reprimand, but to take effective measures.

Turning to Popo, he said: 'Chief Popo, by virtue of the authority conferred on me by the Governor, I herewith relieve you of your duties as chief, until I hear from the Governor whether or not His Excellency approves of this. Not later than tomorrow you are to hand over your uniform and insignias to me, so that I can ask Mr. Van Lier to return them to the Governor. If the Governor wants to retain you, His Excellency will return these objects. For the time being, however, you are no longer chief.' And addressing the meeting: 'Elders, you have heard my decision. Whoever has a matter to discuss with the leader of the Dika Negroes, must apply to me until I have appointed a successor to Popo.' Popo listened to this sentence without a word. The entire *krutu* came to beg Kanapé for forgiveness on his behalf. A son and a nephew of his dropped to their knees. But Kanapé declared that he would not accept any excuses."

From what he said to Van Lier on this matter, it was clear that Kanapé did not intend drawing the Government into it: in case Van Lier should wish to report on it to the Governor, he asked him "to inform His Excellency that the matter has not been clinched yet, and that Popo would probably be kept on as chief, but then no longer with the same authority he enjoyed previously".[19] The other Djukas also understood that the threat of governmental involvement was intended rhetorically, to lend weight to the affront inflicted on Popo. Popo and his followers decided to go to Drietabbetje the next day to offer apologies to Kanapé and Granman, and to ask them to retain Popo as chief. Many Bush Negroes also came to beg Van Lier to forgive Popo.

The form which the punishment took and the reactions of those involved are characteristic of the Djuka legal system. Thoden van Velzen,[20] who cites examples of this kind of judicature, remarks that, in spite of the obvious disadvantages of using the Government as 'bogey-man', this happens regularly. "Threatening the prominent Djukas with heavy penalties and then backing out of it or simply not referring to it again is quite common at meetings and oracle-sessions. Such behaviour is normal for a worthy; it forms part of his social role."

Consequently the threats were not carried out. All the same, the fact that Popo had fallen into disgrace made quite an impression: a chief is partly dependent on the support of the Granman (and in this case also of the Head Chief) for the exercise of his power.

From the whole course of events it is clear that the chastisement of Popo was much more a display of power and a personal act of revenge than a proof of support for Van Lier's authority, as he took it to be.

c Death of Chief Popo

During Van Lier's absence (22 June 1922 – 26 August 1923) Popo died. What happened at the time was thus not known to him, but the consequences became clear to him on his return. The disaster that befell Kanapé's brother-in-law and son-in-law was perhaps regarded by the Djukas as another proof of Van Lier's evil magical practices. They also suspected him, together with Kanapé, of having helped to bring about Popo's death: it had been a result of the reprimand and humiliations he had suffered at Van Lier's hands. The attitude of Amakti and Kanapé at the *krutus* held on 3, 5 and 7 September, when they affirmed that they had full confidence in Van Lier, that the evil spoken of him was slander brought from the city, and that the many deaths were not caused by him but by a *lanti-siki*, an epidemic (of influenza), at first did little to improve the situation. The Djukas kept refusing to send their children to Van Lier's boarding-school. "From the Djuka point of view", he wrote in his report on 1924, "this refusal was well-founded. Indeed, appearances against me as *Wisiman* increased rather than diminished. The number of deaths in the villages was constantly rising. It seems to me worth recording that within three months the death occurred of Kanapé's eldest son, Joveni, shortly afterwards of his widow, and somewhat later, on the same day, of two female first cousins of Kanapé, as well as of a number of other persons." One of the two Indians who came to visit Van Lier suddenly died on his return to his village. In April 1924 the wife of Kanapé's second son died, and soon afterwards one of his own wives.

"For those who are familiar with the customs and mental attitude of the Bush Negroes", Van Lier wrote in the above-mentioned report, "it is easy to see that in all these happenings the hand of '*Masra* Van Lier' was seen. In the meantime these sad incidents were eagerly seized upon by those whose task was apparently to make life impossible for me and rob me of every chance of success. Reports of my wicked intentions and warnings to Kanapé and Amakti against me now arrived practically every day from Cottica and from Albina. Kanapé assured me that he was regularly asked whether his eyes would not be opened till he, too, had become a victim of my witchcraft. To the credit of this Bush Negro and no less of Amakti as well as Gagu I can testify that they paid no heed to these fictions, at any rate they continued to support me."

On 1 September Kanapé gave Van Lier his view on the whole matter. In a report of this conversation Van Lier[21] wrote: "According to Djuka custom Kanapé, who is in mourning for the death of his wife, may not yet take part in *krutus*. He is obliged to stay in his hut all day long – the hut in which the deceased died – and weep for her. He must remain in this condition until the customary feast has been held, on which occasion much food and drink will be offered to the deceased. In view of Kanapé's position and the fact that the late lamented was a young woman who was expecting her first child shortly, the feast will be huge... I found Amakti with violent tooth-ache and a swollen upper lip so that he could hardly speak. The pain grew worse during the following days. The oracle, Grantata, when consulted on the matter, declared that the Granman had uttered imprecations against himself because of a quarrel between his three wives and that the spirit of the predecessor, Oseisie, had therefore slapped him across the mouth. The whole of Drietabbetje was in uproar, offering sacrifices to Oseisie and begging that Amakti be forgiven."

Under these circumstances no *krutu* could be held, but Van Lier did not want to go back without having achieved anything and thus held a discussion with Kanapé, Gagu and a chief, Atuwan, in Kanapé's hut. This brought important matters to light. "Kanapé declared", wrote Van Lier, "that he would stick to his word and that the school would be continued, in spite of the fact that he had been taken in by the *Wisiman*. I asked him if he really believed me to be a *Wisiman*. No, definitely not, but the fact that the *Bakras* liked him was most offensive to the Djukas. From this I gathered that the *Bilo* Negroes are not to be trusted. Since the death of Chief Popo, for which the *Bilo* Negroes hold me and Kanapé responsible, they hate both of us. The opposition the school has experienced all along has been mostly the work of the *Bilo* Negroes who refuse to admit that '*Masra* Van Lier' is not a *Wisiman*... Kanapé's attitude to me seems to have changed. This time his remarks were not frank, as usual, and twice he even tried to lie to me. This in itself does not surprise me. After all, this man, in spite of his liberal views, is still too much of a Bush Negro not to ascribe all he has suffered in less than a year to supernatural forces, of which I am, if not directly, then at any rate indirectly, the cause. From the other Bush Negroes I also learnt that he suspected that he was being 'bewitched' by the *Bilo* Negroes on account of my friendship with him. He is very nervous and suffers from anxiety. In order to regain his confidence I suggested that he should come and stay with me after the sacrificial feast in honour of his wife's memory, so that I could cure him by means of medicine, but chiefly by offering him diversion. He has accepted the invitation and I have to wait and see whether he will come, from which I shall be able to infer how far he still trusts me." On 9 November, after discussion in Drietabbetje, Kanapé did in fact accompany Van Lier so as to put himself in the latter's care at Granman Staalkondré. The High Priest was still feverish and suffered from palpitations of the heart. The chief deity, Grantata, who was consulted about Kanapé's stay at Granman Staalkondré, gave a favourable verdict and this encouraged Kanapé to submit to treatment by Van Lier. His condition did, in fact, quickly improve and he regained his physical and mental vigour. This, added to the fact that he was aware of the Government's backing (during his illness a matter of prestige had cropped up, when Amakti had tried in vain to act on his own, without Kanapé's knowledge) induced him to extend his active support once more to Van Lier.

d Notes on a complicated accusation of witchcraft

According to Van Lier the Djukas ascribed Popo's death, as well as the misfortunes dogging Kanapé's footsteps, to *wisi*. He deduced this from the fact that he himself was regarded as a *wisiman* and furthermore as the agent who – together with Kanapé – had caused this death. He was, however, confusing several different matters here. Neither the Djukas nor Kanapé had explained to him what they actually meant. Popo's death had been, as Kanapé said, the result of the scolding and the humiliation inflicted on him by Kanapé and Van Lier. According to the Djuka this is an instance of death through guilt, but not of *wisi*. The fact that Van Lier was thought capable of practising *wisi* had no connection with Popo's case. It is unusual for a white person to be accused of *wisi*, but Van Lier, so well versed in their religion, was probably regarded as being able to do it; the accounts coming in from the coastal area confirmed his evil intentions. So the belief that the practised *wisi* could be – temporarily – credited.

Kanapé declared to Van Lier that he had been afflicted by *wisi*. Now, a High Priest cannot, according to Djuka belief, be bewitched, just as little as he can practise witchcraft (which also goes to prove that Popo did not die as a result of his *wisi*). Kanapé's explanation of his misfortunes did not indicate *wisi* at all. His view was that Popo's spirit had taken revenge, not only on him, but also on his family and those nearest to him. This explanation clearly meant that he was the victim of a *kunu* (spirit of revenge, Chapter II § 3) and that Popo was this *kunu*, which, in view of the occasion of his death, was obvious to every Djuka. The reason why Kanapé did not call this matter by its true name was that he would then be practically admitting to Van Lier that he had Popo's death on his conscience. He preferred to ascribe his mishaps to witchcraft.[22] Van Lier was taken in by this because, apart form the fact that no one ever used the word *kunu* during the entire discussion of the matter, he probably had not yet become sufficiently acquainted with the phenomenon of *kunu*. In his early writings it rarely occurs and he gives no clear description of it before 1940.

e Medical aid

The Djukas' fear of Van Lier also expressed itself in their initial repugnance to accepting medical aid from him. In his report on 1923 Van Lier wrote: "A proof of the fear I inspired in the Bush Negroes was the fact that the people in the villages where I disembarked on my journey to Granman Staalkondré *literally fled* at my approach."

Gradually, however, probably partly through the reassuring utterances of the Djuka leaders, the sick and the injured started coming to him again for treatment and he was fetched to attend to serious cases. Although he imagined that soon "no fewer patients than before were presenting themselves", it appeared that many ill Bush Negroes went to the balata warehouses and the balata bleeders for help because they were afraid of being 'bewitched' by Van Lier. Malaria was rife in the Tapanahoni and the many deaths did not help to restore confidence speedily in Van Lier.

On 4 December First Lieutenant Weijne, returning from a tour of inspection along the Lawa, visited Granman Staalkondré. He reported this visit to the Governor who asked him to investigate the general state of affairs (without, however, conducting himself like an inspecting official) and learn something of the attitude of the Bush Negroes towards Van Lier.[23] In this report Weijne mentioned that the Bush Negroes were now coming to Van Lier again for medicine and only grumbled at the fact that they had to pay for it.

On 26 February Van Lier replied to a letter of 4 February 1924[24] from the Government Secretary in which he asked how the Bush Negroes felt about buying medicine, that the Djukas had known from the outset that he asked payment from those who were in a position to pay, while medicine was given free to the impecunious. But no one who declared that he had no money was ever sent away by him without being helped. Since supplying on credit was the same as giving free, little medicine was sold. Van Lier received fresh complaints when Kanapé informed him in October that the Bush Negroes had been told in Albina that Van Lier was supplied by the Government with medicine to distribute free and that he was therefore cheating them if asked payment for it.

Van Lier was obviously irritated by this question, which was constantly being raised. Criticism of his action in this connection he regarded as part and parcel of the slanderous tales which found their way to the Tapanahoni. Probably so as to focus attention on this aspect, he made no mention in the letter of the incidental bickering that occurred between him and the Djukas about the matter of payment.

f Education

In spite of all his problems, Van Lier was busy getting his boarding-school in order and cultivating the agricultural plots so as to be prepared to receive pupils, should they actually turn up. They did not come, however, but many visitors came to take stock of the situation at Granman Staalkondré and receive information about the educational plans. One of them, Chief Bobi Staai, gave his view as to why previous efforts had failed: "because religion was taught, but especially because the children were beaten and scolded by the teachers if they did not know their lessons...". Also, most of the time had been taken up by the singing of Christian songs, some of which he still remembered, for instance '*Oranje Boven*' (a Dutch patriotic song in praise of the House of Orange!). At this point Van Lier jotted down in his notebook: "for the time being, preferably no singing lessons". All the chiefs who visited him declared that their confidence in him had been restored. "Nobody is to blame for the wrong done to me", Van Lier wrote in his notebook. "Everybody was upset by the unfavourable reports about me that came from Albina." Probably the chiefs found it wiser, taking into account the attitude of Amakti and Kanapé, not to show their distrust openly. It was clear that the Djuka leaders had been serious in their promise to support Van Lier when Kanapé, accompanied by Granfiskari Gagu, brought his son and a son of Amakti to Granman Staalkondré on 12 October. Gagu also promised to send a child to school, and both undertook to make propaganda for the cause. "Kanapé", Van Lier wrote on 12 October to the Government Secretary, "declared on his own behalf and on behalf of Amakti that they entrusted the children to my care with all their heart and expressed the hope that the school, which had at last been started, would continue to flourish in the Tapanahoni from one generation to the next".

On 15 October 1923 the school was officially opened with the two pupils, and lessons in Dutch were started. It turned out, however, that Amakti and Kanapé were the only two who ventured to confide their children, Atrondee (or Anton, as Van Lier called him) and Koninkje to his care.

Van Lier began teaching his two pupils on 15 October. Two days later, on the 17th, he wrote in his diary: "Started today teaching them to count. Anton can count up to 10, Koninkje only up to 6. After half-an-hour Koninkje still cannot remember the numbers up to 10. Suddenly he bursts into tears. I give them leave to go and play. After a time both come and ask to start again. I ask K. if it would not be better if we have no more lessons today. No, he would rather go on counting. At the end of the lesson K. could count up to ten. That evening I asked him why he had cried in school and he answered that he had been afraid he would never learn to count." On the 23rd he noted: "Koninkje, who had a stiff tot before he came to school, is most obstreperous. When in a bad mood he refuses to answer or to do a thing, etc. I leave him to his own devices." And the next day: "The boys are showing that they are Bush Negroes. Their disobedience gets worse by the day and their laziness grows apparent." In spite of the complaints of their teacher the boys seem to be making progress.

When First Lieutenant J. Weijne visited Granman Staalkondré on 4 and 5 December he also had a look at the school. In his report to the Governor (27 December 1923) he remarked that there were only two pupils so far, but that Van Lier told him that after the Christmas holidays, in January, another eighteen would be coming along. Weijne attended a language and arithmetic lesson and found: "as far as I could judge, the results were not bad. I myself have taught common school subjects for years, so I feel that I am in a position to express an opinion... The result of five weeks' teaching was that both pupils could spell all the words on the reading-plank fluently without making mistakes. Even without the reading-plank they could assemble the words correctly and pronounce all the letters separately. In arithmetic they could count up to 10 and do adding and subtracting with numbers below 7, all of course in Dutch. They have lessons three days a week from 8 to 11, and the rest of the time they learn to work at home and in the fields."

As for the Bush Negroes' feelings about the school, Weijne wrote that they kept it to themselves. They only said that if the Granman decides that the children should go to school, then they go. "They had nothing unfavourable to remark about Van Lier personally. They only found that at times he was inclined to be harsh and scold them soundly, which hardly surprises anyone knowing the Bush Negroes." They also found it strange that he did not carry on with Djuka girls and abstained from strong drink, but (so Weijne ended his report) "this can only reflect to his credit". Weijne struck Van Lier as being "a congenial young man" (Notebook, 4 December).

After the 'Christmas holidays' in January 1924, however, no children turned up. Van Lier sailed to Drietabbetje for a *krutu* to be held on 4 February. On this occasion Amakti and Kanapé exerted pressure on their subjects. "Kanapé stated firmly that he would refuse to be consulted as High Priest by anybody until at least one child from every village was sent to school. Amakti announced that nobody need come and consult him in matters requiring his judgment as Granman, or come with a request that needed his assent, as long as his command to send the children to school was being ignored. Gagu was in complete agreement with Kanapé and Amakti. The result of these measures was that on the following day the parents of nine children sent word that they were prepared to send them to school. But when Gagu, by order of Amakti, arrived at one of the villages to fetch the children, he came up against the passive resistance of the mothers who declared that their children had been taken ill and would have to wait till they were better. From each of three villages, namely Kisaai, Saajé and Clementi, one lad was brought to me. It may be supposed that more will follow."

With Kanapé's Anton (Amakti's son was ill) and these three newcomers Van Lier continued his teaching until he took leave and went to Paramaribo on 15 March.

g Notes on the educational work

It took time before the shaken confidence in Van Lier's good intentions was restored. The first thing to start functioning again was his job as medical consultant. The matter of school attendance, however, was fraught with far more difficulties. To the Djukas it probably seemed a much more drastic commitment to surrender their children completely to his influence, than to procure medical aid from him for themselves and their children. After all, they could wriggle out of accepting this help whenever they wanted to, or seek the simultaneous protection of their own medicine-men and ward off possible dangers by sacrificing to the gods. The children, abandoned wholly to Van Lier, had none of these protective measures at their disposal.

Neither the fact that Amakti and Kanapé entrusted their children to his care, nor their assurance of utter faith in him could remove the fear. The attempt of both leaders to enforce obedience by means of threats did not help either. Probably these threats were not put into effect anyway (§ 2b).

h Agriculture and cattle-breeding

During Van Lier's absence "much had happened" he wrote in his report on 1923: "The *entire hatching* of chickens ($\pm$ 150), except 13, died of a disease that broke out among them. A sow, near farrowing, died after a few hours' illness. My man-servant – paid entirely by me – was not able to keep the provision ground in proper order by himself. (Money for hiring hands was not available.) The result of this was that a large part of the plot was once more overgrown by *kapewerie* (Negro English for brushwood, undergrowth). The coconut-palms, which had been getting along nicely, were choked by the flourishing weeds. When I got back in August 1923 it was a case of having to start again from scratch." Van Lier had received an amount of Fls. 600 for agricultural purposes, part of which he spent to cultivate and replant his field with coconut- and cacao-trees, citrus and other plants, including ornamental shrubs. Since he had lost the Djukas' confidence, he got no co-operation from them at all. Still, he had been able to bring along Bakboord (the forest-keeper whom Gonggrijp wanted to dismiss) with instructions to persuade the Bush Negroes to practise more intensive agriculture, especially by planting coconut-palm and cultivating more expensive types of timber on the neglected provision grounds. Bakboord, too, was out of favour with the Djukas. All the same they succeeded in tidying up Granman Staalkondré, and by December there was quite a display of new plantings. Nor was J. Weijne dissatisfied. "The general impression was not unfavourable. The camp inhabited by Mr. Van Lier was built of light materials, as camps usually are. Around the house the bush had been cleared and beyond that about $1\frac{1}{2}$ hectares had been cleared for cultivation, and here sweet and bitter cassava, corn, coconut-palms, oranges, lemons and other fruit-trees are grown. Then there was a pig-sty with three pigs, a goat-shed with a billy-goat and a nanny-goat, and a hen-coop with some twelve hens."

Van Lier wrote in a report on the year 1923 that this cultivation was intended for the boarding-school. With regard to agricultural instruction he was optimistic, even though he could not report any concrete results. He thought that the Djukas were beginning to devote more care to their planting and tillage and were cultivating larger fields, partly because they were urged to do so by Granman Amakti, and because of propaganda made by the supervisor of forestry. "During the past year much has been achieved in this respect," he wrote "therefore it is all the more regrettable that the drought, also in the Tapanahoni, is threatening to cause great disappointment and a shortage of food is again to be expected this year." About the instruction given at his demonstration plot at Granman Staalkondré, he simply stated that it was being kept up "as far as the means and circumstances allowed."

§ 3 Notes on a report by the postholder

The time spent in the Tapanahoni from 26 August 1923 to March 1924 had affected Van Lier's health, and more especially, his mental vigour. The tone of his notebooks, journals, letters and reports reveals that his optimism and his faith in the success of his plans were ebbing away.

During his period of leave in Paramaribo from 15 March to 7 July 1924 he wrote " A report of the Postholder among the Aucaners during 1923 and the first quarter of 1924". The report gives a survey of the entire history of his postholdership and is pervaded by a tone of pessimism. As to the contents of the report: the factual data given by Van Lier are, on the whole, accurate. The reactions of the disappointed postholder to the events sometimes indicated a sound insight, at other times a faulty view of the position. Sometimes his criticism was apt, sometimes not, sometimes he was too optimistic about the future, sometimes too pessimistic.

a On the relations between government and postholder

The postholder realized that he had landed in a conflict situation as a result of his special status of official executor of the educational project. On the one hand he had to consider the Djuka society which had its own view on the course of events, and on the other hand he had to take into account his employers and the Surinam community that had to finance the project.[25] "The civilizing task" Van Lier wrote, "is one which demands much patience and perseverance and is a lengthy process if one wishes to achieve one's goal. The private person can quietly go his way and regulate and adapt his work according to the prevailing requirements and circumstances. The Government is hobbled by all sorts of regulations that do not allow of a supple modification when practical need arises, but demand lengthy deliberation. Furthermore, the official has to render an account of his labours to the Colonial States or the Government of the mother country, and is dependent on their mood, whether favourable or otherwise, at the same time being exposed to the destructive criticism of the press."

The solution he suggested was to have the work undertaken by a private person, and as a private enterprise. He did not dwell (nor shall I) on the problems with which this private person would be confronted and which would be broadly the same as in the case of a Government enterprise.

He concluded the report with the remark that "in Surinam the civilizing work should be left to private enterprise; a government official would never, for the above reasons, achieve any success, or at any rate none worth mentioning in this field."

As to the 'private person' who would be better equipped for the carrying out of the task, he was (still) convinced that "the wished-for aim would never be realized, if one stressed religion at the outset. The 'private person' – even if he were a missionary – should from the beginning avoid even the faintest suspicion of a specific creed."

b On criticism and slander

On the attitude of the Colonial States and the criticism in the press Van Lier remarked bitterly:

"In the Colonial States no opportunity to express destructive criticism of the Postholder and his work was allowed to pass by, and regular attacks on his person gradually became the rule. Not a single item needed for this work was granted without a hard struggle on the part of the deputy of the Governor.

In the press, particularly in the same periodical[26] in which such appreciative contributions had been published before, nothing but destructive articles appeared later on, some even stooping to direct scorn and hostile insinuations at his person."

According to Van Lier "a time had come when this institution... without a plausible reason, suddenly lost *all* sympathy."

While criticism by the Colonial States harmed Van Lier's position in Paramaribo, the 'smear campaign' did the same in the Tapanahoni. In spite of the co-operation of the Djuka leaders there was, according to Van Lier, "not the slightest chance that the work could be resumed on a sound basis before full confidence in me is restored. But who can tell whether the concealed slanderers will soon cease attacking me, or that no fresh disasters will occur? Who can guarantee, for instance, that not one of the children in the boarding-house will fall ill and die?"

The aim of Van Lier's effort to exonerate Amakti and Kanapé from the charge of obstructionism was:

1. To avoid a repetition of past events. After the subsidized attempt of the Moravian Mission to found a school in the Tapanahoni had failed, the Djukas were accused of sabotage by the Government. When he had heard the Djukas' side of the matter,[27] Van Lier also wrote a plea to show that the fault did not rest with them, or not with them alone. Now he argued, just as he had argued then, that the leading Djukas sincerely desired the improvement of their people and the reasons for the failure lay elsewhere.

Neither Van Lier's plea of 1919, nor that of 1924, could restrain the Government from putting all the blame on the Djukas, as the sequel to these events was to show.

2. To prove that Kanapé's appointment to a position of power which he (Van Lier) had brought about, and the reprimand given to Amakti in Paramaribo in September 1921 had had favourable results.

Together they now saw to it that the Government's instructions were carried out, that 'law and order' reigned in the Tapanahoni, and that even though the school was still empty, Granman and Head Chief gave their full support to the realization of this enterprise, too.

Although the Government's interference in the administrative position in the Tapanahoni doubtlessly had its effect, Van Lier overestimated its consequences. There was, for instance, the matter of burying corpses within three days. This, according to Van Lier, would be observed in future. "The burial of corpses within three days of death has now, with a few exceptions, become the rule. The corpses of so-called *wisimans* are no longer thrown away, but buried. Corporal punishment no longer exists, etc." As mentioned in § 2b of this chapter, Van Lier mentions the speedy burial of corpses only once. It was impossible to control from his post whether or not the regulations were adhered to. The Djukas were well aware of this.

The 'law and order' that Amakti and Kanapé were able to enforce with their limited powers was not as prevalent as Van Lier would have liked to assert. Kanapé's own position, as explained in § 2, could hardly be called strong. Amakti's prestige, already slight, had suffered further as a result of the strike of 1921.

As regards Van Lier's complaints about the attitude of the Colonial States, it is true that the opponents of the educational scheme did not spare their criticism. One should remember that the results of the work were by no means evident. Seen within the framework of the economy drive, the States members found the amounts the postholder asked for rather too high. Yet, although there was much obstinate opposition as a rule, the grants were voted in the end. This was due to the quite important group of supporters of continuation of the 'experiment', especially the Governor and his mouthpiece, the Government Secretary.

As to the 'slander campaign': it is, of course, impossible to ascertain how intense it was or which section of the community was responsible for the spread of rumours. It is noteworthy, however, that Van Lier himself thought that the Djukas' confidence in him was unshaken despite the slander until the 'fate' of the many illnesses which co incided with his return convinced them of his evil intentions. One is inclined to believe that the unrest among the Djukas was also, if not rather, due to the events in the Tapanahoni connected with the conflict between Kanapé and Popo. All the same: the slander did nothing to improve the situation and Van Lier seized upon this action to help explain why the educational plan failed to succeed.

c On agriculture and forestry

Although his often protracted absence destroyed the results of his work in the agricultural demonstration field Van Lier was optimistic about the influence of the instruction given by him and his forest-keeper on the methods of the Djukas. "Fortunately the results of the trouble taken have become evident, although they are not yet conspicuous to the outsider. The Bush Negroes are at last beginning to understand that they must cultivate larger fields and spend more care on them, if they want to be free one day from the recurrent shortage of food... It is noteworthy that they are now selecting planting material with more care and tilling their fields more judiciously."

Van Lier's observations about changes in the agricultural methods cannot be verified in any way. In Chapter II § 4c it was pointed out that changes in that field could only have been achieved by very drastic means. In Van Lier's case the wish was probably father to the thought.

d On the continuity of the educational work

Van Lier was fully aware of the harmful effects of his frequent and often lengthy periods of absence. He observes that he was away for thirty-one months during the five years of his postholdership and was therefore present for twenty-nine months. For this Van Lier blames the circumstances, at any rate he does not blame the administration or the postholder. One could justify the interruptions of his work if one considers the strike, his attempts to obtain a grant for the boarding-school, the distrust shown by the Djukas; still, it must be recorded that nothing was done to facilitate the postholder's return to his work.

A striking feature of the report is that the lack of results is blamed entirely on the Government (and the press and the slanderers). Neither the Djukas nor the postholder are to be held responsible in any way. As regards the latter: self-criticism was definitely not Van Lier's strong point. As to the Djukas: on other occasions Van Lier did not spare them his criticism at all. He often spoke appreciatively of the co-operation of at least certain members of the administration and the press. The reason why he now gave such an exaggerated representation of the matter was probably because he hoped to improve the relationship between the administration and himself by emphasizing the favourable results and possibilities and stifling criticism. His remark that a government official would 'never achieve any success, at least none worth mentioning', seen in this light, should not be taken too seriously, certainly not with reference to what he expected of his own activities. For that matter, Van Lier had no intention of abandoning his task and position, but kept on persevering. The sanction of a new grant for his boarding-school, the discussions with Governor Rietberg and the Government Secretary, Van der Helm, the period of repose and return to health, all these strengthened Van Lier to go back to the Tapanahoni with fresh courage.

NOTES

[1] Van Lier, 1922, pp. 594-612.
[2] Ahrensberg and Niehoff, 1965, p. 117.
[3] Thoden van Velzen, 1966, p. 75. Nevertheless: such cases do occur by way of exception: Van Lier recounts (1919, p. 32) that the High Priest openly called the Granman 'a betrayer of his people, because the latter, Oseisie, was too pro-*bakra*".
Thoden van Velzen, p. 211, also mentions an instance when the Granman was reproached for having gone to Paramaribo without 'divine' consent. He had to ask to be pardoned for that in public.
[4] Van Lier, 1940, p. 150.
[5] Thoden van Velzen, 1965, Chapters VI and XII.
[6] In the Colonial Reports of 1922 and 1923 the number of Djukas along the Marowijne are given as 4498, along the Upper Commewijne as 131 and along the Cottica as 1014, i.e. a total of 5643.
[7] A method used also by Thoden van Velzen in his 1961 survey (1966, p. 13).
[8] Government Resolution, No. 2588, 18 May 1922.
[9] Government Resolution, No. 2696, 29 July 1922.
[10] Meeting on 16 August 1922, p. 45.
[11] Van Lier wrote in his report covering 1923 and the first quarter of 1924 somewhat unjustly that the motion 'was carried merely from political considerations' and that 'the purpose of the civilization of the Aucaners was more or less lost sight of'.
[12] Negro English: Missie, here the Queen.
[13] Negro English for Governor.
[14] Report 1923 and 1st quarter 1924.
[15] Government Resolution, No. 105, 12 August 1923, Highly Confidential.
[16] Government Resolution, No. 7072, 12 September 1923.
[17] Van Lier, 1919, p. 55.
[18] Van Lier, 1919, p. 62.
[19] The chiefs are appointed by the Granman, the Government acknowledges the appointment and supplies a uniform. At that time they did not yet receive a salary; since 1945 this has been changed.
[20] Thoden van Velzen, 1966, pp. 250 and 260.
[21] Government Resolution, 11 September 1924, Highly Confidential.
[22] This last suggestion was made by W. van Wetering.
[23] Government Resolution, No. 157, 27 December 1923, Highly Confidential.
[24] Government Resolution, No. 370, 4 February 1924.
[25] See also Goodenough, 1963, pp. 435 and 429.
[26] *De Surinamer*, a Catholic paper. See Chapter IX § 3b.
[27] Van Lier, 1919, pp. 17-27.

CHAPTER VII

PERIOD 1924-1926

§ 1 FIFTH STAY IN THE TAPANAHONI, 18 JULY 1924 – 18 NOVEMBER 1925

On his return to Granman Staalkondré the Djukas received Van Lier cordially and came again, like formerly, to ask for medical aid. In spite of the efforts of Bakboord and his wife, the agricultural fields and livestock had not prospered. With the planting material and animals (fowls, goats and pigs) he had brought along, Van Lier started to revive his small farm. But on the 24th he fell ill again: a severe attack of malaria and enteritis, from which he recovered after a fortnight.

a Education

Van Lier could not, however, begin teaching: the Djukas did not send any children. Neither Amakti nor Kanapé had succeeded, in spite of their threats of January 1924, in persuading the Djukas to entrust their children to Van Lier. In September Van Lier travelled again to Drietabbetje to discuss the matter. Kanapé declared that the opposition to the school came entirely from the *Bilo* Negroes, as they still mistrusted Van Lier as a result of the conflict between him and Popo. During Van Lier's absence the matter had been thrashed out in Drietabbetje and the decision taken to propose once more, on his return, that he should strike camp at *Bilo* and come and settle in Drietabbetje, or at any rate in the vicinity of that village. If he was prepared to do that, he could also be assured of a flourishing school. All the *Opo* Negroes were willing to send their children to the school as soon as it was started at a place to which the children could travel back and forth daily.

"The above indicated" Van Lier wrote in his report of 11 September, "that the *Opo* Negroes object to confiding their children to my care and would like to have me settled where they can keep an eye on me."

This was no doubt a reason why the *Opo* Negroes came forward with this suggestion. Another – more important – reason was that the school was once more a stake in the political manoeuvres between the two factions of *Opo* and *Bilo* Djukas.

On 7 October First Lieutenant Weijne, who had in the meantime been appointed District Commissioner, arrived at Granman Staalkondré for a tour of inspection. Many discussions were held, especially on the matter of the school. On 10 October a large *krutu* was held at Drietabbetje. Again Amakti and Kanapé maintained emphatically that, in view of the obstinate behaviour of the *Bilo* Negroes, it would be far better if Van Lier moved the school to Drietabbetje.

Weijne and Van Lier, who after this *krutu* undertook a joint tour of duty to the Lawa River, had ample opportunity for deliberating on the matter. In the letters they wrote to the Governor and the Government Secretary both set forth their point of view. It was clear that Weijne had reached more or less the same conclusion as Van Lier at the end of his report on 1923, in which he offered the opinion that a private individual would have a better chance than a government official of making a success of the school.

Weijne wrote, after his return to Albina on 25 October,[1] that he would rather appoint a postholder-government official in the Upper Marowijne, who would exercise control over both the Tapanahoni and the Lawa and be invested with more authority than had hitherto been the case. He would, however, have to act entirely in accordance with instructions from the District Commissioner in Albina.

With regard to the educating of the Djukas, Weijne wrote: "A boarding-school will not be feasible during the first few years. We have been too optimistic in believing that a primitive people would willingly surrender their children to a foreign *bakra*... We started off too ambitiously; let us see first what education can hope to do for them by means of a day-school, for which there will be enough pupils immediately... This day-school will, however, have to be started in the village of Drietabbetje since no Djuka will send his children unless the children of the Granman himself go to school." The private individual who would have to direct the school must be "an ordinary teacher who understands the Djukas and has become acquainted with their ways".

When Weijne wrote this letter, Van Lier and he were probably in agreement on two points: that the functions of postholder and teacher should be separated, and that a day-school should be started in Drietabbetje.

As regards the latter point, Van Lier had allowed himself to be convinced, while Weijne was in the Tapanahoni, by the arguments of Amakti, Kanapé and the *Opo* chiefs that he should move to Drietabbetje for the time being. But shortly after Weijne's departure Van Lier decided to keep to his original plan and continue his attempt to start a boarding-school in the Lower Tapanahoni. Concerning the suggestion to move the school to Drietabbetje, he wrote to the Government Secretary on 18 November 1924[2] that he had told the District Commissioner during the latter's visit that he had, in fact, been inclined to go and live in Drietabbetje for a while, where he would attempt to draw the children so that they would gradually be completely entrusted to his guidance and could later on be taken with him to his headquarters. On further serious consideration, also of the financial aspect, he had decided to abandon this idea. "This plan does not deserve recommendation" he concluded. "From the start the aim has been not so much to instruct the young Bush Negroes in school subjects as to mould their characters, while agriculture and cattle-farming would occupy a primary place in their education. If we start with a day-school in Drietabbetje, we may expect it to be full in a short time, but we may also expect the parents to be very pleased when they hear their children reading a bit, see them writing and hear them speaking some Dutch. In their eyes that would be a tremendous achievement; they would then regard it as quite unnecessary to send their children to a boarding-school. Their education would remain in the hands of the parents. Of character-building, agricultural instruction and so forth there would then be no question." Van Lier did not give up hope that the Djukas would still entrust their children to his boarding-school, especially since Kanapé had expressed the same view and the District Commissioner would bring pressure to bear on the Negroes.

Van Lier travelled to Amakti's headquarters in the company of a number of *Bilo* chiefs, and on 9 December another *krutu* was held. The *Bilo* chiefs asked Amakti and Kanapé to endorse a request to free a Djuka who was imprisoned in Albina for the theft of balata. Both Kanapé and Amakti refused. "Amakti declared that he would have nothing to do with the matter, that he would henceforth adhere firmly to Kanapé's resolve not to give any help to any Djuka before the school at Granman Staalkondré had enough pupils."

Evidently the *Bilo* chiefs now realized that they would gain nothing by their attitude of aloofness. On the contrary: the group consisting of Amakti, Kanapé and other *Opo* leaders, were getting, partly because the Government supported them, too much political prestige to their liking. So they came round completely and brought five children to Granman Staalkondré on 14 December.

The *Bilo* chiefs, amongst others Banda of the village of Sajé and Ajettee of Nikerie, made statements about their changed attitude: Banda said that they now had experienced personally what trouble resulted from a breach with Drietabbetje and Van Lier, and that they had undergone a change of heart. Ajettee requested him to accept the children, "and no ill feelings". Surely, he said, Van Lier had now had his full 'revenge': Kanapé had recovered while at his place (which did much to clear him from the suspicion of practising black magic) and the *Bilo* chiefs now came to beg him to take the children. The whole course of events was God's will and proved that he was not a *wisiman*.

Van Lier enrolled the boys as pupils, but the school would not be opened, he said, until the ten *Bilo* children agreed upon had arrived. So far not a single *Opo* child had been brought.

§ 2 VAN LIER IN ALBINA; TROUBLES WITH THE DISTRICT COMMISSIONER

In February 1924 First Lieutenant J. Weijne was appointed District Commissioner of the Marowijne district. His predecessors, amongst others, De Sanders, under whose administration the strike of the transport workers had taken place, had hardly concerned themselves with the way in which the postholder acquitted himself of his task. Weijne, however, behaved differently, by instruction of the Governor, Baron van Heemstra, whose special protégé he was. Moreover, he and the postholder fell out on account of a number of incidents in Albina as well as in the Tapanahoni. The animosity on the part of the District Commissioner was heightened because the newspaper *Suriname* conducted a sharp campaign against his management of affairs. (This paper supported Van Lier and published his articles.)

From 26 December to 23 January Van Lier was in Albina where he conducted discussions about the wage-demand of the Djuka freight-carriers and an impending strike with the District Commissioner Weijne, who also summoned Amakti to Albina. The latter arrived with his retinue on 16 January. Van Lier advised the District Commissioner to yield to the demands, which he thought were justified. Weijne would not, however, accept this advice, the price for the transport of goods and the wages of the carriers were not raised, the only concession made was in the cost-price of foodstuffs. The Djukas submitted to these decisions. But between Weijne and Van Lier the matter gave rise to friction: Weijne reproached Van Lier for having given poor advice, and Van Lier complained of not having been kept posted about developments in Albina.

After Van Lier's departure on 23 January an incident occurred, the results of which made Weijne doubt Van Lier's reliability.

Amakti stayed on in Albina for another couple of weeks to give his boatsmen an opportunity of earning a bit more with freight transport. During this time Father F. Morssink paid a visit to Albina and vicinity. This zealous priest, who had already made several unsuccesful attempts at obtaining a foothold for his mission work in the Tapananhoni,[3] declared, when Amakti and three chiefs visited him, that, if it was Amakti's wish, he would see to it that a school was started in his area. Amakti avoided a direct reply and merely pointed out that Mr. van Lier already had a school in the Tapanahoni. Morssink awakened Weijne's interest in his project and Weijne asked Amakti, as the latter took leave, whether he would rather have the priests' school in the Tapanahoni than that of Mr. van Lier. Amakti gave Weijne an evasive reply, too, but promised to write a letter to the District Commissioner after he had discussed the matter with his chief and elders. Amakti left, arriving on 24 February at Granman Staalkondré, where he immediately told Van Lier what had happened and asked him to write a letter on his behalf to the District Commissioner. This letter, with an accompanying note, reached Weijne on 4 March. Amakti wrote[4]: "Granman Amakti sends many greetings to the Commissioner. With God's help, Commissioner, I reached the Tapanahoni safely. I arrived at Granman Staalkondré today and found Mr. van Lier with the pupils of his school in good health. Commissioner, when I left Albina you asked me which school I would prefer in the Tapanahoni, whether I would rather have a school of the priests instead of Mr. van Lier's school. Then I replied that I wanted to keep Mr. van Lier's school, but that I would write you a letter on the matter when I had discussed it with the Chiefs and Elders. I am now writing this letter to you, to inform you that I have already talked about the matter here, but that nobody wants to have the priests' school. We have grown used to Mr. van Lier. We know all his ways and he knows our ways. He has just started again with the school. All the people have promised to send him children; many have already brought the children to him, let us now be satisfied and continue like this. There is not a single Djuka Negro who wants a school except Mr. van Lier's...".

In his accompanying letter Van Lier wrote that Amakti had told him that Father Morssink had sent a message to Amakti "inviting him to come and have a drink with him and bring his chiefs along."[5] On this occasion Morssink had asked the Granman whether he would cooperate with him in the founding of a school in the Tapanahoni. Amakti stated that he wished to retain Van Lier's school at all events, and did not make a single promise. The priest then told Amakti that he would visit him at Drietabbetje to re-open the discussion. Amakti advised him not to come "before he had received a message to say that he was being expected".

Amakti told Van Lier that he had no intention whatsoever of asking the priest to visit him, and that this should have been clear to him, for: "if somebody says that he wants to pay you a visit and you ask him not to do so until you let him know that he may come, and you never send him that message, then surely he will understand that he should *not* come".

Weijne forwarded Amakti's and Van Lier's letters to the Governor on 6 March, accompanied by an indignant comment.[6]

It appears from this letter that he had already enlightened the Governor as to Father Morssink's plans and Amakti's promise to write a letter after a *krutu* had been held to discuss the matter. Although Weijne was annoyed at the fact that Amakti had written him his opinion, obviously without having held a *krutu* at Drietabbetje, he put the blame on Van Lier: "...Now Amakti sends me that message as soon as he arrives at Granman Staalkondré, which is a mockery. It struck me, moreover, that this letter which, after all, conveys a most important decision, was not stamped by Kanapé but only endorsed by two of the postholder's labourers. The Granfiskari Gagu and the chiefs Banda and Ajettee, who are here, give me the positive assurance that the Granman was to have held the *krutu* at Drietabbetje, which goes to show that Amakti has simply sent me a bogus letter, to which Van Lier was privy. Whether Mr. van Lier is really reliable is something about which I am beginning to entertain some doubts. Knowing the Bush Negroes better than I do, he must have realized that Amakti was play-acting... I, for my part, am convinced that Mr. van Lier is not quite above board. This sort of thing has been going on for years, they distrust Mr. van Lier[7] and that in itself is reason enough for not continuing the postholdership. Only Kanapé, whose position as High Priest is jeopardized by the Christian religion, is in favour of the school. As soon as there is a school run by a religious denomination, be it Roman Catholic or Moravian Kanapé will lose his influence and income as priest, so that in this matter his attitude is dictated entirely by self-interest."

Weijne, who had gathered from Amakti's vague replies and promises that he was prepared to consider Morssink's plan, probably took for granted that the letter so hastily written by Amakti must have been suggested to him by Van Lier. But this was not the case. According to Djuka tradition it would have been grossly discourteous if Amakti, while a guest in Albina, had given a straightforward refusal in reply to a query and a request of the District Commissioner. As soon as he was back in the Tapanahoni, he could offer his candid view of the situation. He had already held a *krutu* to discuss it in November 1918 and in February 1921 and had moreover given Father Morssink to understand that he was not in the least pleased with his plans. Hence his wily formulation when he wrote that he had already discussed the matter with his chiefs and elders.

As for the role played by Van Lier in all this: when Amakti brought him an account of what had happened and asked him to write the letter in question, he must have been shocked to learn that his already precarious position was being threatened by the Roman Catholic priest in conjunction with the District Commissioner. No doubt Amakti's firm stand pleased him. He certainly felt no urge to reprimand him and was probably glad to help him with his letter.

Amakti had already more than once disregarded the regulation that his letter should also bear Kanapé's stamp. For that omission he, and not the postholder, was then held responsible. Besides, it is quite clear from Weijne's letter that he, too, realized that Kanapé would certainly not be in favour of a school with a religious bias.

§ 3 BACK IN GRANMAN STAALKONDRÉ

a Education

On 16 February 1925 Van Lier finally opened his school, still with not more than seven boys brought to him by the *Bilo* Negroes. Although Amakti repeatedly declared that he would soon send *Opo* children, he evidently could not or would not persuade the parents to do so. Kanapé had been taken ill again. Van Lier personally believed Amakti's promises. In a letter to the Government Secretary he wrote on 27 February[8] that he had started the school with seven boys but presumed that within a couple of weeks the number would be increased to twenty. Amakti had asked Van Lier to give the Government Secretary fresh assurance of this, also in his name. Van Lier added that, to his mind, everything indicated that the Bush Negroes had turned over a new leaf.

Meanwhile a number of chiefs from *Bilo* villages, led by Banda of Sajé, had come to Van Lier with the proposal to move the school further down, midway between *Bilo* villages, since the *Opo* Negroes obviously had no intention of cooperating in the matter. Availing themselves of Van Lier's visit to Pulugudu,⁹ Banda and Ajettee showed him, on his way back to Granman Staalkondré on 13 April, the place they regarded as suitable: Ningre-tabbetje, a relatively large island, fairly high, never inundated during floods, favourably situated within reach of Wanfinga, Nickerie, Malobbi and Vandaaki.

In the meantime the pupils at Granman Staalkondré had lessons regularly and Van Lier was satisfied with their progress. Some of them were a positive nuisance at times, but Van Lier knew how to handle them. Occasionally they groused at having to do so much work in the house or the garden, but Van Lier was able to persuade them and the parents who supported their offspring that this was all a necessary part of the educational program. Minor dramas were enacted, as in the case of Baapa who was brought to school, as he averred, under false pretensions. "When I tell Baapa that he is to stay here, he starts crying at the top of his voice. After I have stood him in the corner and threatened him with a ruler he stops it... All day long he was quiet and withdrawn, then in the evening he suddenly began to behave as cheerfully and boisterously as the rest, as though he had been here for days." The next day Baapa ran away. On 20 April Van Lier mentioned with satisfaction that he had distributed 'slates and books' to the boys.

b Governor and States decide to discontinue the boarding-school

The letters of criticism which the District Commissioner wrote to the Governor and the Government Secretary no doubt contributed to the fact that Van Heemstra ceased defending the postholdership in the States. In spite of the optimistic letters of Van Lier, who had seven boys at school since 16 February and reckoned on getting more, the Governor instructed Weijne to "handle this matter as tactfully as possible"[10] during his next visit to the Tapanahoni, but "if it should appear from the various data of appeals made to parents, and, if necessary, from indications of passive resistance, that the Administration has done everything in its power to fulfill its promise and that it cannot be held responsible for the failure, then I authorize you to close the school, after having explicitly recorded in a written interrogation of Kanapé, Amakti, and if need be of others, their admission that the Administration has kept its word but the Bush Negroes have opposed those efforts and thus shown themselves unfit to act as cooperating party.

If the above is not clearly evident, then Your Honour might consider continuing the experiment for some time and on such conditions as are to be determined by yourself, after having issued written warning that if the experiment does not succeed, the Bush Negroes will have to accept full responsibility for the closing down of the school."

The decision as to whether Van Lier would retain his position as postholder was likewise left to Weijne's judgment: if he should decide to discontinue the school, "then the question arises whether the Postholdership is to be retained. From the point of view of possible cultural development that office then becomes redundant and if, moreover, you see no valid reason for keeping Mr. Van Lier in that position, you may consider yourself justified to instruct him to return to the city for good." In this case, too, it would have to be stated in writing that the abolishment of the administrative function which had been created in the interests of the Bush Negroes was the result of their own opposition, and "that they were fully responsible for the betrayal of their earlier promises made in Paramaribo and confirmed by protocol". The Governor concluded the letter in which he had thus in advance repudiated all governmental responsibility for the failure of the experiment, with the remark that Weijne could, if necessary, state on his behalf that "consideration will not be shown in future and henceforth the slightest opposition or resistance will be severely dealt with".

On receiving this letter, the District Commissioner did not waste any time: the statement made by a number of *Bilo* chiefs who happened to be present at the time in Albina is dated 4 March, two days after the despatch of the letter from Paramaribo, and ran as follows: "The undersigned, Granfiskari Gagu, Chief Banda and Chief Ajettee and others here present, declare that the Government kept its word with respect to the school and even exceeded their promise, so that, should the school not succeed, this is to be blamed on the Djukas themselves. Especially after what has been done for the school during the past six months and discussed by the District Commissioner, the failure is to be imputed solely to the recalcitrance of the Djukas, so that the Government cannot be accused of anything like breach of faith."

On 19 March the chiefs returned to the Tapanahoni with the message of the District Commissioner that 'if within four weeks there were not at least twenty children in the Boarding-school, His Excellency would definitely close down the establishment",[11] and visited a number of villages to announce this ultimatum. Chief Ajettee came on 17 April and brought a boy, and Gagu assured Van Lier on 28 April that the remaining twelve pupils would soon be brought. While on 5 April another child was brought from the *Bilo* village of Powie, on the 3rd of this month the only child from an *Opo* village was fetched back by Gagu "because his mother objects to her child living here as the only *Opo* child among *Bilo* Negroes" (Journal, 3 April).

Meanwhile the District Commissioner did his best to terminate the matter as soon as possible. After receiving the required statement from the three chiefs in Albina on 4 March, he wrote on 1 April[12] to the Governor that, notwithstanding the fact that he had not yet been able to go to the Tapanahoni because of the floods, he advised him "to close the school down at once. From Gagu, Banda and Ajettee I have already obtained a statement that the Bush Negroes are to be blamed for the fact that the school is to be discontinued. Amakti will also make such a statement, as he already conveyed this by word of mouth when he was in Albina".

This letter makes it clear that Weijne had gone ahead with the matter before receiving an official communication from the Governor, and also that he did not find it necessary to await Amakti's personal statement but regarded those of three of his chiefs as sufficient. No mention was made of Kanapé or of Van Lier.

The Governor curbed this excessive zeal and wrote back on 9 April[13] that he "did not believe the time had arrived for the closing down of the school at Granman Staalkondré. Although the statements by Gagu, Banda and Ajetee constitute the beginning of a proof, Amakti and Kanapé will have to give evidence that they agree, and furthermore, a positive statement from Mr. van Lier is necessary." Weijne now came forward with a new suggestion, namely that "a military patrol of about six men under command of an officer should be sent via the Sara Creek to Drietabbetje".[14] He assumed that the *Bilo* Negroes had been compelled by fear to bring seven children to school, since they realized that he could easily reach their part of the Tapanahoni below the big falls. "The *Opo* Negroes, however, living above the 'Granhollo Falls' feel safe to do as they please... Fear can drive the Bush Negroes to send their children to school. But since this was never the Government's intention, for the Bush Negroes had asked for the school themselves, I do not regard this as the correct way, albeit efficacious." Weijne, who evidently did not seem quite sure of his personal power and authority, added to this letter: "Apart from the school matter, a patrol sent to Drietabbetje via Tosso Creek would have an excellent effect, so I request Your Excellency humbly yet urgently to order this patrol for next October, if you do not consider it necessary just yet."

This proposed military stunt of the District Commissioner – First Lieutenant did not appeal to the Governor and in his reply to this letter he repeated the instructions to obtain the required statement personally from Amakti and Kanapé. "When this has been done, you may announce the closing of the school", he wrote, "and inform the Bush Negroes that the Government has no intention of conducting any civilizing work among them for the time being."

For that matter, it was no longer necessary to try and persuade the Bush Negroes to alter their attitude, for in the Colonial States meeting on 5 May the post for the boarding-school as well as the postholdership had been struck off the budget. "I do not believe", the Governor wrote in the above letter, "that there are grounds for asking the Minister to restore the former in the definitive budget, because it is clear that nothing will come of a boarding-school". He was still in favour of a continuation of the postholdership as a merely administrative function, "but I regard the present dignitary unsuitable because the Bush Negroes still look upon him as an ex-balatableeder and do not trust him in the least." (A balatableeder is a labourer who extracts the rubber sap from the balata-tree. Van Lier was a prospector, that is an overseer of balatableeders. The title was thus – intentionally? – derogatory.) At the said meeting of the Colonial States[15] only two members were in favour of a continuation of the experiment. The opponents still toned down their criticism by remarking that they had nothing against the person of Van Lier. The advocate R.D. Simons, for instance, emphasized the fact that for this difficult task "an unusual sense of calling and great self-confidence are essential".

In an ironical philippic he argued that the whole enterprise was a failure. Discussing the reports Van Lier submitted on his work, he said: "The reports always deal with the condition of the livestock and make no mention of the penetrating civilization or development of the inhabitants, which, after all, was the issue at stake. In order to prove this, the speaker could read aloud all the reports. He will, however, confine himself to a few quotations:

'17 December. A she-goat gave birth to twins, a male and a female kid. Unfortunately the male kid was stifled during birth.' Let us shed a tear at this case of infant mortality and take comfort in the thought that 'those whom the gods love die young'. Somewhere else we read a harrowing description of the suffering of some pigs, evidently after an attack of indigestion. And again: 'Today a sow gave birth to a farrow of five. Activities are being continued.'

The speaker does not understand the hilarity in the hall and on the platform. He is absolutely serious and is reading aloud from the official reports that have to keep us posted about the progress of the civilizing work along the Upper Marowijne. In reading these quotations the speaker has no unfriendly intentions towards Mr. Van Lier, but he wishes to point out how complete the failure is and to convince his fellow-members that there is no longer anything to prevent us from closing the school and the boarding-school."

"This school!" he exclaimed in the course of the same speech, "We were given to understand that the entire Tapanahoni was burning with eagerness to be educated, a fire that could not be quenched by all the waterfalls in that part of the world. The school came, the boarding-school came, and Mr. Van Lier was all set to start civilizing the Bush Negroes. An utter fiasco! After much travail and endless trouble the pupils came along in a horde of... one. The student who was going to slake his thirst for knowledge at the Alma Mater of Granman Staalkondré answered to the august name of Koninkje (Little King), Amakti's son. And so Mr. van Lier, instead of becoming a teacher, was appointed private tutor to this stripling who would save the situation and become the torchbearer of civilization in the uncivilized country beyond the Falls. And with a variation on the well-known saying, Koninkje would be one-eyed in the land of the blind. It has become as clear as noonday that the Bush Negroes have not kept their promise to send their children to the school and boarding-school, the Administration is fully justified in closing both these establishments. In the Preliminary Report it is asked whether the Administration has any information on the 'state of prosperity' of the school. The Administration will not have missed the irony of this question. School and boarding-school have practically ceased to exist, as is best demonstrated by the reports of Mr. Van Lier which the Governor forwards regularly to the Colonial States. These reports have more in common with what one would expect from some farming enterprise than from a person who has been charged with a civilizing mission. This entails no reproach to Mr. Van Lier. He is faced by a situation he is powerless to alter."

Meanwhile, on 29 April, Van Lier received a letter from the District Commissioner with the Governor's instructions that he was to obtain a statement from Amakti and Kanapé that they were responsible for the failure of the school, and that he, Weijne, would arrive at Tapanahoni on 14 or 15 May and wanted to hold a *krutu* at Drietabbetje on the 21st "to stage the last act of the boarding-school affair".

On receipt of this letter, Van Lier wrote in his diary on 29 March that "from the letter received from the D.C. I must conclude that His

Excellency the Governor has decided *to abolish the Postholdership*".

Van Lier had not yet had any official communication from Paramaribo, neither about the statement he was to obtain from Amakti and Kanapé, nor about the Governor's plans with regard to him and the boarding-school, nor about the outcome of the Colonial States meeting on 5 May.

On 5 May Van Lier held a *krutu* with Amakti and Kanapé in which he informed them of the Governor's demand that they should make a statement to confirm that the failure of the development plan was entirely the Bush Negroes' fault. "Kanapé", Van Lier wrote on 5 May in his diary, "had definite objections to submitting this statement without commentary. The discussions resulted in a request that I should write a letter dictated by Kanapé to the Governor". This letter ran as follows:

Drietabbetje, 5 May 1925

Granman AMAKTI of OTTERLOO and Head Chief KANAPÉ of OTTERLOO to His Excellency the Governor of Surinam

Granman Amakti and Head Chief Kanapé send many greetings to the Governor.

Your Excellency! Mr. Van Lier has come here to Drietabbetje and has asked us on behalf of Your Excellency to make the following statement:

1. That the failure of the school is to be blamed entirely on the Bush Negroes themselves.
2. That the Government has done everything it promised toward the establishment of the school.
3. That in spite of all the trouble taken by the Administration, the Bush Negroes refuse to send their children to the boarding-school.
4. That there is every evidence that the school, in its present state, will have no chance of succeeding either.

We beg most respectfully to state that only point *two* can be fully endorsed by us.

As regards points 1 and 3 we humbly beg to state that, although this appears to be the case, it is definitely not true that all the blame for the slow progress of the school lies with the Bush Negroes. On the contrary, Governor! The chief culprits are to be found in the city, in the Cottica, and especially in Albina.

I, Kanapé, wrote long ago already to inform Your Excellency how the Djukas are being incited against Mr. Van Lier. At the time I asked Your Excellency to make a law forbidding the people in the city, in Albina and in the Cottica to blacken Mr. Van Lier's character and to frighten the Djukas into believing that Mr. Van Lier came here to do us harm. Since then the condition has remained the same, or rather, its has grown worse, much worse. For instance, the Djukas' attention is drawn to the fact that Mr. Van Lier is not a trained teacher and not capable of teaching the children properly. The children will learn nothing, no matter how long they remain at school. It is also pointed out to the Djukas that in all other districts where there are schools for the Bush Negro children, professional teachers are employed who are under supervision of proper authorities. Here Mr. Van Lier is alone and no one exercises control over him. He can do as he likes and the Djuka children will no doubt become his slaves. By means of witchcraft he will gain the children's affection so that he can do with them what he pleases[6] and they will work for him as slaves. But they will not learn anything that will be of any advantage to them in later life because Mr. Van Lier is no teacher and therefore not competent to teach children. Mr. Van Lier knows how to deceive the Government with many wiles, so as to be able to continue earning money and achieving his object of making slaves of the Djuka Negroes for his own benefit.

The Djukas are also told that they will soon be rid of Mr. Van Lier if they just have some more patience; because the Administration is getting tired of paying him a salary for doing nothing.

We can swear that it is true before God, Governor, that all this slander is regularly brought here from the Cottica and Albina and that it has become steadily worse since it appears that the school is at last on the point of being established.

In point 4 it says that we must declare that it is clear that the school, in the way it is being run at present, will have no chance of future success either. To this we respectfully reply that we cannot make this statement because we are convinced that a school will NEVER succeed here *except* in the way it is being conducted by Mr. Van Lier at present.

We therefore deeply regret the fact that Your Excellency has now decided to close down the school. In Albina the Commissioner said to Chiefs Banda and Ajettee that if there were not twenty pupils enrolled at the school by the end of four weeks, he would come here to close down the school. And now we have received from Mr. Van Lier Your Excellency's order to make a statement declaring that it is the Djukas' own fault that the school cannot be established, we begin to believe that it was true what the Commissioner said.

We deeply regret that Your Excellency has taken this decision at the very moment that the school was to be started in spite of all the tales being spread among the Djukas by Mr. Van Lier's enemies.

Governor, there are already 8 pupils in the school who are making good progress. The example of the parents of these children would definitely be followed by others. They, too, would send their children to school. But now, alas, the school is to be closed down.

It is true that the Djukas have been lax in the matter of the school and have repeatedly misled us with promises that they would send their children, so that we have repeatedly passed on this assurance to the Administration. But this is the way the Djukas behave, no one speaks his mind openly. Consequently we hoped that, the school having now at last got fairly under way, Your Excellency would not insist on the number of children being twenty, but would wait and see how matters develop. We respectfully beg Your Excellency to take into consideration the fact that the school was started only *three* months ago and that it is too early to state that it will not succeed, either now or in future. No one can prophesy that, Governor.

We also beg Your Excellency respectfully to call to mind that when we held a *krutu* with you in the city and you promised us the school, it could not be started immediately because Your Excellency had to obtain permission from Her Majesty.

Thus Mr. Van Lier remained here for many months before the school was opened. Then he went to the city and stayed away much more than a year. The school was not started. During this time the Djukas were stirred up against him. And when he returned, so many misfortunes occurred that the Djukas were bound to believe that it was true what they had been told, namely that Mr. Van Lier was a *wisiman*.

Now his enemies no longer say that he is a *wisiman*, but what they say now is just as bad and is making the Djukas lose their faith in him.

And yet, Governor, there are already many who no longer pay any heed to the slanderers' tales and have entrusted their children to Mr. Van Lier. For three months the children have been staying with him and all is going well. These children would become the precursors of others and the aim, a school among the Aucaners, would be realized at last. Alas! At this very moment Your Excellency orders the school to be closed. Governor! A curse seems to be resting on the Djukas preventing them from ever obtaining education for their children. This time the desired end seemed in sight and now it is disappearing once more like smoke in the wind. Your Excellency, we ask you to await developments a little while longer. By doing this you would bestow a favour on us. If the school is abolished, we fear that there will not be any further chance of education for the Djuka children.

The people have already disappointed us so often that now we no longer dare give any positive assurance. But we are convinced that, if Your Excellency will still have some patience, the school *is bound* to succeed.

We send respectful greetings to Your Excellency and to the Government Secretary and pray that God may bless you and all who are helping Your Excellency to govern the country.

Amakti of Otterloo
Kanapé of Otterloo

At the same *krutu* of 5 May the *Bilo* chiefs sent word officially through Banda of the village of Sajé "that they would oppose the closing down of the school with every means within their power. The *Bilo* Negroes had suffered enough for the sake of the school. It was a well-known fact that they wanted it all along even though they did not dare admit it openly for fear of what the *Opo* Negroes would say. Then, too, they lacked someone to assume leadership in the matter: he, Banda, now wished to state clearly that he regarded himself, notwithstanding the fact that he was the youngest among the chiefs (in seniority: he had been elected only a year ago) as leader of the *Bilo* Negroes as far as the school was concerned. The *Bilo* Negroes could have sent twenty children long ago, but they did not wish to do it, lest they should give the *Opo* Negroes opportunity of saying afterwards that they would have entered their children if they had not been forestalled by the *Bilo* Negroes".[17]

Banda went on to describe the advantages of the proposed new site among the *Bilo* Negroes, so that those children for whom there would not be room in the boarding establishment, could attend school daily. Amakti thanked Banda for his support and remarked that it was now quite clear that by no means all the Djukas were opposed to the school. The matter was left at that.

Van Lier, ill and exhausted, returned to Granman Staalkondré, where Banda and the other *Bilo* chiefs came to visit him and declared that they were willing to assume responsibility for the removal of the school to Ningre-tabbetje, with everything it involved. Van Lier duly noted their promise.

On 12 May Gagu came to bring a boy from Drietabbetje to the boarding-school and reiterated the assurance that others would be following soon. There were now nine boys, the school was getting along in spite of Van Lier's illness, and his workman-assistant, Johan Bieslijn, took charge of the lessons.

On 8 May Van Lier received a letter from Weijne [18] to say that he would arrive at Granman Staalkondré on 19 May, and wished to hold a *krutu* on the 20th. Concerning his conversation with Weijne, before the meeting with the Djuka chiefs, Van Lier simply jotted in his notebook on 19 May: "Various discussions with W. I point out the chances of success to him. He has the right to postpone. I myself am tired out! Etc....". True to habit, Granman Amakti did not turn up on the appointed day and allowed himself to be fetched the following day. Kanapé was gravely ill and did not come at all. The *Bilo* chiefs, under Banda's leadership, availed themselves of the absence of the *Opo* chiefs to draw Weijne's attention sharply to the fact that it was now no longer their fault that the school did not have enough pupils; the required number of *Bilo* children had come, and if it were not that they wanted to allow the *Opo* Negroes a chance of delivering their quota of children also, the school would have been filled long ago by *Bilo* children. Once more Banda vigorously pleaded that the entire school should be moved to the centre of the *Bilo* villages, promising Weijne moreover that his people would be responsible for the removal and the expenses it entailed. Weijne, rather strangely under the circumstances, agreed to this proposal on condition that there should be twenty children within a fortnight and that school and boarding establishment would be moved to the new site within three months.

Amakti, summoned to attend the meeting on the 21st, was reprimanded for coming late. Six questions to determine where the blame lay for the failure of the school were submitted to him and he was told of the plan of the *Bilo* Negroes and the extension of time Weijne was prepared to grant so that the school might still have a chance of increasing its numbers. Amakti and his following accepted this but declared that "they were now really going to send the children". To prove the sincerity of their promise, two boys from Drietabbetje were brought to be enrolled.

The meeting reached a dramatic culminating point in the statement of the Djuka leaders, regarded by the Governor as essential for guarding the power relations, in which they took the entire blame for the failure of the project upon themselves.

Amakti declared:

that the Governor had kept his word as regards the school, and no blame attached to the Government;

that the failure of the school was due to the opposition and ill-will of the Bush Negroes, particularly those of *Opo*;

that he, Amakti, did not have enough influence on his people to persuade them to send their children to the school, which would thus not have any chance of future success either.

"Amakti", Weijne wrote in a report on the *krutu*, "called everyone present to witness, when he had to sign, that the *Opo* Negroes alone were to blame, and that if his signature were to bring on misfortune there was no help for it; he could not do otherwise, he declared. The *Bilo* Negroes have scored a great victory over the *Opo* and they aver that there is not one of them who would not rather be the slave of a *Bakra* than of another naked nigger (*Opo*) like themselves (*Bilo*)".

Once again, as during his previous visits, Weijne was impressed by what Van Lier had achieved in spite of tremendous difficulties and opposition. With respect to the school he noted in his report: "The postholder with his pupils, nine in number, stood waiting for me at the landing-stage. It was not a pleasant thought for me that I would have to tell these children, now grown used to the school, that it was to be closed down, but in the Tapanahoni all the Bush Negroes knew that I had come for that purpose. The next day (May the 20th) a number of *Bilo* chiefs came to hold a *krutu* and begged me not to take Mr. Van Lier away...

I am positive, now that the school is here, that the *Bilo* Negroes will part with their children and the *Opo* Negroes will do the same from envy... As to the school, Mr. Van Lier gave lessons for a couple of hours to show what the children knew already, and it struck me that the Bush Negro children are not dull at learning, as I have mentioned in an earlier report."

As soons as he got back to Albina, Weijne sent a wire to the Governor asking for two weeks' extension, which was granted.

Weijne's visit, and the decisions taken at the time, made a deep impression on the *Opo* Negroes. Obviously the *Bilo* Negroes had gained a political victory and at the eleventh hour the *Opo* Negroes tried to better their position. Chief Asodé took trouble to enlist more *Opo* children for the school and brought along two boys. He asked "what the Aucaners could do to retain the school and not let me go away from here", Van Lier wrote in his notebook on 31 May. He had decided, however, not to express his view on the matter any more and replied to him and to the many Djukas who came with the same question that the decision did not rest with him, but with the Government.

On June the 2nd a number of *Opo* chiefs came to Van Lier with the news that they, too, were willing to fix up a new site for him at their own cost and suggested Puketi.[19] If Van Lier agreed to this they would start work immediately, so that the *Bilo* Negroes would not be ready before the *Opo* Negroes.[20] To this Van Lier merely replied that he had no personal authority to grant them permission.

Meanwhile the work in connection with the building of the new camp at Ningre-tabbetje was proceeding briskly under Van Lier's regular supervision and instructions.

At the end of June, after many *krutus* in the course of which the tension between *Opo* and *Bilo* was in no way lessened, Amakti tried to make his influence felt by ordering the *Bilo* Negroes who were on the construction job at the new camp to stop working. "Banda duly noted the message and stated that he would continue the work which he had pledged himself to deliver to the Commissioner. The *Opo* Negroes could likewise, if they saw fit, construct a new site, and when both were ready, *Masra* Van Lier would then decide for himself where he wished to settle" (Journal, 2 June 1925).

For the *Opo* Negroes there was little to be done now except resign themselves to the situation. On 30 June they came to hold another meeting with Van Lier, and declared that, even if Van Lier should now settle among the *Bilo* Negroes, they would still start a provision farm on a small island facing Puketi as well as at Ningre-tabbetje, where a school could eventually be built, with the Government's permission. If it would be impossible to procure a separate teacher for the school, Van Lier could divide his time between teaching at Puketi as well as at Ningre-tabbetje. Chief Jenta of Puketi, who proposed the plan, once again expressed the general appreciaton of the fact that Van Lier had founded a school after all the futile attempts in the past.

The *Opo* Negroes further declared that they would write a letter on the subject to the District Commissioner (Van Lier did not wish to be involved in this) in which, moreover, they would again ask pointedly that Van Lier should not be taken away from them. With this show of initiative and activity they tried to save their face to some extent in the eyes of the Government, but especially toward the *Bilo* Negroes. After a *krutu* held at Drietabbetje by the chiefs of *Bilo* and *Opo*, Chief Banda came to Van Lier on 4 June to tell him that, as far as that matter was concerned, a 'divine peace' had been established.

On 9 June Van Lier reported to Weijne that there were twenty pupils at his school, and the District Commissioner who, before his visit to the

Tapanahoni, had repeatedly advised the Governor and the Government Secretary in his letters not to put off the closing of the school any longer, sent this information to the Governor, adding the remark: "I regret that the States members have not been willing to wait until I had returned from the Tapanahoni before taking a decision, all the more since they have been patient for so long (practically five years) and it was now only a matter of some weeks.

I am fully convinced that the school, as far as its numbers go, may be regarded as having succeeded. I do not share the fear that the children will be fetched home again when the danger of discontinuance is past. While I was at Granman Staalkondré, it happened that two children of *Opo* Negroes were brought, and the persons who brought them declared that Mr. Van Lier might, if need be, take the children along to Albina or Paramaribo, they were surrendering their children unconditionally to Mr. Van Lier...

Therefore I beg Your Excellency humbly but urgently to consider the replacement of the boarding-school on the budget so that its results may be watched during one more year."[21]

The Governor, impressed by Weijne's plea, made one more attempt at persuading the Colonial States to change their mind. He forwarded the District Commissioner's report, adding the written observation: "If this report should incline your Board to request me to invite the Minister of Colonies to reinstate the annulled posts on the definitive budget, I should be glad to be informed as soon as possible."[22]

The Colonial States, however, saw no reason for retracting their decision. The fact that the number of children had suddenly soared to twenty after Weijne's visit did not restore their faith in the cause, and in view of past experience they doubted whether the number would be sustained. They did not think there was any guarantee whatsoever that this would be the case.

c The school

Because of the sudden increase of the number of children at the school, Van Lier was faced with the problem of food shortage. In order to eke out the small supply of rice he undertook a journey to a number of villages, as far as Pulugudu, to buy some tinned food despite the fact that he was in very poor health. The inhabitants of Granman Staalkondré lived, in addition, on bananas and *kwak* (cassavameal, diluted with water) until fresh supplies arrived from Paramaribo and Albina. Van Lier was suffering from attacks of vertigo, feverishness, boils and especially insomnia, and he let his assistant, Bieslijn, take over the school from time to time. He found the many and lengthy *krutus* about the removal of the school and the measures to be taken in connection with it particularly exhausting.

On 27 July they started moving from Granman Staalkondré to Ningretabbetje, and on 4 August Van Lier, the children and his labourer Bieslijn moved into the new camp. Banda and others gave their active assistance and promised to help out with food supplies until the new fields yielded enough for their needs.

In a letter dated 27 August and in a report of 9 October Van Lier gave a survey of the position. Of the twenty boys there were thirteen of *Bilo* and seven of *Opo*. Van Lier described the ration usually given per child per meal: 200 gram rice or 150 gram flour, or 200 gram *kwak*, or a quantity of ground cassava or cassava bread, and 50 to 100 gram sugar. The quantities supplied of cured meat, fish and ham respectively were: 75, 75 and 50 gram. For the frying of pancakes or cod each child received 30 gram of oil.

In the report he explained why he had deviated from the original plan of accepting only boys below the age of ten. (Of the twenty boys he estimated the age of five at under ten, of two at ten, of one at eleven, three at thirteen, two at fourteen, two at fifteen, two at sixteen and two at seventeen.) The intention had been that the boarding-school would be self-supporting by the end of three or four years, with the help of food-cultivation and cattle-raising. "But now", Van Lier wrote, "that various circumstances have impeded the hoped-for development of agriculture and cattle-breeding, and with the fact in mind that the credit for this work might well be stopped on account of the country's stringent economic policy and the unfavourable attitude of the Colonial States, necessity had to be turned into a virtue and as many older boys as possible accepted from whom some useful labour for the purpose of food-cultivation might be expected.

The admission of older boys was not free from risks. The fear of reprehensible conduct on the part of these lads still existed, of course, but since I had no other means of gaining my objective, I had to overcome this fear in the hope of being able to deal judiciously with the situation. It is gratifying to be able to report that things have gone better than I had expected and that, with a single exception, I have had no reason to complain of the conduct of my pupils. This exception applies to three of the older boys: Jacopu, Angele and Adenaai, who ran away during

Clemens, ex-pupil of Van Lier, on Stoelman's Island, where his family was nursed in the hospital. He earned his keep by working for the boarding-school of the Moravian Brothers. Here he is depicted stamping cassava, regarded by the Djukas as woman's work. (photograph by the author)

the night of 30 September. The reason they gave, as I was to learn later on, was that I had made them work too hard. I may mention here that Jacopu, since the day of his arrival until his 'escape' never touched an implement and was always suffering from severe syphilitic pains. Angele, suffering likewise, did next to nothing. Only number three, Adenaai, a strong, healthy but utterly lazy youth, worked hard enough, being constantly prodded on by me." The two first-mentioned boys came from *Opo* villages and were seventeen and sixteen years old.

In this report Van Lier offers his opinion of the Djuka children and describes the boarding-school's daily routine.

"Although I have little cause to complain of the boys' behaviour, especially in the matter of obedience – which is worth mentioning since disobedience is the chief characteristic of Djuka children[23] – their great vice, a constant headache to me, is their inveterate slovenliness. It is the usual thing for them to leave lying around and lose the tools they work with and the few bits of clothes they bring along from home, etc.

The rules these boys have to observe are the following: At half-past-five they have to rise and go and bathe in the river. After that they may warm themselves at a small fire which they build themselves. This I allow to make up for the lack of a camp-fire at night. (To warm themselves at a fire is an ingrained Djuka custom which many of them cannot do without.)

While two of the eldest (they have to do it in pairs, turn and turn about) are getting breakfast, the others sweep the yard, the camp and the place where the animals sleep. School starts at nine and continues until noon. Those whose turn it is then go and cook their midday-meal, while the others are occupied with various chores. After having had their meal they may go and play. Most of them wander along the river with bow and arrow and come back, especially during the dry season, with a couple of small fish. A favourite pastime of theirs is hollowing out canoes or carving oars. At three o'clock they all have to start work, which is usually carried out under my personal guidance.

On the old site most of the work used to consist of the cultivation of crops, here it consists of the care or the clearing of newly laid-out provision grounds.

At five o'clock the boys knock off. Then they have to help stable the goats, fetch water for household use, cooking, etc. At seven o'clock it is time for supper, and then they may go and play again, tell each other stories (*anansitoris*) and at nine o'clock the whole camp has to be quiet.

At school they are taught to read (Hoogeveen method) and cipher

(Boosman and Bos method). I have not started with writing lessons yet. I take great pains to enlarge their stock of ideas and develop their powers of observation. Since my aim is rather to civilize their manners and improve their characters than to furnish them with book-learning, I occupy myself with the boys as much as possible also after school hours. I try to stimulate their interest in '*Bakra* life', I do my utmost to cure them of their inherent sneaking, underhand Bush Negro ways, their propensity for lies and deceit. I am glad to be able to report some improvement in this respect. One is pleased when, after some mischievous act, the culprit owns up at once, while there is less tale-bearing than formerly.

Fortunately the pupils' health has been quite satisfactory up till now.

From the parents I am getting more cooperation than I had counted on, and it is clear that they have full confidence in me and that they take the school quite seriously.

Since I have settled here and the school has been started on the new site, I am regularly asked to accept more children as day-pupils. Chiefs Banda, Ajettee and Madoné even remind me that this was the reason why the school was moved to the new position. I have not been able, however, to comply with this request since there is no seating accommodaton for more pupils.

In my note No. 2 of 24 September 1919 'on the proposed plan for the carrying out of the Postholder's duties among the Aucaners', which plan, without any alterations, received the approval of His Excellency Governor Staal, I included the following remark: 'If I succeed in bringing together a number of children under my guidance in a boarding-school, then the first step towards the civilization of the Aucaners will have been achieved.' With deep satisfaction I may now point out that, despite numerous difficulties which presented themselves and at times seemed insurmountable, I have succeeded in taking this first step, which would not have taken place if I had not moved in the matter.

At the same time it is disappointing to realize that the Government's effort at civilizing the Tapanahoni has proved a fata morgana.

For the sake of the rising generation here it is to be sincerely hoped that the work will be continued by means of private enterprise. To my mind this should be possible, seeing that the foundation has been laid already, on condition that religion is kept in the background at the outset. Even though there may, fortunately, be many here who would, individually, like their children to be baptized and receive a Christian education, I fear that if one of the missions who wish to carry on with the work starts with religion at once, it will cost endless trouble before the same progress is made as has been achieved by the Government. The opposition of 'those in power' here who have much to gain materially from the heathen customs of the people, will not be put down easily."

d Agriculture, cattle-breeding and fishing

During this last period nothing whatsoever was done about instruction in agriculture and cattle-breeding. On his return Van Lier had to tackle the job once again of getting his neglected provision fields and livestock going so as to meet his own needs. When children came to the boarding-school, he had the greatest trouble in providing them with food. The removal of his entire station made it necessary for him to start all over again. By buying food in various villages, transporting provisions from Albina and putting the older boys to work hard on the school-grounds, he managed to come out. This was not an attractive example for the Djukas, who did not feel any need to exert themselves so strenuously.

Nothing came of Van Lier's efforts to teach the Djukas new fishing methods. The *tramaille* (drag-net) he had brought along got torn on the rocky river-bed almost every time it was used. The Djukas thought (rightly) that they knew more about fishing than he did.

e Medical aid

Van Lier hardly mentions this at all, although it is clear that the Djukas still consulted him. He made no more efforts to improve their concepts of hygiene. All that had been achieved was that the Djukas had 'promised' to bury their corpses within three days, and not throw the bodies of (deceased) witches into the forest any more. There was no check on this. Van Lier could not persuade the Djukas to give up the habit of catching fish by using poison (*ponsu*), nor did he manage to instruct them in new methods of meat preservation.

f More disagreement with the District Commissioner

The relationship between Van Lier and District Commissioner Weijne had meanwhile deteriorated considerably since the easing of tension which had taken place during Weijne's visit to the Tapanahoni in May 1925. The Djukas, irritated by a number of steps taken by Weijne, complained to Van Lier. Chief Akrosi of Albina handed in his resignation, while Van Lier had difficulty in dissuading Kanapé from doing likewise. The first step was that Weijne, after failing to obtain a wage rise in Albina for the transport workers with the *Compagnie des Mines d'Or*, had had a refractory Djuka put into prison. The other measure which caused a commotion in the Tapanahoni was that the Government had set up a custom-house at Pulugudu, without warning Van Lier or the Djukas beforehand.[24]

Amakti and Kanapé asked Van Lier to write a letter to the Government in which they expressed their dismay at this course of events. Van Lier sent this letter, accompanied by a personal comment, to the Government Secretary. Weijne blamed Akrosi's resignation and the Djukas' indignant reaction on Van Lier and not only reproached him for not having supported the Government and the District Commissioner, but accused him of breach of faith.

These events may be inferred from the two defensive letters written by Van Lier, since the Government's and the District Commissioner's contributions to the correspondence on the matter are not to be found in the archives.[25]

From Van Lier's replies it appears that he had found it indeed difficult to justify the two above-mentioned measures towards the Djukas. He could not do so with genuine conviction and his arguments had little effect on the Djukas, themselves past masters in the art of disputation. In his letter of 12 October 1925[26] he wrote: "It is incorrect to say that I have not defended your policy; the opposite is the case. The reason why you found no mention of this in the report is the fact that I felt justified in assuming that it would, without explicit mention, be taken as self-evident." Van Lier, who in his report on this affair (appended to the letters by Kanapé and Amakti) had endeavoured to enlighten the Government about the unrest and irritation among the Bush Negroes, thought that Weijne did not regard the situation seriously enough. "I suppose that is the result of being insufficiently acquainted with the character of the Aucaners, while you are too much guided by your opinion, so often expressed towards me, 'that all primitive people resemble one another mentally and morally'. Even if this should be the case with the peoples of the Orient, it does not apply to the Bush Negroes of Surinam. I have already pointed out on earlier occasions that even the various tribes differ from one another with regard to their character, as, for instance an Englishman differs from a Frenchman." Weijne who, intensely annoyed, forwarded this letter to Paramaribo with numerous marginal comments, scribbled next to this remark: "Rubbish, there is a marked resemblance between all primitive peoples and Mr. Van Lier is no judge in the matter."

One of Weijne's reproaches towards Van Lier was that he had not been 'grateful' enough for the help he had received from Weijne in the school affair. Van Lier countered this charge in the same letter. "That I received a great deal of help (I may even say a *very* great deal) and cooperation from you in the establishing of the school I have more than once mentioned with gratitude in official communications. But that 'without you' the school would still have stood empty I do not believe. I presume that you would not either, on carefully considering the history of its development, maintain this claim. So much then for the reproach for my ingratitude (as though you were rendering me a personal favour) 'after all that you have done for me'."

Weijne wrote in the margin: "Without my intervention in October 1924 and May 1925 the school would never have come into being, that is not to be denied."

To Weijne's remark in the letter (to which the above quotation was a reply) that Van Lier's prestige had been 'nil' before his, Weijne's, arrival, Van Lier retorted that this was "absolutely inaccurate and to my mind already *utterly* refuted by the fact that His Excellency the Governor maintained me in this position, *where prestige is of paramount importance*, during FIVE years before your arrival, while I had the great privilege of hearing from His Excellency when I last met him (that was just about the time that you assumed the post of District Commissioner at Marowijne) that-he-had-absolute-confidence-in-me."

Van Lier explained the whole matter once more in a letter to the Governor (21 December 1925), in which he defended himself against Weijne's accusations. In the last paragraph of this letter Van Lier discussed Weijne's remark in his insulting letter of 21 September in which he asserted that Van Lier's prestige was 'nil'. (Weijne sent a copy of this letter to the Governor.) "The reason why I bring this again specially to Your Excellency's notice is so as to emphasize that Mr. Weijne cannot have formed *any* opinion of my prestige among the Bush Negroes. He has never had an opportunity of observing my relationship with or behaviour toward these people. On the *very* rare occasions that I came into contact with the Bush Negroes in Albina in the presence of the District Commissioner, I have always had to fulfil the passive role of interpreter; while Mr. Weijne's visits to my station were *always* extremely brief and all negotiations were rushed along at such a pace that there was no time for him to form an impression of my conduct in the performance of my official functions."

g Abolishment of boarding-school and postholdership

On 2 October Van Lier was instructed by the Government Secretary, on behalf of the Governor, "to return to Paramaribo by about 1 December, after having handed over everything belonging to the Government, with an inventory, to the District Commissioner".

On 22 October Van Lier received a letter from Weijne to say that he would come to the Tapanahoni on 16 November to hold a *krutu*, and on 5 November a letter to say that Mr. Zangen would come along to take over the school and boarding establishment.

Van Lier took the necessary measures. By Amakti's request and with the District Commissioner's permission it was decided to hold the *krutu* at Puketi.

On 26 October Van Lier received a missive (Highly Confidential, No. 75) from the Governor[27] informing him that he was to be dismissed on retaining pay on 1 January 1926. In the same letter the Governor wrote with reference to Van Lier's report of 13 September in which he conveyed the complaints of Amakti and Kanapé, that he considered that Van Lier had failed in his duty as administrative official.

Van Lier did not reply to this letter until he had returned to Paramaribo on 19 December.[28]

He felt, Van Lier wrote after he had received the Governor's missive,[29] that he was "under a moral obligation to inform those who had supported me with such loyal affection (Kanapé, Banda, Ajettee, Madoné and others) that I shall soon be leaving. But above all I regard it as my task to make propaganda for the continuance of the school and pave the way for whoever later on succeeds me."

He tried to do this among the *Bilo* as well as the *Opo* Negroes. The *Bilo* Negroes assured him that the children would be fetched back on the day that he left. But, Van Lier wrote: "I may be able to bring them to a different way of thinking by appealing to their views on property and rights of succession." They did want Van Lier to promise, though, that the children would not be baptized. "To this I replied that I could not make a positive statement, but that for the time being there would be no question of baptism or Christian education, for the good reason that three years ago the Moravian Brothers had been willing to give secular education to the Aucaners in Cottica. Why should they not do the same here in the Tapanahoni?"

While making propaganda for the continuance of the school among the *Opo* Negroes from 10 to 12 October at Drietabbetje, he warned them "that the present generation would bring down the curse of the next on their heads, if it was *now once more* denied a chance of education, after all that had preceded the establishment of the school".

On this occasion he only obtained the assurance of Amakti (Kanapé was not present) that he was willing to continue supporting the school himself, but that the people would not place the same confidence in Van Lier's successor as they had in him at present.

Kanapé sent word to Van Lier that he would not attend the *krutu* and asked Van Lier to write a letter on his behalf to the Governor to hand in his resignation as Head Chief. "With a view to the bitterness now prevalent among the Aucaners", Van Lier wrote in his journal on 9 November, "added to the fact that I am being recalled at the very moment when, to my mind, it is of the utmost importance that the Administration has at its command the services of someone who can be trusted absolutely, I have decided to go to Drietabbetje tomorrow to try and persuade Kanapé to cancel his resolve." On 11 November he had an interview with Kanapé. In his report of 19 December he wrote to the Governor that Kanapé would not consider withdrawing his resignation. He gave as reason the disappointments he had experienced: "he had done his duty faithfully; he had kept the promises he had made to the Governor! His attachment to the *Bakras* had even cost him his health." On the other hand there was the fact that nothing had been fulfilled of all that the Administration had promised the Djukas. Moreover he suspected that he had lost the confidence of the Governor since District Commissioner Weijne had been appointed. The latter 'did not like the Aucaners' and misinformed the Governor. The fact that Kanapé was unwilling to cooperate with Weijne was even, Van Lier thought, the main reason why Kanapé had decided to resign. Van Lier's efforts to make him change his mind were of no avail. "It would be psychologically unjustified", Van Lier wrote, "to keep on with it and I thought it would be better to give him a few days in which to calm down, and then try and convince him of the error of his decision and bring him round to a different way of thinking." As to the school, Kanapé at first firmly declared that he would not support any but Van Lier's. He would, however, offer no active opposition to his successor. "I may be able", Van Lier wrote in the said report, "to persuade Kanapé on this particular issue. I pointed out to him that he would later on reproach himself if he stuck to his resolve. His opponents, who have so often called him a hypocrite who only pretended, for the sake of personal benefit, to support the school, would then appear to be in the right because nobody would believe that he was taking this stand on account of my discharge, but would prefer to assume that he was only too pleased of a chance to back out completely."

Upon this Kanapé declared that he would regard the school as a matter in itself, for the sake of the Djukas, and from 'love' for Van Lier, even though he were no longer Head Chief. This he would convey personally to the District Commissioner and Mr. Zangen when they arrived at Granman Staalkondré.

When he got back to Granman Staalkondré II Van Lier found a missive from the Governor[30] on 12 November instructing him to reply to Kanapé's and Amakti's letters of 13 September. It was too late, however, to reach them before the District Commissioner's arrival, and he let them know that he had received a message from the Governor which proved that they were wrong to assume "that the Dutch Administration no longer appreciated them" (Journal 12 November 1925).

In the "Report to His Excellency the Governor on the *krutu* held by the District Commissioner of Marowijne on Monday 16 and Tuesday 17 November 1925 in the village of Puketi and on the Postholder's discharge from the Tapanahoni", written on 19 December in Paramaribo, Van Lier gave a detailed description of the events in question.

On 15 November the District Commissioner, together with the minister of the Evangelical Moravian Brothers, M. Kersten, Van Lier's successor Zangen and the latter's wife, arrived at Granman Staalkondré II.

Kersten described Granman Staalkondré II in a report[31] on this journey as follows: "The island, about one square kilometre in size, lay opposite Malobbi and three other villages under surveillance of Chief Banda. On the southernmost point stood a shed where travelling Djukas could find shelter for the night and where the sick could stay. Van Lier's house stood about ten metres away, and was 20 metres long and 8 metres wide. The roof was of plaited palmleaf, the walls of split-poles. The front part of the house was divided into Van Lier's workroom which contained a desk, and wooden shelves with medicines, also some cases. Next to the room a bedroom and a small bathroom. Behind these rooms across the entire breadth the schoolroom with benches, reading-planks, reading-books, slates, exercise-books, etc. On the back wall a large portrait of the Queen, with, on the right, ex-Governor Staal, on the left, Governor Van Heemstra. Behind this room the boys' dormitory, with a storeroom and a kitchen built on to it. The estate, as well as the children, looked well cared-for, the small stock of animals likewise". Kersten, whose report was written in German, concludes: "*Die Arbeit des Herrn van Lier hatte damit seinen Abschluss gefunden, 6 Jahre hat er dort oben ausgehalten, mit viel Geduld und allerdings auch hohen Kosten, doch einiges erreicht."*

The next morning the company set out to Puketi, where Amakti with many chiefs and elders had gathered.

The District Commissioner opened the meeting with the statement "that a great deal of misunderstanding had arisen between the District Administration and the Aucaners, which he now wished to clear away, this being the main purpose of his coming here. He had come to realize that this misunderstanding had been caused by correspondence and therefore he was now instituting the rule that he would visit the Tapanahoni at least once a year and that the Granman would reciprocally visit Albina once a year to discuss matters touching the interests of the Djukas." Thereupon the Commissioner informed the meeting, on behalf of the Governor, that Mr. van Lier had been recalled. His Excellency regretted this decision, but he had to obey the wishes of Her Majesty the Queen (sic). Van Lier's departure would not, however, mean that the school would be abolished. On the contrary, the Governor wished the school to be continued, but as a day-school, which meant that the parents would have to provide the children with food themselves. They might, however, stay on at Granman Staalkondré. Mr. Zangen had come to take over that task. The District Commissioner now asked the Djukas to promise that they would respect the Governor's wishes in this matter, in which case the customs station at Pulugudu would be removed.

Amakti expressed his regret that Mr. van Lier, to whom the Djukas had grown attached, was leaving them. As regards the school, he was sorry to say that he could not promise that it would be kept up as a day-school. The difficulty lay in feeding the children. Those who lived nearby could have their meals before and after school, but the children whose parents lived a long way off could not do so and would therefore have to stay without education.

The District Commissioner replied that in that case the customs station[32] would *not* be removed, and the Djukas would have themselves to blame for it. To this the Granman objected that the District Commissioner should not confuse two unrelated matters. He had said at the beginning that he had come to clear up misunderstanding, and there was nothing that he, Amakti, would welcome more; he respected the authorities but would nevertheless speak his mind clearly. It was not on account of lack of goodwill on his part that he did not want the children to make use of the school, but it was impossible for the parents to provide them with food. Why then should the custom-house be kept on as a punishment? Therefore he asked the Government to continue feeding the children.

He feared that if this request were not granted the school could not be kept up.

Kersten replied that the problem of distance could easily be solved by starting schools in other centres as well. If Amakti should, for instance, wish to have a day-school in Drietabbetje, he could, by way of speaking, promise that it would "be started tomorrow".

Amakti replied that he would rather not have two schools in the Tapanahoni and continued to plead earnestly for the provision of food by the Government, so that it became obvious to every one that this was the reason why "he would rather not have two schools".

Chief Sona "who had a flair for finding loopholes at awkward moments during transactions with the *Bakras*", pointed out to the Granman that the matter was too weighty to be settled off-hand. He suggested that the children living within easy reach of the school should continue to attend it as day-pupils, while the question of food provision would be discussed later on. The Granman accepted Sona's proposal, but now wished to know whether the teaching would remain neutral. Upon this Kersten stated that there would be no attempt to baptize the children as long as the parents did not ask for it themselves. The District Commissioner made a similar statement in the name of the Government. Then he declared that the customs station was to be abolished.

On the second day of the *krutu* Kanapé turned up. He waited at the village landing-stage and asked to have an interview with Van Lier. He declared that he had yielded to Van Lier's request that he should come to the *krutu*, but that he was now going to recount all his grievances to the District Commissioner. When Van Lier told him that he had been instructed by the Governor to state that Kanapé enjoyed the Government's confidence and expected that he "would show that he was a loyal subject of Her Majesty the Queen", this was evidently enough to make him give up his resolve to unburden his heart and hand in his resignation. His desire to remain on as salaried Head Chief was strong enough for him to be pacified by the Governor's statement.

His encounter with Weijne went without a hitch. However, he declared that "not knowing what obligations Amakti had undertaken at the *krutu*, he reserved the right to disagree on such points as he could not identify himself with".[33]

On the same day, 17 November, Van Lier and his company returned to Granman Staalkondré II and handed over the boarding-school and the inventory to Zangen. The District Commissioner delivered a farewell speech in which he praised Van Lier for the way in which he had fulfilled his task, despite the many difficulties that attended it. His pains and efforts had not been in vain: the school had been called into existence. For this he thanked Van Lier in the name of the Government and in his own name. He declared that he was happy "to be able to presently submit a favourable report on the person and the work of Van Lier to the Governor".

In his reply to this eulogy Van Lier expressed his satisfaction that someone had come to take over his work so that he was spared the distress of having to lock the door behind him when he left.

He pointed out to his successor that he had suffered much physically, and even more morally, during the six years that he had exercised his official duties. That he had succeeded, in spite of all, in laying the foundation of civilization among the Djukas, he owed to his motto: "My strength is in God!" which he always kept in mind, even at the most difficult moments, and his wish was that Zangen might find strength from the same source to continue the constructive task.

On the 18th Weijne and Kersten left Granman Staalkondré early in the morning, Van Lier at three o'clock in the afternoon. In his journal he wrote the following about his departure: "Kanapé, who had come from Puketi to Granman Staalkondré to see me off, was deeply moved by my going. The leave-taking from my pupils threatened to become sentimental; some of them started weeping, so I found it better to embark without saying goodbye to each in turn."

At Pulugudu Van Lier had an attack of influenza which kept him there for another day. A number of *Bilo* chiefs came to see him off and Banda told him that Kanapé had called a *krutu* with the *Bilo* Negroes at Granman Staalkondré to exhort them to let their children continue to attend the school as a day-school. On this occasion Kanapé firmly announced that he would keep on supporting the cause. He had directed Banda to keep a watchful eye on developments there and to report to him if there were *Bilo* Negroes who tried to oppose Zangen in any way.

On 24 November Van Lier arrived at Albina. "The District Commissioner and his wife received me most cordially and offered to put me up. At the midday-meal Mr. Weijne was kind enough to propose a toast to my health, and once again made appreciative mention of my labours and of all that I had achieved in the Tapanahoni. He regarded it as a pleasant duty to bring out a *most favourable* report to His Excellency the Governor" (Journal 24 November 1925).

Van Lier left on 25 November on the steamer 'Prinses Juliana' for Paramaribo, where he arrived on the 26th. About this departure and his first days in the city he wrote: "Some thirty minutes before the departure Chief Akrosi came to tell me that all the Aucaners in Albina wished to see me off. They intended accompanying me from my home – I was staying with Dr. Hiemcke – while guns would be fired as the ship left the harbour.

I replied that, although I appreciated this gesture very much, I would prefer to leave without any ostentation. All the same, many salvoes re-echoed as the ship took the water."

On 26 November he arrived in Paramaribo. "As a result of all the fatigue and excitement of the past weeks I felt exhausted and rather overwrought," he wrote "On my doctor's advice I spent three days resting in bed." On 30 November he concluded his Journal with: "I feel my usual self again and went to pay my respects to the Government Secretary today."

Weijne, who had repeatedly assured Van Lier that he would submit a 'most favourable report' to the Governor, performed this obligation in a hand-written letter.[34]

In this 'Report on the person Van Lier' the District Commissioner wrote: "Your Excellency, although unasked for, I should like to mention some facts which throw light on seemingly contradictory aspects of Mr. van Lier.

Since I happen to have given you, especially lately, several items of information concerning Mr. van Lier which were not to his credit, I do not hesitate, where this is necessary, to rehabilitate Mr. van Lier.

The assumption that he might be carrying on some action against his successor is entirely unfounded and I do not believe that anything of the sort has taken place. As far I can gather from my talks with Kanapé and his associates, he has spoken favourably of his successor. It is, however, an undeniable fact that Mr. van Lier sometimes invents things, or gives a representation which is not absolutely accurate, or which is incomplete. He does not do so with the evil intention of lying or deceiving, but he has become too much the Djuka in his way of thinking. He is no longer capable of rising above the Djuka mentality, he can no longer think and act like an enlightened person. And that is why he, by manipulating a matter in true Djuka fashion, brought me under the impression that he was a liar. I know quite well that Van Lier, since his youth, has been regarded as a compulsive liar (*fantast*), but this aberration has grown worse since he has been living among the Djukas. There is no question of malicious intent, at least in most cases, I believe."

Weijne demonstrates in this 'rehabilitation', by citing some examples, how Van Lier had acted like 'a liar, but unintentionally, at least in most cases'.

The first example deals with the already mentioned trouble with Chief Akrosi of Albina.

The second and final example to prove that Van Lier was a liar concerned his remark towards his successor "that he had spent 17 months in succession in the upper parts, while he had been in Albina from 20 December 1924 - 23 January 1925."

The letter continues: "But the stupidest thing Van Lier did was to seal the blood-oath with Amakti.[35] As an official he should have kept himself above the Djukas and not become their equal. No wonder they called him the white Djuka, which has lessened rather than enhanced his prestige.

All these things combined to make him totally unfit for the function of postholder and it was time Van Lier returned to the civilized world. In his case it is difficult to distinguish between fact and fiction, and this tendency has grown much worse in the Tapanahoni."

At the end of the letter there are some appreciative remarks: "Still, I am firmly convinced that he stayed there all these years from a sense of calling, and for that I admire him, for no one who is not familiar with the interior can have any idea of what such a life is like. With that alone he has proved that he came here for the Djukas and without any motives of self-interest. In spite of his faults and unfitness for postholdership, he, as an inhabitant of Surinam, has tried to do more for the Bush Negroes than many others who have a great deal to say about it. He has actually been able to hand over a school to his successor, the school is there largely as a result of his perseverance, and the Government has him to thank for it."

Van Lier's financial management was also regarded by Weijne as having been dishonest.[36] After much writing back and forth about this, no charge could be laid at Van Lier's door. The accounts he submitted were paid, and the money still owing him was refunded. (Albeit with a complaint scribbled by the Governor in the margin of one of the accounts: "Van Lier has been an expensive customer".)

§ 4 NOTES ON THE FIFTH STAY IN THE TAPANAHONI

a The influence of power tactics

Kanapé continued his efforts to consolidate and enlarge his position of power when he had recovered completely from his temporary mental and physical set-back. This time he used the school as a pawn on his chessboard, for he regarded it as an effective means of procuring for himself the badly needed support of the Government. He saw two possibilities: if he succeeded in getting a school at Drietabbetje, filled with *Opo* children, he would win the Government's approval, and moreover he would bring the *Bilo* Negroes into disrepute, thus strengthening his power over them. He favoured this line of action. If this did not succeed, he could still manage to stay in the Government's good books by actively supporting the boarding-school at Granman Staalkondré. Amakti backed these manoeuvres of Kanapé, because he, too, wanted more goodwill from the Government and greater authority over the *Bilo* Negroes. For a short while (in October 1924) it looked as though Kanapé's first plan would succeed. But Van Lier decided to continue with the boarding-school instead of moving the school to Drietabbetje.

The *Bilo* Negroes probably saw through Kanapé's plan. When it appeared, moreover, that their own obstinacy would cost them the support of the Djukas administration (without which they could not manage either, neither in the religious nor in the civil sphere) as well as that of the Government, they did their utmost to keep the boarding-school on their own territory and supply it with children.

Neither Kanapé (who became ill again) nor Amakti succeeded in carrying out the second plan: they could not persuade their *Opo* subjects to send their children to school.

The *Bilo* chiefs, encouraged by their success, now went a step further. So as to free themselves more completely from their *Opo* rulers, they tried to make the boarding-school their own exclusive affair by moving it still deeper into their terrain. In May 1925 the situation was favourable for this manoeuvre: the Government's threats to discontinue the boarding-school and the position into which Amakti and Kanapé were forced by accepting the entire blame for the failure, improved their chances. The statement by the young Chief Banda, no doubt also bent on improving his own position, at the meeting of 5 May 1925 indicates the heightened self-confidence of the below-stream Djukas. The District Commissioner's visit and the *krutu* of 20 May did much to strengthen their position further: thanks to them the school was given another chance, and it was agreed that the boarding-school might be moved.

Kanapé found it hard to swallow the new political defeat. After his futile effort in October 1924 he kept himself in the background; at any rate, judging from the documents, he did not take active part in public affairs. He comes to our notice only when he tries to exculpate himself from all guilt in his letter of 5 May 1925 to the Governor. The closing of the boarding-school and the departure of the postholder, to whose co-operation and support he owed his position, made him fear that he might also be deposed as Head Chief. In order to guard his status and his self-respect, he played for high stakes: he declared his intention to resign. He complained bitterly to his friend Van Lier, knowing very well that the latter would do everything in his power to prevent him from carrying out his threat. He explained to Van Lier that he believed he had lost the confidence and support of the Government. Van Lier passed this on. The Governor, probably realizing that the influence of the Government on the Djukas, however slight, would diminish further without the services of Kanapé as paid go-between, sent him a motion of confidence. Kanapé immediately decided to stay on. In his extremity he even made a fresh attempt at strengthening his postion among the *Bilo* Negroes by assuring the up-and-coming Chief Banda that he would help him to support the the school of Van Lier's successor.

From the above it is clear that internal complications also did much to hamper the development of the school. If the Djukas really wanted to see the number of pupils increased, as they said they did, this was further impeded by animosity and lust for power. Van Lier was not able to control these internal conflicts.

b The role of the District Commissioner

The District Commissioner J. Weijne had been, before he came to Surinam, a first lieutenant in an infantry division in the Dutch East Indies, where he was one of those military men drafted into the civil administration who held executive posts in the outlying provinces. During the time he spent at Albina he had a road constructed from the Marowijne to the Cottica river, called the 'Weijne Road'. His policy did not meet with general approval. The newspaper *Suriname*, in particular, accused him more than once of bad management of affairs and of personal misconduct. The editors of this paper regularly supported the work of the postholder.

Even if he was not entirely responsible for the Government's decision to abolish the boarding-school and the postholdership, he did play quite an important role in this affair. Two factors helped to bring about strained feelings between the District Commissioner and the postholder: the personal, and the administrative relation between them. Weijne's personality, as it emerges from the documents, was unsuited for the elegant solution of problems. He showed a lack of mental suppleness in this matter and did not possess the psychological insight to come to a satisfactory agreement with the Djukas or with the postholder. His policy was calculated – with the approval and at the instigation of the Governor – to make an end to the postholdership and the development project. And he did achieve this aim, while changing his views repeatedly in the course of one year, making impracticable proposals and bringing the postholder into disrepute with the Governor. Now, Van Lier was not the sort of man to knuckle down meekly to Weijne's actions. Just like his superior, he, too, was convinced that he was in the right. He reacted violently to criticism of his work as administrative official as well as of his educational work. In their administrative relations the problems appeared that have been discussed in Chapter VI § 3. Goodenough[37] indicates a number of problems in an analysis of administrative relations. On p. 433 he remarks that while one "should expect administrators to be concerned primarily with providing the kind of support that field personnel find they need, and with keeping information and supplies flowing freely", in reality quite a different situation presents itself. In this connection it strikes him that:

1. "Administrators (a) tend to feel they must enjoy unquestioned authority and (b) have power to invoke strong sanctions" (p. 432). Examples confirming this occurred in the case in question:

    a. Weijne's pronouncement on 25 October 1924 that an administrative official should behave "in complete accordance with the instructions of the District Commissioner at Albina"; his reproach to Van Lier (in September 1925) that he did not support his (Weijne's) policy and that this management of affairs was at fault.

    b. His "tendency to apply strong sanctions" is shown in his proposal to send a military patrol to Drietabbetje (April 1925), mainly as a demonstration of authority. He threatened (16 November 1925) to keep the customs station as a punitive measure if the Djukas did not show their readiness to patronise a day-school. Goodenough goes on to say that:

2. "Administrators regard their field personnel professionally less competent than themselves to judge the tactical requirements of the field situation" (p. 434). This conviction was also illustrated in Weijne's reaction to Van Lier's refutation of his view "that all primitive peoples resemble each other as regards mental and moral capacity". Van Lier was "no judge in the matter" (12 October 1925). Weijne held that "without my intervention the school would never have come into being, that is

not to be denied." Another example of Weijne's opinion that Van Lier failed to employ effective tactics was his remark that the latter's prestige was nil. Given the extraordinary weight attached to the possession of authority and prestige in the world of administrative officialdom, this was a grave reproach.

3. "Administrators", Goodenough says further, "believe that they (their field personnel) are constantly disturbing administrative routines by their sudden shifts in tactics" (p. 343).

This cause for conflict did not occur in the relationship between Weijne and Van Lier. On the contrary: Weijne could not deny that Van Lier stuck to the views he held and expressed in his plan of work, for instance that the school should be a boarding-school and that his station should be in the Lower area. (As to this, it would be easier to accuse Van Lier of what Goodenough calls a lack of flexibility (p. 377).)

The reason why I touch on this point is that here the 'Administrator' is the guilty party. His frequent change of opinion regarding the development work could well have had a bewildering effect on the administrative activities of the government (if they had paused to consider it!) The following serve as examples of this tendency: When he first visited the Tapanahoni (4 December 1923), Weijne gave a favourable verdict on Van Lier and his work. On 25 October 1924 he thought that no results could be expected from the way the 'experiment' was being carried out. In April 1925 he pressed for the immediate abolition of the postholdership, in May 1925 he thought that the school would now be started and asked for postponement, in June 1925 he called the school a success and wanted to have the experiment continued for another year. In September 1925 he thought that Van Lier was not capable of obtaining results(without his mediation). On 17 November 1925 he decared that Van Lier had completed his task: the school had been founded. Finally, in his letter of 'rehabilitation' to the Governor on 23 November 1925 he wrote that Van Lier was unfit for his task but also that, 'thanks to his perseverance', he could hand over a school to his successor.

4. Finally, according to Goodenough, "administrators believe that those whose task it is to put their plans into practice are disorderly, wasteful, (and) sloppy in their bookkeeping" (p. 343). In this respect Weijne goes a bit further: he accused Van Lier of bad faith (March and September 1925), untruthfulness (23 November 1925) and of fraudulence in his financial administraton. The correspondence bearing on the facts in question shows that these accusations were unfounded. As for the

economic situation: this also gave rise to trouble. As regards the low wages earned by Djuka freight carriers, the (for them) unfavourable rates of exchange and the institution of customs control, the attitude of the District Commissioner and that of the postholder were diametrically opposed.

c The abolishment of boarding-school and postholdership

1 The role of the Government

By 1925 the negative facets in the design of the development plan had completely superseded the positive. The Colonial States had accepted only temporarily (and not without protest) the view of Van Heemstra's predecessor Staal that the development project should be regarded as a lengthy affair and that the postholder should be allowed time to prepare for the execution of his plans. Governor van Heemstra, however, agreed with the Colonial States that the experiment had lasted long enough and had not yielded any results. The fact that it was now at last beginning to show some progress (on 16 February Van Lier started his school with seven children) did not change this view. The way in which the course of events was regarded excluded the reflection that only now, after a period of preparation, could the *execution* of the development scheme be started in earnest.

From the remarks made by the Governor and the members of the Colonial States it appears that they were badly informed of the facts and so drew the wrong conclusions.

Governor van Heemstra went on leave from 21 May 1924 to 21 February 1925. On 2 March 1925, eleven days after his return, Van Heemstra authorized the District Commissioner to wind up the whole affair, after having compelled the Djukas to confess to sabotage. Thus his decision to put an end to it had been taken *before* the Colonial States had to decide on the future of the 'experiment'. We have seen that the District Commissioner carried out his orders with fervour. Under these circumstances the members of the Colonial States could not be expected to offer Van Lier and his work yet another opportunity.

A single remark on the speech by Advocate R.D. Simons. The fact that the reports reminded him of those of a 'farming enterprise' was an unintentional tribute to Van Lier's conscientious efforts at teaching the Bush Negroes something about cattle-breeding. This was part of his task of 'civilizing' the Djukas.

Granman Staalkondré II, 1965, situated opposite Malobbi. The landing-place and the road that led to the house and boarding-school have been reclaimed by the jungle.

(photograph by the author)

When Simons observed that Van Lier was 'private tutor' to Amakti's son, he should have known from the postholder's report that on 16 February there were seven boys at the school. Not much to boast about, but hardly a corroboration of Simon's statement that school and boarding-school "had practically ceased to exist".

2 The reactions of the Djukas

From § 1 it appeared that after the conflict between the Upper and Lower factions the latter at last started sending children to Granman Staalkondré. The three chiefs (all of them *Bilo*) who had signed the confession of guilt in Albina had much to gain by proving that, if it was a matter of sabotage, this was to be laid at the door of the *Opos*. They saw, at least Banda and his followers did, that it would be to their advantage if the boarding-school and the postholder were to be retained, and Weijne's threat to close the school had a marked effect on them. They could not provide the necessary twenty children either. Yet Banda knew how to make political capital out of it, as was apparent from his remark at the *krutu* of 5 May that the *Opo* Negroes should not be given the opportunity of saying later that "...the *Bilo* Negroes had outdone them". Naturally Amakti and Kanapé had no desire to be branded saboteurs and reacted with the aforesaid letter (§ 3 b).

Once more they put the blame on the slanderers, who had come this time with fresh scandal-mongering. Although the letter certainly reflected Kanapé's and Amakti's thoughts at the moment, Van Lier must have had influence on its formulation. Its impassioned tone could no doubt be partly attributed to his way of translating spoken Djuka into written Dutch. It proves that the Djukas, as well as Van Lier, were very well acquainted with the beliefs and rumours being circulated in Paramaribo and Albina; and that Amakti and Kanapé wanted to show, by their emphatic request not to have the school closed down yet, that they still hoped for an improvement in the situation. They did not mention that all the children now attending school came exclusively from *Bilo*. To admit that they could not persuade the *Opo* Negroes to send their children would be a concession of weakness. (The malicious gossip had a two-sided effect, moreover: even the Governor was not immune from it. He, too, began to think that the Bush Negroes themselves had hit on the idea that an ex-balata overseer could not be a good teacher. Hardly a considered pronouncement; the Djukas regarded Van Lier as a 'learned *bakra*' who certainly knew how to teach the children to read and write. Besides, hardly any of the teachers of the mission schools had been trained for the profession. And finally: even Weijne did not regard this as a criterium. In his first report on Van Lier (4 December 1923) he remarked that the latter was a capable teacher; he himself was competent to judge, for, as an officer, he had also taught in a school!)

The Djuka chiefs were perfectly aware of the fact that Van Lier did not approve of the Government's demand that they should make a statement confessing to sabotage, but the fact that the postholder had no influence with the Government in this matter made them realize that he did not really count any longer. His obvious loss of prestige with the Government also damaged his reputation among the Djukas.

Kanapé withdrew from the humiliating exhibition and Amakti, cornered and anxious about his paid position, admitted everything (§ 3b). The hard fact that he, the Granman, could not compel his subjects to obey his order was undeniable, as well as the fact that it was the *Opo* Negroes who refused and the *Bilo* Negroes who agreed to send their children. Even in the case of questions with which he disagreed, for instance those demanding that the Government should be exonerated on every count, he took all the blame on himself.

The Government did not bother about such subtleties as trying to protect Amakti against the loss of his eyesight, soothing the animosity between the inhabitants of the Upper and Lower Tapanahoni, or considering the Djukas' rules of social etiquette at meetings.

Although Van Lier had made the Djukas promise that they would entrust their children to his successor, it appeared that they were unwilling to do so when they realized that no more food was to be provided: if they showed their willingness by sending children, it was surely not too much to expect a reciprocal gesture to relieve their precarious food situation. The Government did not realize the importance of this demand for the Djukas; neither did they realize that the success of future development plans also depended on it.

d Notes on the development project

Van Lier was convinced that the transmission of 'western civilization' was the only means of educating the younger generation to achieve greater prosperity. In Chapter IV § 6 the resistance apt to be aroused by the introduction of western standards and customs is described. But now a number of factors had also come into operation which weakened this resistance somewhat.

1. The 'western civilization' propagated by Van Lier was, for the

Djukas, that of the inhabitants of the Surinam coastal parts. This Surinam was (and is) for them a reference society. "When he compares his lot with that of the foreigners – and he frequently does so – then the comparison is to his disadvantage. The Djuka believes that he is deprived in the Tapanahoni. Besides, he "knows that the Bush Negroes as a group are much weaker than the foreigners, at whose mercy they have been put".[38]

By 1925 the Djukas were already keenly aware of this, because of the Government's threats and coercive measures. Thus the Surinam culture had a high prestige value for the Djukas. Even though they were not at all prepared to sacrifice their own free existence and own culture for the sake of it, they were not averse to learning ways of increasing their prosperity within their own community.

2. The confidence in Van Lier had been almost completely restored. Illnesses and accidents were no longer ascribed to his influence.

3. In spite of Van Lier's clear preference for the pattern of western culture, he showed an interest and respect for that of the Djukas. Here an aspect came into play, indicated by Ahrensberg and Niehoff. "To meet Westerners who are interested in their culture for the purpose of learning rather than of criticism is an experience few non-westerners can resist".[39]

4. Van Lier treated the Djukas as 'fellow human beings'.

5. The result of these combined factors was that he could allow himself to criticize certain aspects of their culture and to try to change it. Various examples from Van Lier's pedagogical practice corroborate this.

i. Both children and parents complained that Van Lier made his pupils work too hard. Even Chief Banda came to voice his disapproval of this: the Djukas surrendered their children, the white man now had to provide them with food and shelter. They seemed to accept Van Lier's argument that this was part of the system of education, perhaps because learning to till the fields and help in the house was also part of the education of Djuka children at home.

ii. The fairly severe daily discipline to which Van Lier subjected his pupils was also accepted. The reason for this was that, on the one hand, he seemed to have a marked ascendancy over the boys, and, on the other hand, he left them free to amuse themselves in Djuka fashion during their leisure time.

iii. They accepted his strictures on certain characteristics they displayed. No doubt their parents also accused them of disobedience and untidiness.

It was not so easy to accept the odium of 'inborn slyness and meanness, as well as lying and deceitfulness'. That they accepted it again indicates that Van Lier could allow himself certain liberties, but also that he probably expressed himself more tactfully towards the Djuka children and their parents. Unfortunately Van Lier does not elaborate on the way in which he tried to arouse their interest in the '*Bakra* life'.

NOTES

[1] Government Resolution, No. 58, 25 October 1924, Confidential.
[2] Government Resolution, No. 65, 18 November 1924, Highly Confidential.
[3] In spite of Governor Staal's request in 1918 to Monseigneur van Roosmalen not to allow any mission work to be done while a postholder was carrying out this educative task in the Upper Marowijne, Father Morssink had already taken several trips up the river.
[4] Government Resolution, No. 11, 4 March 1925, Highly Confidential.
[5] According to Father Morssink he had invited the chiefs, and Amakti had come along of his own accord (Morssink, MS 1932, p. 54).
[6] Government Resolution, No. 21, 6 March 1925, Highly Confidential.
[7] An illogical conclusion!
[8] This letter is not to be found in the State Archives. In Father Morssink's notes, however, it is mentioned and quoted in part (MS 1932, p. 72II).
[9] Pulugudu is a village situated at the confluence of the Lawa and the Tapanahoni.
[10] Government Resolution, No. 7, 2 March 1925, Highly Confidential.
[11] From Van Lier's Journal, 19 March 1925 (Morssink, MS 1932, p. 72).
[12] Government Resolution, No. 27, 1 April 1925, Highly Confidential.
[13] Government Resolution, No. 16, 9 April 1925, Highly Confidential.
[14] Government Resolution, No. 22, 1925, Highly Confidential.
[15] Records of the Colonial States, meeting of 5 May 1925, p. 68.
[16] A crime which is regarded as being almost as evil as the practice of black magic.
[17] Journal, 6 May 1925 (Morssink, MS 1932, p. 49).
[18] Not in the archives.
[19] The proposal was an attempt at a compromise. Puketi is the furthermost village lying just within the border of the *Bilo* territory.
[20] Morssink, MS 1932.
[21] This letter, undated, is appended to the Government Resolution, No. 49, 29 May 1925.
[22] Government Resolution, No. 1822, 17 June 1925.
[23] Köbben, 1968b, p. 79, remarks that the schoolgoing children in the Cottica are 'docile and calm'.
[25] Government Resolution, No. 3, 13 September 1925, Highly Confidential.
[26] Secretary's Agenda, No. 634.
[27] This letter is not to be found in the archives.
[28] Government Resolution, No. 4, 19 December 1925, Highly Confidential.
[29] Report, 19 December 1925.
[30] Not in the archives.

[31] Archives Moravian Brothers Paramaribo.
[32] The customs station was started in August 1925 at the confluence of the Tapanhoni and the Lawa.
[33] Report to the Governor, 19 December 1925.
[34] Government Resolution, 23 November 1925, Highly Confidential.
[35] See Chapter V § 1. The 'blood-oath' was taken without shedding a single drop of blood.
[36] Government Resolution, No. 131, 30 November 1925, Highly Confidential. Government Resolution, No. 3, 10 December 1925, Confidential. Secretary's Agenda, No. 121, 29 January 1926.
[37] Goodenough, 1963, pp. 429-453.
[38] Thoden van Velzen, 1966, p. 27.
[39] Ahrensberg and Niehoff, 1965, p. 190.

CHAPTER VIII

SHORT SURVEY OF THE EVENTS AFTER 1926

§ 1 BROTHER ZANGEN AT GRANMAN STAALKONDRÉ

H. Zangen, who took over Granman Staalkondré in December 1925 from W.F. van Lier, had come to Paramaribo in about 1900, at the age of twenty-three. He was a watchmaker by trade, worked, among other jobs, as a pharmacist, as supervisor at the gold-placer 'Toeval', and in October 1919 trekked with his wife, a Surinam woman, into the Bush. He wanted "to help the Bush Negroes" he wrote in 1927[1] in a brochure, by giving medical aid and doing mission work.

When he got into financial difficulties, he accepted a post offered by the Moravian Brothers (or Herrnhutters, as they are usually called in Surinam) and became a mission-teacher at Abenaston, a Christian village on the Surinam River, among the Saramaccaners.

He had thirty-five pupils in the school, but "with the villagers", he wrote in his brochure "I did not get on so well. There were too many who wanted to boss the show. My way of teaching did not please them, either. They wanted the old method, where the teacher says something once and the whole class drones it after him in a chorus fifty or a hundred times. And I used to try and mould people who can think for themselves and also understand what they are saying. They likewise resented the fact that I spoke up against their evil ways from the pulpit. Still, I managed to bring about that nobody took a second wife during the fourteen months that I worked there, and only once did a man lay hands on a sixteen-year-old schoolgirl. But after I left, almost everybody, including the most faithful church-elder, took a second wife!"

After this period he was appointed by the Moravian Brothers to succeed Van Lier. Not, as he had hoped, at the latter's salary of Fls. 4800 per annum, but on his former basis of Fls. 600, to which the Mission added another Fls. 200.

About the educational project at Granman Staalkondré he wrote in the aforesaid brochure: "During the first weeks I still had thirteen boarding-school boys, but when the food left by Mr. Van Lier was finished, they soon disappeared. After that, meetings were held for weeks and months on end with the village leaders and during all this time I could only teach such children as were brought along by the sick. At last, in the second half of January 1937, two pupils turned up, and a month later two more, so that now I have four regular pupils at school, and hope more will be following."

The reasons why Zangen could not make a success of the school were: in the first place, the children were not given food, and in the second place, he could not resist trying to convert them to the Christian faith, for, as he wrote: "for me the school is not the most important matter! Not that I neglect it; no, on the contrary I take a great deal of trouble to get hold of the children and to really teach them something. No, that is not what I mean. But I want above all to be a missionary and so I have the welfare of the entire Negro population at heart. To help them in their misery and in their disease; to liberate them from their foolish conceptions, that is my striving, the task for which I exert myself and for which I have endured wretchedness and privation all along. And this trouble has not been in vain. My buildings are too small to house all those who are ill and who come and ask for help."

As early as January 1926 Van Lier made another trip to the Tapanahoni. Under instructions of the Surinam Bauxite Society he left on 11 January to convey the body of an employee of the S.B.S., who had died at Pulugudu, to Paramaribo. A record of this is contained in Van Lier's notebook covering 1926.

At Pulugudu Chief Banda and others came to greet him. Kanapé also came from Drietabbetje, specially to see him. Together with Kanapé he visited Granman Staalkondré on 25 and 26 January. "I am spending the night at Zangen's place. The man is very ill. His wife is also ill and he will not consider leaving... The place is in a state of utter squalor... Most of the animals have died etc.... Kanapé is going on to D.T. (Drietabbetje). I stay behind at Granman Staalkondré. Zangen has a large number of patients every day to be treated." Unfortunately he did not make a note of talks with Banda and Kanapé.

It was clear, however, that Kanapé, despite his promises to Van Lier, dissociated himself from Zangen's efforts to continue Van Lier's work.

He was offended by the fact that, after all the trouble taken (also by himself), Van Lier had been recalled when the school had at last got going with twenty pupils. Moreover, he bitterly reproached the Government that he had not received written notifications of all their plans. Several facts became evident when Kanapé visited Paramaribo and a *krutu* was held on 14 June 1926, at which the acting Governor Nijsingh, Kanapé and his adjudant (his son-in-law), Government Secretaty van der Helm and an interpreter were present. Van der Helm took 'brief notes' of this meeting.[2] From these it appears how inadequate the Governor's replies were to Kanapé's grievances, which centred round the fact that he had not been kept posted officially, that is to say in writing, as to the decisions the Government had taken with respect to the Djukas. He felt aggrieved because the Government had failed to recognize his official dignity as Head Chief – a position he had not solicited. He was especially sore at the closing down of the school, which had been done without official notification to him: when, after much laborious effort, there were twenty children at last, Van Lier suddenly left.

The Governor had nothing to say except that it was not stipulated in the 'protocol' that Kanapé had to be kept informed by letter, but that this would happen in future. (It appeared that the Government Secretary had promised it to Kanapé, but that the District Commissioner did not know about it.)

The Governor remarked further that after all, there was a school, to which Kanapé replied that he had no official knowledge of that either. The meeting was concluded with the assurance to Kanapé that in future he would be notified by letter of every decision, and that he had the Government's full support in his capacity as Head Chief.

In September 1926 District Commissioner Weijne visited the Tapanahoni. As early as 23 April 1925[3] he had proposed a military patrol through the interior to the Tapanahoni (via the Surinam River and its tributary the Sara Creek, and the Tosso Creek which flows into the Tapanahoni about thrity kilometers above Drietabbetje) which would have a 'brilliant' effect, namely the heightening of the Government's prestige. This now took place. There was no meeting between the patrol and Weijne in the Tapanahoni, for the troops were delayed and the District Commissioner had returned to Albina. Weijne did hold a *krutu* with the Djukas during which the school matter was also discussed. In his report of 10 October 1926[4] Weijne wrote: "The school matter... After discussion not much was changed. The *Opo* Negroes do not want to support a school for the *Bilo* Negroes. The

Bilo Negroes dared not send their children, for fear of the *Opo* Negroes.

Mr. Zangen had already told me the same. But he had very good results with the treatment of the sick... Those who required nursing were accommodated in the old schoolroom. Generally speaking this is a success and the Bush Negroes are beginning to have confidence in Mr. Zangen. Since he cannot entice the Bush Negroes by providing food, as his predecessor did, and they have to bring their own rations along so as to be able to stay there, the success is doubly remarkable." Especially from the last phrase it is clear that Weijne received (or gave?) a quite erroneous presentation of the facts. Zangen's predecessor had supplied the school children, not the patients, with food. One of the main reasons why Zangen's school declined rapidly was that the children no longer got food. The treatment of the sick (without providing meals) had been equally successful with Van Lier as with Zangen.

According to Weijne the patrol had achieved its aim: "the knowledge that a military patrol, in spite of difficulties ... can get to them, will do a great deal to keep them out of conflict with the Government. As a matter of fact the Bush Negroes thought the soldiers had come to fetch Amakti (guilty conscience, of course)".

In August 1931 two missionaries undertook a tour of inspection to the Upper Marowijne (Tapanahoni) by order of the Evangelical Moravian Brothers. In his report on this journey W. Fliegel[5] described Zangen's activities at Granman Staalkondré. He, too, mentions that Zangen's main business was the giving of medical aid. There were no pupils. "There can be very little question of medical mission work, since he himself does a lot of bungling with that temperament of his", Fliegel wrote, "he is too irascible and moreover deeply pessimistic about the Aucaners". As to Granman Staalkondré itself, Fliegel mentioned that Zangen had built on many additions to the original buildings: a dwelling-house with a dispensary, and a hospital shed. The island was swarming with parasol ants. "Everything Brother Zangen has taken the trouble to plant, young fruit-trees from the nursery, etc., have been demolished by the parasol ants that do not even spare the pine apples".

In 1933 Zangen returned to Paramaribo and Granman Staalkondré was abandoned.

§ 2 ESTABLISHMENT AND GROWTH OF THE MISSION POST AT SAJÉ

One of the aims of the above-mentioned tour by the Moravian Brothers' emissaries, Fliegel and Sprang, was to investigate the possibility of establishing a mission post with a school at Sajé.[6] They visited this village, where Brother Leerdam had settled after an unsuccessful attempt to obtain a foothold in the village of Malobbi, a short distance south of Granman Staalkondré. But here, too, the work made very little progress. Banda, chief of Sajé, gave his active support to this project, just as he had done during Van Lier's tenure of office in the Tapanahoni. It appeared, however, that the approval of the acting Granman, Kanapé (Amakti died in 1931), was needed before the work could be started in earnest. Fliegel and Sprang left for Drietabbetje, where they were received by Kanapé. First he vented his ill humour towards Zangen, with whom he could not get on and who was supposed to have insulted him; but when it emerged that Zangen was leaving Granman Staalkondré, he came round. He declared that he had nothing against the erection of a new hospital and school in Sajé. As for being baptized, he said he would not forbid anyone who wanted it, but that he himself was too old for baptism.

Neither did he have any objection, he said, to the building of a hospital on an island opposite Drietabbetje. Both the brothers were delighted at Kanapé's obliging attitude, and Fliegel wrote in his account of the journey: "Will God open the door for the Gospel to be brought to the Djukas under the reign of one who, since he combines the functions of Head Chief and Granman, has greater authority than any other Granman? Will that which we behold in our mind's eye now become a reality? Drietabbetje with hospital and school, Piketti, Sajé, Malobbi, each with its own school, and in one of these places an ordained brother who will zealously serve all these villages, or is it nothing but a fine dream?"

It was indeed a dream. Only in Sajé did the brothers manage to establish a medical aid post with boarding facilities. Kanapé did not object to this. It was in a certain sense the Government's wish to continue the work begun by Van Lier, and Kanapé had promised his support in the matter. It was a good thing for his position to cooperate with the Government in this.

He would allow a hospital with school at Drietabbetje but only by the same procedure: with express permission of the Government. He informed the District Commissioner of the Moravian Brothers' request, but added that he did not know "what to do with them, since they could produce no letter from the Commissioner".[7] The result of Kanapé's letter to the District Commissioner (who was a Catholic) was the establishment of a Catholic boarding-school opposite Drietabbetje (see § 3).

The missionary Leerdam left Sajé to go on leave, and his place was taken by G. Helder, who had five children at school in 1932. Helder had tried to teach in Drietabbetje from 1909-1913, under Granman Oseisie, who supported him at the outset. His efforts failed, just like those of his predecessor Spalburg, because he tried to convert the children to the Christian faith. In Sajé Brother Helder also took a sombre view of the position. He had no confidence in the Djukas whatever. In his annual report on 1932 he wrote: "To trust and rely upon an Aucaner will always lead to disillusionment. An Aucaner who knows how to lie is an honourable personage and is greatly respected by the people. The Head Chiefs, leaders and elders are 'wise men' because they are past masters in the art of lying and deceit. One who does not want to lie is a cheat and is held in contempt." According to Helder, Chief Banda also belonged to the category of liars.

Helder went on to complain about the activities of Father Morssink, the Catholic priest, at Sajé. The latter had bitterly reproached Banda and his brother Abena[8] because they favoured the Moravian Brothers. "The charming Father Morssink", wrote Helder, "warned the children that, if another teacher came, they were not to receive him... If the teacher called them to come to school, they should refuse." Morssink promised the people food and clothing if they would accept a boarding-school from him. "This Roman Catholic yeast has thorougly soured our Sajé population", Helder remarked resentfully.[9]

Leerdam was back at Sajé from October 1933 till December 1933. He called himself an evangelical hospital attendant and in his annual report he complained of the difficulty he had in getting paid for the medical aid he gave. The Djukas regarded his help not as "an act of charity, but as an obligation". Most of them, accordingly, refused to help keep the grounds in order by way of compensation. Leerdam tried to let the Djukas "feel and see that it was not a matter of money and possessions, but of moral principles". According to him the Djukas actually believed in western medicine, but this "did not detract from their faith in the gods. They believe our medicine is most effective, but not before the gods no longer hold the whip-hand, and extend their cooperation". He observed furthermore that, although there was a great deal of malaria, the sufferers of this disease did not come for treatment. Fever was, according to the Djukas, more than all other ailments, a scourge in the hands of the gods.

E.M. Koorndijk, who took over the work in 1934, began in November 1934 to build a house with boarding-school and polyclinic, partly from the timber and sheets of corrugated iron left behind when Granman Staalkondré was abandoned. Chief Banda provided transport and granted a high-lying piece of land. In February 1935 Koorndijk started his work: evangelization, conducting church services, baptizing, medical aid and education. He remained in Sajé till 1946, and had the assistance of one evangelist. He undertook trips to neighbouring villages to preach the gospel and in his report on the year 1935 Koorndijk expressed optimism. At the end of that year there were 67 baptized members in the congregation of Sajé.[10] In 1946 there were 152. In 1952 there were 103 who received baptism, in 1962 there were 157.

A certain amount of medical aid was provided in a clinic built with the help of patients. In Sajé and the neighbouring villages this aid was gladly accepted, and the Brother regarded the sick who had been cured as propagandists for his mission work.

In the school, which did not have boarding facilities as yet, Koorndijk had 29 pupils at the end of 1935, of whom 7 were girls. Koorndijk was satisfied with his pupils' zeal for learning, but all the same expected better results from a boarding-school. The evangelical teaching – naturally – occupied a very important place. In 1954 a boarding-school was built on a higher-lying island, situated slightly to the south, and called Carmel. Now, in 1969, it occupies a roomy building and has at least 50 pupils, boys and girls.

§ 3 LISIEUX, A CATHOLIC DAY- AND BOARDING-SCHOOL IN THE TAPANAHONI

On 27 June 1932 Kanapé concluded an agreement with the Apostolic Vicar, Monseigneur van Roosmalen, to establish a Catholic boarding-school in the Tapanahoni. On 8 November 1932 a school was opened opposite the chief village, Drietabbetje, "dedicated to the little Saint Theresia, hence the name Lisieux".[11] M. Melcherts, former cook-choir-boy in Father Morssink's service at Albina, was appointed teacher. With his wife (he married in 1934) he directed the school and boarding department until the school was closed down in 1938. From 1932 to 1935 there were seven to ten male boarders. After the entire building was burnt down in 1935 and re-built, there were twenty-four boys in 1937 (the data for 1936 are missing), while the following year there were only four. The "Annual Report of the Roman Catholic Congregation in Surinam"[12] mentioned in this connection: "the deposed Head Chief Kanapé has exerted his influence and persuaded the people through intimidation to remove their children from the day- and boarding-school".

The lavatory door of corrugated iron in Karmel bearing the words 'Granman Staalkondré via Albina' is the only visible remainder of Van Lier's boarding-school. Karmel, diagonally opposite Granman Staalkondré II, is a boarding-school of the Moravian Brothers and lies near the village of Sajé where a school was founded about 1932 by the Moravian Brothers. The remains of Granman Staalkondré were utilized for its building.

(photograph by the author)

Why did Kanapé accept a (Catholic) boarding-school right opposite his headquarters in 1932, and why did he boycott the same boarding-school in 1937? A reply to these questions can be found if one considers the history of the boarding-school in the light of the power politics Kanapé practised during those years in the Tapanahoni, and the way he utilized the aspiration of the Roman Catholic Church to obtain a foothold on his territory. Since Amakti's nomination to the Granmanship in 1916 Kanapé had been High Priest; and, as we know, Head Chief since 1921. When Amakti died in 1931, his sister's son, Amatodja, was nominated to succeed him. The latter, however, pleaded that he was too young to accept the post of Granman. It is likelier that he, together with the faction supporting him, felt incapable of challenging Kanapé's strong position and did not relish playing second fiddle to him. This became clear during a *gran krutu* in 1933: Kanapé, who had been acting Granman since Amakti's death, declared that he was prepared to cede his power to Amatodja, providing the latter would have no authority over the elders (including Kanapé), nor alter any laws of Grantata (the god whom Kanapé served as High Priest) and, furthermore, not take any important decision without informing Kanapé beforehand.[13] Amatodja refused to become Granman under these conditions, and his supporters were powerless to prevent Kanapé from insisting on them. But what Kanapé did not feel free to do was to become Granman himself: Amatodja had been designated officially, and probably even Kanapé's followers would not have tolerated it if he had usurped the position.

Despite Kanapé's great authority as High Priest, because the entire population depended on him for religious support and as Head Chief, because in that capacity he could count on the Government's loyalty and – no mean consideration – on a salary, he still kept doing his utmost to consolidate his power. He was well aware that neither the Djukas, nor the Government, would accept a Granman-less state for long. His policy consisted chiefly of making sure that as many of the Djukas as possible were on his side, and to gain the Government's unwavering support and goodwill. For instance, he assured himself of the backing of the *Bilo* Negroes by extending his approval and cooperation to their wish for a school run by the Moravian Brothers.

He had noticed that the Government was in favour of schools in the Tapanahoni, but that a school supported by only the Government was doomed to fail. So Kanapé wanted to get a Christian school with the express approval of the Government. It was true that in the past, during Granman Oseisie's reign, this combination had been a failure, but

Kanapé probably thought he was strong and astute enough to fare better. It did not matter to him whether it was a Protestant or a Catholic school. The fact that it happened to be a Catholic school was due to the chance circumstance that the delegates from the Moravian Brothers could not produce a permit from the Government when they came to talk about a school with Kanapé, whereas the Catholics – probably warned that this was what Kanapé wanted – could.

An important role in the matter was played by Father Morssink, who, as has been mentioned, had already made an effort in this direction in 1918. In 1931 he was appointed pastor in Albina, with what he termed 'carte blanche' from the Apostolic Vicar in Paramaribo to attempt to establish a school in the Tapanahoni.

With envious eyes he perceived the success of the Moravian Brothers who had managed to start a boarding-school at Sajé. When he heard that Kanapé had refused to grant the Moravian Brothers a school at Drietabbetje because they did not have an official letter from the Government on the subject, he knew what to do. The Apostolic Vicar sent him a letter advising him to obtain the 'utmost cooperation' from the District Commissioner Van Hecke, 'a sound Catholic'.[14] At Morssink's earnest request the District Commissioner advised Kanapé, with whom he was on excellent terms, to accept a Catholic school. Together they drew up the following statement:

> Commissioner of Albina to Head Chief Kanapé of Otterloo.
>
> I, District Commissioner of Marowijne, agree, and give my immediate consent, to the plan of the Catholic pastor to open a school in the Tapanahoni.

Van Hecke, yielding to pressure from the pastor, thought he could venture to take this step on his own authority without consulting the Government.

In June 1932 Kanapé travelled to Paramaribo where he had an interview on the 27th with the Apostolic Vicar van Roosmalen, and, among others, with the District Commissioner Van Hecke. By Kanapé's request the interpreter on this occasion was W.F. van Lier!

Morssink's *Evangelization of the Djukas* (1932) contains a short report on p. 240 of this meeting where, broadly stated, it was agreed:

1° that Kanapé gave his approval to the establishment of a Catholic school in his country, and would back it.

2° that he objected to the establishment of a church. He and his family would remain 'heathens'; others were free to be baptized if they wished, including children, if their uncle gave his consent.

3° The mission priest had to provide clothing and food. The transport of foodstuffs would be undertaken for a small consideration by Djukas who travelled up the river.

4° The mission had to pay for the clearing of the grounds by the Djukas.

The Catholic mission wasted no time, the school was already opened, as has been mentioned, on 8 November 1932.

Kanapé got what he wanted; the Upper Tapanahoni had a school to counterbalance the school in the Lower Tapanahoni. He thought the agreement concluded with the District Commissioner had assured him of the official approval of the Government that owed him their support as long as he held to his side of the agreement, and, above all, would have to maintain him in his position. His lack of insight into administrative tactics and in the relationship between administration and Catholic mission would, however, cost him dear. The District Commissioner's independent statement had no binding force whatsoever as far as the Government was concerned, nor were they particularly interested in a Catholic school in the Tapanahoni. The Government did not even subsidize the school like that of the Moravian Brothers at Sajé.

Moreover, the pressure exerted by Amatodja and his followers on the Government to have the Granman officially installed did not diminish and in 1937 the Government thought the time had arrived to put an end to Kanapé's interregnum and force Amatodja's nomination. With this in view the then District Commissioner, Mr. Raue, left for the Tapanahoni and called a *gran krutu*. In his letter on this matter to the Governor (5 March 1937, Highly Confidential) he wrote that Amatodja, after long hesitation, wished to accept the Granmanship, Raue having indicated that the Government had no intention of appointing Kanapé to the post, and was not satisfied either with an intermediate form "in which the latter virtually had full control of affairs". "I managed to put Kanapé in his proper place from time to time and gradually shoulder him out of the way", Raue wrote. He recommended that Kanapé should be dismissed, but be put on a sort of pension in recognition of services rendered. He had noticed that Kanapé was very keen on an allowance and he thought it would be easier in future to keep the High Priest in hand if he was given a grant. Raue found it unwise to offend him, for, after all, "he remains an influential person whose favourable disposition is worth cultivating".

Raue's advice was followed: Amatodja was intalled, Kanapé dismissed as Head Chief, his allowance was reduced from Fls. 400 to Fls. 360 per year (Amatodja's salary was Fls. 500 per year).

Kanapé still retained his very important position as High Priest (with the sugar-coating of an allowance). It was now a matter of strengthening his position as much as possible. This had an immediate effect on the Roman Catholic boarding-school. Whereas Kanapé had probably thought up till now that he could control the menace of Christianization sufficiently through his twofold position of power, he could henceforth count only on his religious authority. As Granman, Amatodja would be able to decide on the future of the school, and his decisions would have the support of the Government. It was important to exhibit his religious power at once.

As it was, this religious authority was being undermined by a Djuka medicine-man, Wensi, who had been active since 1933 in the region above Drietabbetje. He destroyed sanctuaries, professed a sort of Christianity, and succeeded in gaining so much influence that even Kanapé had difficulty for a while in asserting his position with regard to his people as well as to the Catholic and Protestant missions. The fact was that Wensi tried to insinuate himself with the above-named missions, both of whom, after a preliminary response to his advances, dropped him when it appeared that he was double-faced and kept up 'idolatrous practices' as well as 'Christianity'. Early in 1936 he left the Tapanahoni for the Cottica.

Kanapé began to put pressure on those responsible for the care of the schoolchildren, probably uttered threats concerning the evil consequences of their straying away from the faith of their forebears, consequences affecting not only the children but also others who belonged to the same lineage, and very likely warned them that he would extend no more religious help if the children were kept at school.

As to the school itself, all that need be mentioned is that the pupils were not taught through the medium of the 'Afaka' script (Chapter IX §3) which Morssink propagated with such enthusiasm. Apparently Kanapé, too, preferred to have the children read the writing of the whites rather than that of the handful of Djukas.

§ 4 STOELMAN'S ISLAND

In 1954 the medical work was concentrated exclusively on Stoelman's Island, situated at the point where the Tapanahoni and the Lawa converge to form the Marowijne. Here the Moravian Brothers established a well-equipped hospital, with medical staff, who also travel up the river to visit the Djukas in their villages.[15] Since a small airport has been built on the island, the city of Paramaribo can be reached within an hour. The trip by boat still takes three to four days.

On Stoelman's Island there is also a boarding-school under the direction of the resident clergyman, A.J. Axwijck. The pupils number at least forty (1969).

§ 5 DRIETABBETJE

For some years now there has been a small polyclinic, with a nursing sister, also run by the Moravian Brothers. In 1965 the Government started building a day- and boarding-school on the same island, this time after consultation with the Granman, the parents and mother's uncle of the children, and with their approval. Special wishes were fulfilled: the school provides transport, a meal and a set of school-clothes for the children. The school was opened in July 1966. The boarding establishment has not come into operation yet. From the data[16] I could gather about the 'Akontu Felanti' school it seems that the Djukas are showing a satisfactory degree of interest. They realize that school-learning enhances their chance of finding employment in the city. (An important employer, *Suralco*, demands that a test should be given.)

Lessons in arithmetic, writing and reading, singing and physical culture, are given in Dutch by five trained teachers. The number of children, including girls, varies from hundred to hundred and forty. (One of the causes of the marked fluctuation is the fact that they have to help their mothers on the provision grounds.) They are exclusively children of above-stream Djukas. The boarding-school seems to be intended for children living still further south than Drietabbetje.

The relationship between the Granman and the principal leaves much to be desired: according to a newspaper report (*De West*, 29 December 1968) Granman Gazon declared that the principal 'had undermined the local authority' and demanded that he should leave Drietabbetje immediately, which actually happened. This is probably connected with the fact that the Surinam Government is trying to obtain political influence in this area.

Whereas between 1917 and 1926 an attempt was made to create manpower by raising the standard of development, the striving nowadays seems to be to activate the Djukas politically. The Bush Negroes, comprising 8 to 9% of the population, could throw a not insignificant weight into the political balance.

NOTES

[1] Archives Moravian Brothers, Zeist, The Netherlands.
[2] Government Resolution, No. 3, 14 June 1926, Confidential.
[3] Government Resolution, No. 22, 23 April 1925, Highly Confidential.
[4] Government Resolution, No. 71, 10 October 1926, Confidential.
[5] Archives Moravian Brothers, Paramaribo.
[6] Data from Archives Moravian Brothers, Paramaribo.
[7] Morssink, MS 1932, p. 232.
[8] Abena had previously declared that he wanted to join the Catholic church.
[9] At that time such reproaches were continually bandied about. Protestants and Catholics accused each other, usually with good reason, of 'stealing' the children from their schools. In his excitement Morssink spoke of the Moravian Brothers as vultures setting out on predatory expeditions (MS 1932).
[10] The congregation consisted of Sajé and two adjacent villages, Clementi and Powie.
[11] Morssink, MS 1932, p. 235 et seq.
[12] Archives, Secretariat of the Surinam Mission, Amsterdam.
[13] Morssink, MS 1934, p. 54.
[14] Morssink, MS 1932.
[15] Doornbos, 1966.
[16] These data were obtained from, among other sources, the former principal S.A. Charry.

CHAPTER IX

CONCLUSION

§ 1 VIEWS OF THE PARTIES CONCERNED; A SUMMARY

a The Government's view

The final view of the results held by those responsible for the inception and launching of the project may be inferred from a comparison of their initial expectations with what, in the end, they considered as having been achieved.

As has been pointed out in Chapter IV § 4, the Governor and the Colonial States expected a material and ethical result of the development work. Material benefit would accrue, they hoped, from the gain in labour and the heightened productivity of the Djukas. On the ethical side it was hoped to promote the welfare of the Djukas by helping them to develop, and to discharge a 'moral debt' towards a neglected population group. They hoped attain these results within a couple of years.

Most of the members of the Colonial States thought that the achieved results were nil. The school, when it finally got started, was not given a chance of survival.

The Governor was of the same mind. Still, he was prepared to consider giving the school an opportunity and making provision for it, as well as for the postholdership, in the next annual budget.

The District Commissioner (who played a role during the last year) also believed that the school had a chance of succeeding in due course.

The lack of success was (naturally!) blamed on the executor of the project and on the Djuka community. The postholder had not come up to expectations. He had neither the necessary 'authority and prestige' nor the required ability to make a success of the project. In other words: the qualities he possessed and had been credited with had not proved adequate to the task. The Djuka community had sabotaged the measures adopted for the sake of their welfare and had not shown any appreciation of the Government's good intentions.

b The postholder's view

The postholder anticipated the same material results as his employers but laid more stress on the ethical side of his work. He was emotionally involved in it and felt called to raise a group of people, whom he pitied deeply, out of their material and spiritual misery. He hoped to achieve this in the first place by educating the younger generation. This he regarded as his life work. Consequently his view of the duration of the project differed from that held by the Government. At the conclusion of a development project which he thought had been ended prematurely, Van Lier believed that, although the visible results were indeed meagre, something of great importance had been achieved. The first steps on the way to further success had been taken: the Djuka distrust with regard to his person and the plans he fostered had been largely overcome. As a result of this, children had been brought to his boarding-school. His medical help was called in and appreciated. He believed (erroneously) that a number of hygienic measures had caught on. (Burial of the dead within three days and the interment of witches.) Training in methods of agriculture, cattle-breeding and forestry had not had a proper chance owing to circumstances, but Van Lier thought, if he were able to devote more attention to these matters, the Djukas would display greater interest in them.

c The view of the Djuka community

At first the Djukas' opinion of what the Government hoped to achieve by their endeavours was mostly unfavourable. This was, on the one hand, the result of their profound mistrust of the Government's intentions in general, on the other hand the result of their ignorance concerning the development plan in particular (Chapter 10 § 6). As long as this opinion prevailed and was clearly voiced by the Djuka leading figures, the postholder's work encountered opposition. With the gradual decrease in their mistrust and heightened pressure by the Government, the chances of the development work improved. Its effects were diminished, however, by internal conflicts and unforeseen circumstances (Chapter v § 2, Chapter vii § 4d).

The Djukas believed, like the postholder, that when the 'experiment' was ended the development work had only just been begun. A number of prominent Djukas had offered their loyal cooperation. They considered that the Government had lost patience, after the difficulties that had been overcome, with the slow progress of the development project and were withholding the support needed by the postholder for its execution. In their opinion the postholder deserved their confidence when all was said and done, but they thought that his work suffered from his frequent and lengthy absences, from smear campaigns, and from the wrong choice of headquarters.

§ 2 VIEWS HELD BY CONTEMPORARIES

a Father Morssink

Father Franciscus Petrus Morssink (C.s.s.R.) was born in 1876, arrived in Surinam two years after his ordination to the priesthood in 1906 and died in 1945 in Paramaribo[1].

In 1914 he was put in charge of the mission work in the Marowijne district and stationed in Albina. Although he limited his visits by river to the Indians and the Paramaccaners during the first three years, he came into contact with Djukas in Albina. In 1917 he became acquainted with Afaka, a Djuka belonging to the below-stream Negroes and the Bry-*lo*. This Djuka had compiled an alphabet of syllable-writing consisting of fifty-six signs, by means of which he could write the Djuka language.[2] Morssink, "as a missionary who availed himself eagerly of every favourable opportunity for spreading the faith" thought that Afaka's 'book', which gave proof of attachment to the '*Sante Katoliki kerki*', offered a golden chance of disseminating the Catholic creed among the Djukas. There were some thirty Djukas who knew the writing. Morssink also learnt it and began, with consent of Monsignor van Roosmalen, Apostolic Vicar at Paramaribo, to try and get the system adopted by the Djukas, first together with Afaka and, after the latter's death in 1918, with his brother (or nephew) Abena. After a couple of trips to the Upper Marowijne and the Lower Tapanahoni, where he was received with general friendliness and interest, he left on 3 November 1918 for the Upper Tapanahoni to pay an official visit to Granman Amakti on behalf of Msgr. van Roosmalen. His effort to enlist Amakti's help for the spread of the Afaka writing (and simultaneously of the Catholic faith) met with a curt rebuff: Amakti felt aggrieved that Afaka had not brought the matter to his attention before approaching anybody else, especially the whites. He expressed contempt for that *wisiwasi* (nonsense) book, whose practitioners could not even read aloud a letter from Msgr. van Roosmalen. Although Morssink, on his return journey, encountered great indignation among the Djukas on account of Amakti's obstinacy, and found that they were willing to start a school with him without Amakti's consent, nothing came of the plan.[3]

Back in Albina, Father Morssink fell seriously ill and went on leave until 1921.

Meanwhile postholder Van Lier's experiment of doing civilizing work among the Djukas had been started. In spite of the Governor's request to Msgr. van Roosmalen to undertake no mission work in the Tapanahoni during the experiment, Father Morssink left once more in 1921 for the area with this object in view. He did not proceed beyond Powie, the below-stream territory opposite which Van Lier's Granman Staalkondré was situated. This trip yielded such poor results that the area was not re-visited by the Roman Catholic mission workers before 1931. As a matter of fact, Father Morssink stayed away from the Marowijne area until that year.

In 1931 he was appointed pastor in Albina and began trying to enlist the interest of the Tapanahoni Djukas in a Catholic school, especially since he was vexed by the growing influence of the Moravian Brothers.

He wrote a treatise on the 'Djukas or Aucaners' in which he described their history and religion[4] and one on 'The Evangelization of the Djukas'. In the latter he discussed the Government's attempt at developing the Djukas along non-Christian lines at some length. In the first chapter, on 'A Postholder's Bush Negro Boarding-school' he describes the early history of the postholdership, in the second, 'On this high-flown but ineffectual Civilizing impulse, or Postholdership in the Tapanahoni' he gives a chronological rendering of Van Lier's notes during that period. He had procured the notes in question from the referendary, Esser, who had filched them from the Secretariat of the Colonial States. Then follows 'Something about Van Lier's *idée fixe*' in which he offers his views on development without religion. He concludes with an 'Apotheosis of the government's civilizing impulse with the inglorious interment of the notorious xxth Century Postholdership'.

After starting the first piece with the exclamation: "A comedy? A tragedy? Let us stick to the golden mean and style it a 'cheerful drama' or perhaps rather a 'sad comedy'... But the matter is too painful", he goes on to write that, after the unsuccessful attempt by the Moravian

Brothers, in spite of the fact that the Catholic missionaries were diligently occupying themselves with the Djukas, the Government imagined that it could dispense with the Catholics by keeping them out of this territory and civilize the Djukas without the aid of religion. It was a 'no popery' undertaking.

From the outset Morssink's criticism is apparent in the titles (and introductory phrases) of the parts of his argument. He goes on to complain that the Government wanted to keep the Catholic mission away from the Tapanahoni area, without mentioning the fact that the Government had likewise asked the Moravian Brothers not to meddle with this territory for the time being (a request with which they complied). With some malice he mentions Amakti's reluctance to receive Van Lier in the Tapanahoni and minimizes the fact that he did receive him eventually.

After emphasizing the fact that the Djukas, or at any rate Amakti and his followers, were not in the least pleased with the plan and only agreed to receive Van Lier in their midst because the Government brought strong pressure to bear on them, Morssink describes Van Lier's reception on 13 December 1919 at Puketi. He states that the Djukas gave quite a different version of the event than Van Lier. According to them, Van Lier had said: "I am coming here to live among you and to do some teaching". To this Amakti had replied: "If that is Van Lier's purpose, he can stay here; but if he intends doing other things, he had better clear off at once." Morssink recounts disapprovingly how Van Lier took the oath after Djuka fashion. "And he had to squat down next to the *gran-jorka* (ancestral) flag while a libation of water was poured. He swore that he would live among the Djukas like a brother."

The text of Van Lier's inaugural speech in the w.i.g. of 1921 actually tallies with what Morssink was told by the Djukas, namely that "Van Lier had come to live among them and to do some teaching". The first part of Amakti's reply also agrees with their account. The Djuka version which, according to Morssink, differs completely, applies to the second part of Amakti's reply indicating that "if Van Lier intended doing other things he had better go back at once". In the w.i.g. (1923) Van Lier tells that "a member of a committee of wise men" replied on Amakti's behalf to Van Lier's speech, saying that "what the *bakra* has said admits of no criticism." After the solemn oath taken at the ancestral pole, Amakti declared that the Djuka tribe had accepted him. It is quite possible that some Djukas attributed to Amakti the concluding reply as given by Morssink. Morssink regards it as proof that Van Lier was *not* accepted after all. However, the meaning of this reply evaded Morssink completely: the suggestion of 'other things' Van Lier might intend doing undoubtedly applies to the propagation of Christianity.

With Van Lier's acceptance a good deal more was achieved than could be managed by Morssink, who had been turned down flat by Amakti the year before.

After describing Van Lier's initial difficulties in search of a suitable dwelling-place and the building of his house, the first – slight – success and subsequent failure of his efforts at running a school in his temporary shelter in Powie, Morssink concludes this part of his account with 'the first tableau of our play', the solemn opening of Granman Staalkondré in 1920. A year later Morssink visited Van Lier, still without pupils, and "was able to take a personal look at this pathetic loneliness". This took place in 1921, on the occasion of Morssink's vain attempt to gain access to the Tapanahoni territory.

In the second part, dealing with Van Lier's *idée fixe*, Morssink writes in the preface that he is sure all the *Bilo* Negroes want a school, as may be deduced from the 'large following' the Afaka script enjoys. Van Lier's *idée fixe* consists in his conviction that only a school without religion would be likely to succeed. Morssink then quotes a number of Van Lier's utterances and diary notes which illustrate this.

On 19 February 1921 Van Lier writes "that the teaching of religion should be regarded not merely as a hindrance but as an arch enemy of civilization work among this tribe" and on 3 April 1921 "everything boils down to the Djukas' fear that the children will be baptized by the school".

With reference to this Morssink remarks: "But it seems to me sheer quixotry of Van Lier, tilting against windmills, as he contradicts his own argument with subsequent notes", meaning the examples Van Lier gives of a number of Djukas who did in fact evince an interest in the Christian religion. "What is more", he continues "Van Lier indicates by various facts he quotes that the Djukas have Catholic leanings". The following (single) anecdote is supposed to be an example of this: the mother of a dying child comes to Van Lier, repeatedly begging for help which he is unable to give to her. On 21 January 1922 Van Lier writes: "This morning she went down on her knees before the portrait of Her Majesty the Queen, whom she took to be the Holy Virgin, and prayed that Anéné might be restored; I explained to her that this was a portrait of the Queen, but it made no difference to her: "then I have prayed to the Queen; surely all of us belong to her. Anéné also, and God will raise her up for the Queen's sake."

Morssink mentions another example of Van Lier's *idée fixe*: after deploring the maltreatment of victims suspected of *wisi* and its frequent occurrence he exclaims ('pathetically' according to Morssink): "It is my earnest resolve to put an end as soon as possible to this appalling situation" and Morssink adds: "and that by the sole means of a school without religion!!!"

"To crown it all", Morssink writes, thus weakening his own argument, "it seems as though the Djukas themselves have no clear idea of what religion means". In this connection he quotes the utterance of a Bush Negro, jotted down by Van Lier on 20 September 1923 (Chapter VI § 2f): "The previous schools were a failure because of the teaching of religion: the day was completely taken up by the singing of hymns which the children repeated so many times that he even remembers one of them: '*Oranje boven! Oranje boven!*' he sang to me." Another example: Van Lier tells of a Djuka who expresses his satisfaction at the fact that the school is being started now. He used to be one of its opponents, because he thought the children would be baptized. Now, however, his view of the matter has changed: "The young people no longer profess the faith of their forefathers; that is why so many of them die. So they may as well go to school and become Christians, for people cannot live without religion."

He offers no further commentary on the shortened version of Van Lier's notes up to 1925.

From the above it is plain that Morssink's chief grievance was Van Lier's *idée fixe*. It was quite impossible for the good priest to grasp Van Lier's point of view. This is demonstrated by his illogical reactions to the latter's statements about education without the Christian faith. One should also take into consideration the fact that he not only regarded a divorce between these two matters as impossible, but also condemned a combination of school and Protestant teaching as heresy. This attitude explains why he makes absolutely no mention of Van Lier's 'backdoor' theory, with which he was definitely familiar.

In the concluding section of his argument, the 'Apotheosis', Morssink does mention in his résumé of Van Lier's notes that the latter had twenty children at his boarding-school from June till December 1925, but he does not draw any conclusion from this. He expresses indignation at the fact that the Government once again chose a non-Catholic successor to Van Lier, namely the Moravian Brothers. This had, in fact, been the policy of the Government all along.

The later history of educational development in the Tapanahoni contains a partial justification of Van Lier's standpoint: the Moravian

Brothers, who only managed to keep going with great difficulty along the Lower Tapanahoni, where far more value was attached to education than along the upper part of the river, had to promise never to baptize a child exept by explicit request of its mother or uncle. The number of Christians in the Tapanahoni is, however, still below one-fifth of the population and the conservative older people still hold the same view on Christianity that was prevalent at the time of Van Lier.

b The press

In Chapter VI § 3b Van Lier's complaint about the destructive newspaper articles is mentioned. He was referring to the Roman Catholic journal *De Surinamer*. On one occasion it had published an animated review of Van Lier's booklet *On the Bush Negroes of the Marowijne* (1919); but as early as 1921 an anonymous journalist started writing his hostile criticism of the postholder's experiment in the column *From Week to Week*. He thought at the time that it was "absolutely necessary for the civilization of these people to teach them a better, more elevated religion". However, this could not by any means be done by Mr. van Lier, "whose position is that of administrative official, a representative of the state, who does not deal in religion". According to 'v.w.t.w.', as the columnist was called by one of his colleagues, the whole affair was bound to end in a fiasco.

In 1923 'v.w.t.w.' wrote in connection with the grant allocated in 1921 for building a house for Van Lier (who had stated that "he wished to bring a Surinam woman to the Bush Negro community and found a cultured family in their midst"): "Oh, the amiable naïvety of our Administration! Two and a half years have passed and the cultured family Mr. van Lier was going to found is still in the making." (The lady involved in the case rejected his offer of marriage.) 'v.w.t.w.' remarked with reference to the grant for the boarding-school: "Mr. van Lier had to have a school with a boarding establishment to civilize. He has moved heaven and earth, written interminable perorations to prove the necessity, and the Bush Negroes' fervent longing, for a boarding-school. That boarding-school was a *sine qua non*. The Home Government... has given its sanction." At the very time that 'v.w.t.w.' was writing this, Van Lier was in Albina, where the Djukas refused to convey him to his headquarters. (see Chapter VI § 2). 'v.w.t.w.' also commented on this: "It seems true, after all, what is being said out loud in Albina: that the Postholder's authority among the Aucaners is nil." He quotes a remark made by the

Da Kodjo Kanapé (left), priest in Drietabbetje. Round his neck a *libi-tete*, safeguard and amulet, on his head a red plastic cap. Next to him two village headmen, in the foreground an *apinti-drum*, used on religious occasions. (photograph by the author)

States Member Terheggen on 27 February 1922 to the effect that Mr. van Lier had not elevated the Bush Negroes to his own level, but had lowered himself to theirs, and had even expressed sympathy with their practices. "That is condescension in the bad sense of the word" wrote 'v.w.t.w.', "a descent which necessarily undermines all prestige".

In 1925 'v.w.t.w.''s successor revived the latter's criticism, expressed in 1921, with regard to the appointment of an administrative official and added: "for success can only be had by someone who is above the parties, of whom we all know that he is not acting from personal material interest. The only person fulfilling these requirements is the missionary. No one else can gain full confidence. And without confidence nothing can be achieved". The journal *Suriname*, faithful defender of Van Lier, replied with a commentary entitled "The cloven hoof at last".

In connection with an impending strike by the Djuka freight carriers in 1925, *De Surinamer* raised the question: "Should a position (of postholder) which is absolutely worthless and surely costs the country some Fls. 10,000 be retained?" All the same, the journalist of *De Surinamer*, just like some State Members, added to his criticism: "these objections do not apply to the person of Mr. van Lier", but he could not refrain from adding: "Anyway, he does not bother us with his authority, which is non-existent".

§ 3 THE VIEW OF A DJUKA PRIEST

During my visit to the Tapanahoni (August 1965) and more particularly to Drietabbetje, the chief village, I spoke to a number of Djukas about the activities of the postholder Van Lier. Most of them had only misty recollections of the events of forty or fifty years ago. Of those who had attended his school only a few could be traced. They could neither read nor write and remembered only vaguely what had happened when they were at school. A nephew (the son of a sister) of Chief Banda (who had taken pains to further the cause of the school) told me that he remembered the reading plank (he could still repeat a couple of the words on it), the slate and slate-pencil. Also that he had learnt to plant maize in rows, tend goats, pigs and poultry, and that the children obtained their meals from Van Lier. He still recalled, in somewhat mutilated form, a few lines of a little song he had learnt: "If you want to join the soldiers, you've got to have a gun". In his opinion Van Lier cared well for the children, although he occasionally beat them with a stick. Sometimes the children ran away, but he had been forbidden by his Uncle Banda to do so.

A number of Djukas still remembered medical aid received from Van Lier and some of them could show scars of injuries cured by him.

I got most of the information, however, from the son of the High Priest Kanapé, who, though he had never attended the postholder's school, had outspoken views on the events during the latter's stay in the Tapanahoni. His father had told him about the course of events, and he was also acquainted with the opinion of Granman Amakti and other prominent persons of the period.

This man's retrospective objections and the reasons he gave for the resistance to the introduction of western civilization in general and the activities of postholder Van Lier in particular reflect, separately and in conjunction with each other, the factors discussed above.

Da Kodjo Kanapé is about fifty years old, belonging, like his father, to the Oto-*lo* (of which his mother must also be a member, then), a priest of the Great God and also *Bassia* of Drietabbetje. He is intelligent and vivacious and also very candid.

The interview I had with him on 27 August 1965 lasted a full two hours and was recorded on tape. Dr. H.U.E. Thoden van Velzen – on a visit to Drietabbetje for anthropological research – acted as interpreter and translated the interview which was conducted in the Djuka language.[5]

A few days prior to this interview I had told Da Kodjo Kanapé that Van Lier had written down everything he had experienced in the Tapanahoni and that I had read his record. I had also explained to him that I had thus been able to learn what Van Lier's view of the matter was, but that I imagined the Djukas might have a different opinion. I had asked him to think it over and then tell me what he remembered, what he had heard about it and what he himself thought of it.

The information he gave me during the interview served largely to confirm the conclusions I had been able to draw from the material I had consulted in the archives.

Da Kodjo Kanapé started by saying that it was indeed so that Van Lier and the Djukas had different views of the matter. As the Djukas put it: they did not travel along the same road. No meeting had been held to examine each other's standpoint and come to an agreement. Moreover, Van Lier as a 'paper man' (that is to say that he could write) was able to record his views of the matter. The Djukas had not had an opportunity of expressing their opinion.

The following topics were raised:

1 How did the Djukas feel about Van Lier's plans for a school?

The answer to this was: the Djukas did not want Van Lier's school. They did not know where it would lead for they had not been informed of the plan and they dreaded the results of the experiment. This was why they had not given Van Lier a cordial welcome and had not wanted to let him have their children.

2a What were the objections to the school?

The objections to the school were two-fold: the Djukas were afraid that, as soon as the children could read and write, they would leave their tribe and move to the city. The whites thought the Djukas were stupid and wanted to educate them with a view to enticing them to the city. This they tried to prevent. The exodus of their younger members would harm the Djuka tribe.

A graver objection was that the children would be baptized as soon as they had received some education. What would the consequences be? Suppose that such a boy, Da Kodjo explained, is doing some job or other (for instance, helping his mother on the provision ground) and 'disturbs something' (that is to say, he gets into trouble with supernatural forces by transgressing a taboo: killing a sacred snake, felling a sacred tree), then, as a baptized Christian, he cannot offer a sacrifice or pray to the offended god. He adds one sin against the Djuka gods to another and is no longer capable of dealing with matters affected by a religious taboo. And, continued Da Kodjo, his mother has committed transgressions and now he, too, is going to commit transgressions. By which he meant: whereas forgiveness might still have been asked and obtained for the sins of his mother – and of his entire lineage – he has damaged the friendly disposition of the gods through his own ignorance and powerlessness so that his mother and the whole lineage might well suffer for it. When you have been baptized, you can no longer tell the cause of illness or of death. You are unable to find the suitable herbs and other things which could protect you from harm.

In reply to my remark that Van Lier himself had stated that he would give secular education and would not baptize his pupils, Da Kodjo admitted after some hesitation that that was indeed the case. Van Lier was no *leriman*, no missionary teacher, even though he could teach the children something. "If he baptized them, he baptized them on the sly, but he did *not* baptize them, because not a single pupil told us that he had been baptized by Van Lier; if it had happened, we should certainly have known it."

But then Van Lier did give them such education as would have made it possible for them to be baptized later, had they so wished.

So, although Da Kodjo Kanapé admitted that Van Lier did not provide any Christian tuition and certainly did not practise baptism, he believed all the same that Van Lier acted in such a manner as to open the way for the possible later conversion of his pupils. As we know, his insight was quite correct in this case. Van Lier, with his 'backdoor theory', had not been able to conceal his attitude from the Djukas, and, though he does not mention it anywhere, it may be assumed that he at least made indirect propaganda for a Christian way of life in talks with the older people and in stories told to his pupils. The experience the Djukas had had of schools during the period of Amakti's predecessor had, moreover, tended to make them suspicious.

The Djukas' objections to the school were founded on a justified and real fear: the Government's aim was indeed to attract the children who had received some training to join the labour force in the coastal area. The Djukas saw (and still see) the danger of the disintegration and decay of their traditional society. The services for which youthful workers are needed (clearing of provision grounds, freight carrying on the rivers, building of houses, hunting, etc.) would be affected, there would not be enough young people to be trained to succeed the older men of high position (priests, *obiamans*, chiefs) and the population would dwindle.

2b Why did they send their children to school after all?

To this question Da Kodjo Kanapé replied that Granman Amakti, High Priest Kanapé and Van Lier had gone to Paramaribo and reached an agreement with the Government that Van Lier would come to Djuka to teach the children and abolish ignorance.

The fact that the school did not come into existence then he put down to the fact that Van Lier did not get started. (As a matter of fact, Van Lier let a propitious moment pass, waiting for the subsidy he hoped to obtain for the boarding establishment.)

At last Van Lier began to look around for pupils for the school. The Government exercised pressure and Van Lier held many and lengthy *krutus*, but still the Djukas held out, fearing that the children would be baptized, and that they would emigrate after leaving school. "Then the river will deteriorate, even if it does not die"[6] said Da Kodjo Kanapé, "Well, this is the river where we found refuge. That is why they resisted." But Van Lier persisted: he kept on holding *krutus*, discussed the matter with everybody, "continued steering deliberately", tried to convince the people and pointed out the weak spots in their arguments. Until in the end there were people who said: let us pretend to approve, and see what he teaches them, but he must not baptize them. And when they had given their consent, all the villages were obliged to send children.

3a What was the relationship like between Amakti and Van Lier?

The relationship between Granman Amakti and Van Lier was bad, Da Kodjo Kanapé declared. Amakti's standpoint was that the request for a school should have emanated from him, the Granman, and not have been imposed by the Government. As exponent of the administration, Van Lier received the brunt of Amakti's indignation at the injury his dignity had suffered.

Furthermore it was known that Van Lier was not in agreement with Amakti's appointment as Granman; he would have preferred to see Kanapé in that position. This was indeed the case. Van Lier had publicized his opinion on the matter in writing (Van Lier, 1919), probably also in talks with the Djukas themselves. Amakti regarded the friendship between Kanapé and Van Lier and the – likewise contrived – promotion of Kanapé to co-responsible leadership as a clear proof of this attitude.

Besides, Da Kodja Kanapé said, Van Lier came to the Tapanahoni with the airs of a governor. "The clothes he had brought along from the city to come and work here were those of a governor. He told the people that there were two Granmans: Amakti of the Djukas and Van Lier of the *Bakras*. These two were now supposed to exercise joint authority over the river. That is not what it should be like. Not a single Granman, including Amakti, would tolerate that, hence the constant squabbling between Amakti and Van Lier." On this point, too, the Djukas were not entirely in the wrong. The administrators in Paramaribo also feared a loss of prestige, just like the Djukas. They were constantly preoccupied with this in their dealings with the small Bush Negro community and the measure of Van Lier's prestige was often weighed by his success, or otherwise, in the enforcing of instructions. So Van Lier needed prestige and had to be supplied with as much of it as possible. Hence his fine uniform (with sabre and tricorn, although the Governor's uniform was much grander!) and the Governor's statement at Van Lier's installation that he was sending Van Lier to do what he himself could not do for lack of time.

Da Kodjo concluded his exposition with the commentary: "Wasn't it the Granman who had to rule over the country? If he kills nobody, isn't he a good ruler then, isn't he powerful then? If you come to the river to work, you should restrict yourself to your job and not meddle with the task of the Granman."

3b What was the relationship like between Kanapé and Van Lier?

As regards the relationship between Van Lier and his father, the High Priest Kanapé, Da Kodjo Kanapé said that they had been friends already long before Van Lier came to the Tapanahoni as postholder, while he was still travelling in that area as balata prospector. During that time they had met and had formed a friendship. (On one of these occasions Kanapé had hauled the bodies of a couple of Creoles, who were drowned when their boat capsized, out of the river and buried them. Van Lier, as well as the District Commissioner and the Government, had appreciated this action very much.)

When Van Lier wanted to start his school, Kanapé agreed with everything he suggested, and if Van Lier had not explained everything so carefully and convinced him, the school would never have come into being. He sent his young son (or nephew?) to the school, just as Amakti had sent his son.

When I asked whether Kanapé had backed him up to the end, Da Kodjo Kanapé replied that the support had ceased when Van Lier got into difficulties with the Government and was recalled. Kanapé had helped to set the school on its feet and it was not his fault that it was a failure. The Djukas had sent their children, and, so Da Kodjo concluded: "The success of the school depends on how you treat the children and how you teach them".

The friendship between Van Lier and Kanapé was in fact of long standing. This friendship did not prevent Kanapé from using it and even subordinating it to his own thirst for power. For that matter, Van Lier also made use of Kanapé's friendship in order to achieve his own ends. At first this did not harm the friendly relations between the two men and Kanapé actually cooperated in the founding of the school. His indignation at the Government when they abolished the school and the postholder-ship in 1925, and moreover forced Amakti and himself to sign a statement admitting that the Djukas were to blame for the failure, was in fact fully justified. When the Government dissociated itself from the development plan and from Van Lier, he saw no reason why he should continue to support his friend in the matter.

4 Van Lier's headquarters and the controversy between the *Opo* and *Bilo* Negroes

To my question why the school was not built in Drietabbetje but on the lower Tapanahoni, Da Kodjo Kanapé replied that there were two reasons for this: Granman Amakti, who was in any case already opposed to the school, did not want it at his residence. If he accepted it, while the suggestion had not come from him personally, "people would think that he did not rule the country well".

The second reason was that the decision as to where the school should come depended on the Government: Van Lier proposed a site belowstream and was supported in this and other matters by the Government. They also agreed to his wish to move to a station still further down the river.

According to Da Kodjo, Van Lier did in fact get some children of the *Opo-ningre*, but when he moved further they did not wish to let their children go along. "At that time one did not let your children go so far from home with a *bakra*, you never knew what could happen to such a child."

Da Kodjo Kanapé's view of the settlement of the school on the Lower Tapanahoni was the same as Van Lier's: he also realized that Amakti would have sabotaged a school at or near Drietabbetje. Among the *Bilo* Negroes the school had at least a *chance* of success, since they had declared themselves in favour of it. Those who came to ask Van Lier at the eleventh hour to come to the Upper Tapanahoni still (or at any rate to the boundary) had not been sent by the Granman but belonged to the Missiedjan-*lo*, who were for the most part opposed to him.[7]

It was also true, of course, that Van Lier could have started the school wherever he wanted to with the Government's support.

5a The attitude towards the mission school before Van Lier's arrival

Da Kodjo Kanapé thought that the failure of the mission school at the time of Granman Oseisie was due to the religion which the teachers (Spalburg from 1898 to 1906 and Helder from 1909 to 1912) tried to force upon the children. He referred once more to the danger of baptism, putting it as follows: "If he (the teacher, Helder) had taught them to write, everything would have gone well, but he was determined to baptize them. We who live in the bush must be able to hold our own. As soon as baptism is introduced, we get into trouble. Helder said that they had to give up the *afkodrei* (idolatry). Suppose there are two brothers, the one is baptized and the other one isn't. If the baptized one does something wrong, he gets into trouble with the *afkodrei*. What is more, the supernatural punishment will not strike the baptized one then, but his brother."

Just like Van Lier, Da Kodjo Kanapé thought that the missionary zeal of Van Lier's predecessors (1896-1909) was the reason why these efforts at starting a school came to nothing. The suspicion against Christian teaching was still very strong during the twenties and Van Lier, realizing that, tried to act accordingly. Van Lier's school at Granman Staalkondré II gave rise to a permanent Christian school and up to this day (1969) the suspicion it aroused has not disappeared among the above-stream (and to some extent among the below-stream) Djukas. It is inadvisable for the teachers to baptize the children on their own initiative.

5b The attitude towards the neutral school now being built (1965)

Da Kodjo adopted an expectant and resigned attitude towards the school which was being built and would shortly be opened opposite Drietabbetje, waiting to see what would happen in the matter of baptism: "it has been agreed that there won't be any baptism" he said, "but if they come and baptize after all, they will be sent packing".

He accepted the possibility of the schoolchildren leaving the territory when they grow up. Nowadays they leave, even without attending school, so rather let them learn something, then they won't 'loaf around' but can work.

"At my age it is no easy matter" Da Kodjo concluded on a note of acquiescence "but let these young fellows do it if they must".

From Da Kodjo Kanapé's attitude to the secular Government school it appears that the two main objections of the Djukas still exist: the fear of troubles of a supernatural nature and the emigration of young men who are indispensable for the continuation of the Djuka tribe. They realize, however, that the process of modernization cannot be checked and they have resigned themselves to it to a certain extent.

§ 4 THE DEVELOPMENT PROJECT OF THE DJUKA COMMUNITY WAS NOT A 'COMMUNITY DEVELOPMENT' PROJECT

The endeavour, described in this case-history, to improve the Djuka society systematically has been called community development. This development of the Djuka society is not, however, Community Development in the modern sense of the concept as it has been named since the second world war. The term community development[8] has been used here in the sense which T.R. Batten (1964, p. 2) attributes to it: "any action taken by any agency and primarily designed to benefit the community." Here 'community' means a traditional, isolated society. Batten believes that the principles on which community development is founded are not new and were "in fact applied by a multitude of individual government officers and missionaries long before anyone had thought of such a term" (p.3). What *is* new, according to Batten, is "that these principles are now becoming more widely recognized than ever before... It is the emphasis that is new, rather than the principles, and it is all that is implied in this major development – in some cases almost a revolution – in government or agency policy that we now find convenient to term Community Development" (p.3). I believe, however, that in the project described here, despite a number of similarities, it is really a question of essentially different principles. So the political relationship between groups receiving and groups offering development has undergone a complete change: before the second world war the relationship was determined along colonial lines; afterwards, with the progressive decolonization, the contact has been laid, and takes place, between independent countries. Another new phenomenon is that the necessity for development aid has been internationally accepted and the principles have been formulated in an international forum, the United Nations. When a summary is made of a number of differences between 'Community Development' (C.D.) and Van Lier's community development project (d.p.) it should be kept in mind that the principles of C.D. are ideal criteria, which often cannot be or are not applied in practice.[9, 10]

1 C.D.   is based on the fundamental equality of all human groups (but at the same time on the superior quality of western civilization).
  d.p.   The colonial society was based on the inequality of human groups (although Van Lier himself held less orthodox views on the subject).
2 C.D.   offers development aid on request by, and in deliberation with, the receiving country. Although in theory this applies also to the receiving community, it is often omitted.
  d.p.   gave development aid on the initiative of the donor group, while the receiving group had no say in the matter.
3 C.D.   disapproves of compulsory measures during the carrying out of development programs.

	d.p.	resorted to coercive measures, even military threats, and the refusal of favours and facilities whenever signs of resistance were shown.
4	C.D.	aims in the first place at diminishing the discrepancy between prosperity in various parts of the world.
	d.p.	aimed at increasing the prosperity of the colony mainly for the sake of augmenting the affluence of the mother country.
5	C.D.	is prepared to make great financial sacrifices.
	d.p.	was not prepared to make great financial sacrifices.
6	C.D.	believes that the international balance of power should not determine the place, form or degree of aid (once more: in theory!).
	d.p.	aimed at the maintenance of the existing colonial balance of power.
7	C.D.	projects are planned by experts, executors are specially trained for their task.
	d.p.	In the case-history under discussion none of those involved possessed such a training.

Similarities of aims and problems are:

1	C.D.	regards the increased prosperity of development areas necessary for the preservation of world peace.
	d.p.	saw in the increase of prosperity a method of preserving law, order and authority.

2 Both regard the improvement of living conditions and the promotion of prosperity as a moral duty.
3 Both hope to improve the export and import opportunities of both the donor and the recipient areas.
4 Both hope to promote group and individual initiative of the recipient groups by means of development aid, so that outside help will become redundant in the long run.
5 Both hope "to integrate these communites into the life of the nation and to enable them to contribute fully to national progress" (U.N. E/2931).
6 In the carrying out of projects both are confronted with what Ahrensberg and Niehoff (1965, p. 127) call "the weight of the past". In the case of both it may be said that "the past history of contact between the West and the underdeveloped areas is long and has not always been pleasant. It has given rise to certain important and widespread attitudes which it would be folly to ignore." (A number of these attitudes causing resistance to westernization have been discussed in Chapter IV § 6.)

7 c.d. and d.p. have, during the carrying out of development projects, to do with the relationship between the employer (Government or other administrative body) and the executor(s) of the project. The problems arising out of this in the present case-history have been discussed in Chapter VI § 3. In the second place they have to do with the relationship between the executor(s) of the project and the group to be developed. (Problems arising here have been discussed in the notes in Chapter IV § 6a and exemplified in the various conflicts described in the case-history.)

8 In both c.d. and d.p. the technical and mental capacities of the executor of the projects play an important role in determining the final results obtained.

In modern literature on c.d. many recommendations are made which aim at the moulding of an ideal executor so that failures will be reduced to a minimum. The nature of the recommendations indicate the possible shortcomings of the executor. The training of the 'ideal executor' is a many-sided and difficult task. Goodenough (1963, p. 377) remarks: "Obviously, his job is anything but an easy one, calling for a combination of capacities that many of us lack." The capacities of the executor-postholder in the present case-history can be tested by similar lists of recommendations. This is done in § 5c of this chapter.

§ 5 CONCLUDING REMARKS

In order to explain why the effort to bring social and cultural change in the Djuka society described in this study could not be expected to yield better results, a few relevant facets may be outlined as follows:

a The design of the development plan

1 No clear conception was formed of:
– the duration of the project. The Colonial States called it an 'experiment', which only indicated that they did not wish to regard it as a long-lasting affair. The postholder called it a 'life task' (demanding at least twenty years). The Governor was prepared to call it an 'experiment', but made a point of mentioning that quick results could not be expected (Chapter III § 4).
– the costs of the project. Only the salary and a few fixed items of expenditure of the postholder were determined. Each new financial

consequence had to be deliberated on. The costs (about Fls. 10,000 per annum) were always found to be too high (Chapter VI § 1).

– the execution of subdivisions of the project; a demonstration field was thought to be useful, but the costs needed for planning and for hiring a labourer had to be paid by the postholder; the idea of a boarding-school instead of a day-school was not brought clearly to the attention of the Colonial States; it was not fully recognized how necessary it was to discuss the plans with members of the Djuka community (Chapter IV § 5).

2 Insufficient attention was paid to:

– studying the possibilities offered by the physical milieu of the interior for the Djukas to earn a livelihood, and of the measures which could bring improvement in this field.

– the far-reaching social and psychological consequences which every change would entail: plans to re-partition the grounds and move the *los* to new sites, the removal of children from their parents, the introduction of hygienic measures, were examples of this (Chapter IV § 4).

– the likely resistance against change, and the necessary measures to overcome this (Chapter IV § 6).

3 It was insufficiently realized that:

– the task with which the postholder was charged was far too comprehensive to be carried out by one person. It was a full-time job for an administrative official, an agricultural tutor, a medical officer and a teacher.

b The policy of the employers

The realization of the project plans were, inasmuch as the taking of decisions did not fall within the immediate competence of the executor, dependent on the policy of the employers. This policy showed a number of aspects which affected the development work unfavourably (Chapter V § 1).

The problems arising out of the hierarchical administrative relationship between employers and executor led to stagnation of the work. When conflicts arose, the administrative officials usually declared that they were right, and disavowed the policy of the executor.

Proposals submitted by the postholder to his superiors were sometimes given no sanction, sometimes sanctioned only after a long delay. Relevant examples are: grant for a demonstration field (Chapter IV § 4), the request to appoint Kanapé as Head Chief (Chapter V § 1), funds for the boarding-school (Chapter VI § 1), sending a doctor to the Tapanahoni (Chapter IV § 4).

The employers repeatedly failed to give proper moral support to the executor and his work. Growing criticism and cases of slander were not effectively refuted. The postholder's work was made more difficult as a result of the consequent mental tension.

The employers regarded the Djuka community as immature and lacking in culture. Their comparative independence within the colonial scheme was looked upon as an anomaly. The Government thought the resolutions issued by them should be put into effect immediately. They were loth to yield to or investigate wishes or objections, or to conform with the behaviour patterns of the Djukas. This attitude acted unfavourably on the hoped-for confidence in the plans which the postholder, as exponent of the Government, had to carry out.

c The capacities of the executor

The achievement of a successful result in development work is largely dependent on the capacities of the executor. His skill in carrying out his plans and having them carried out and his ability to solve the problems confronting him demand a combination of psychological and technical qualities. Cleveland, Mangone and Adams[11] led an investigation relating to these qualities and came to the conclusion that they could be clustered into five general elements: "technical skill, belief in mission, cultural empathy, a sense of politics, organizational ability".[12] In judging Van Lier's capacities with reference to the above specification, such circumstances as could lead to success or failure which are unconnected with personal ability are no more taken into consideration than was done by those who drew up the list.

1 Technical skill

By this Cleveland and co-authors (p. 131) do not primarily mean 'narrow specialization' but rather 'a breadth of education and experience that will allow an adaptable general practitioner to play a versatile role'. Van Lier was not specialized in any of the three facets of development work: education, agriculture (cattle-breeding, forestry) or medical aid.

As regards education: he took a brief training course but had no experience of teaching. For the limited scope and simple form of the task in hand his capacities were not insufficient. The fact that it took so long before there was any sign of success was due to (among other reasons) the policy he followed: his choice of headquarters, his refusal to start a day-school at a psychologically suitable moment, his adherence to the view that only a boarding-school would yield the desired results. There were also some faulty judgments made by him. He thought, wrongly, that "all Djukas are pining for education"; that the young schoolchildren would influence their parents; he took for granted that they would derive the most benefit from education modelled on western lines. He did not pay enough attention to the role played by women, who are a determining force in education.

As regards agriculture and forestry: he had acquired some knowledge and experience in this field by following a course in agriculture, managing a plantation, being associated with balata gathering. Mistakes in policy and judgments were among the reasons why the plans failed. Here, too, it was an error of policy not to include the women in his guidance program: they were the chief agricultural workers. He could have offered instruction, not only on his own provision ground, but on the provision grounds of the women, who might have been expected to show an interest. Another shortcoming in the policy carried out was the frequent interruptions of the work. Consequently the demonstration field yielded no results which impressed the Bush Negroes. The postholder did not achieve any better results with the way in which he provided in his own needs. It was an error of judgment to suppose that the provision grounds and *los* could be re-divided without sweeping changes in the Djuka society. The fact that a market for staple products was extremely difficult to find was not taken into account either; nor the serious difficulties connected with the transport of these products along the river and the impossibility of exporting wood in large enough quantities to make the trade profitable.

As to medical aid: Van Lier's capacities and previous experience were adequate for his purpose to 'do some doctoring', relieve suffering and create confidence. In this field he was successful. He did not, however, succeed in persuading the Djukas to discard their own methods of medical practice and adopt more progressive hygienic measures. Here, too, he was guilty of an error of judgment. Neither of these changes could come about without drastic social and religious changes in the Djuka community.

2 Belief in mission

This was something Van Lier possessed to a high degree. He has what Cleveland and co-authors (1963, p. 131) regard as commendable: "a wholesome understanding of the purpose of the operation". He had helped to draw up the aims and plans that were to be carried out. (It is irrelevant here whether this concept included a consideration of the ability of the group at whom the operation was directed to understand or appreciate the aims in question.) Van Lier showed evidence of "a frank recognition of its frustrations". As regards "the ability to overcome inherent difficulties", in that he was by no means lacking either. Sometimes it was accompanied by discouragement and nascent doubt as to the likelihood of eventual success, and sometimes by a certain lack of 'organizational efficiency', but he never lost his 'self-respect' in the process.

3 Cultural empathy

By this Cleveland and co-authors (1963, p. 136) mean "the skill to understand the inner logic and coherence of other ways of life, plus the restraint not to judge them as bad, because they are different from one's own ways. A certain involvement in alien ways – well short of going native – may become the most effective device for building a bridge from one culture to another". Goodenough (1963, p. 378) calls 'cultural empathy' a subsidiary product of the required attitude: "to accept other people as fellow human beings, as entitled to the same respect for their wants, felt needs, customs, values and sense of personal worth, as he expects for his". This generalized concept enables us to judge Van Lier's attitude: he did in fact understand the "inner logic and coherence of the Djuka world" and did not write if off as bad, but he believed that the western way of thinking was superior, and he did not fail to impart this view to the Djukas, and he did his best to persuade them to be converted to western civilization. Although he regarded the Djukas "as fellow human beings" and certainly displayed 'a certain involvement' in their way of life and thought, his undisguised preference made it impossible for him "to build a bridge from one culture to another". He did not gain more than confidence in his person and in his benevolent intentions.

4 A sense of politics

It was most important to possess this quality, especially in the Djuka society in which, as has been pointed out (e.g. in Chapter VII §4) the political game is highly developed. Goodenough (1963, p. 347) summarizes it as follows: "the development worker must be sensitive to the local political climate and be able to discover and reckon with political currents and cross-currents". As to Van Lier: he was fairly well acquainted with the political currents and manoeuvring in the Djuka community. He did not succeed, however, in obviating negative consequences of the development work nor, by means of counter-manipulation, in diverting their influence into a favourable direction.

5 Organization ability

This means "a talent for combining personnel and resources into dynamic, self-sustaining enterprises, an ability to utilize skills and forces to make the desired happen" (Cleveland, 1963, p. 150). In order to be fruitful, this talent should be concentrated on three phases of the development work. During the first phase the group should be informed about the plans that are to be carried out and the way in which one intends going about it. During the second phase the members of the group should be absorbed into the process of carrying out the project. Although Van Lier did, in fact, suggest informing the Djukas about the plans, nothing came of it. It was not, however, part of his intention to let them join as fellow-workers and executors in the actual carrying out of the plans. He supplied the example, the instructions, the demonstrations, and the Djukas were supposed to modify their way of life accordingly. During the third phase the talent for organization should be manifested in "the capacity to develop viable organizations within the framework of the local social system" (Goodenough, 1963, p. 377) which will in due course be able to take over and continue the development work. In other words, "working yourself out of a job" (Cleveland and co-authors, 1963, p. 167). According to the authors this "is far from an easy assignment. The temptation is great to get things done by doing them yourself, rather than training others to do them" (id. p. 167). Although the development project had to be discontinued before reaching the third phase, it can be stated that Van Lier had no insight into this organizational need. As regards education, all he could achieve was that a few Djukas promised not to boycott his successor. He did not manage to train the Djukas to the point of opening the way for the gradual adoption of a new agricultural method. Nor did western hygienic conceptions catch on.

d The reactions of the Djukas

The resistance of the Djukas aroused by the acceptance of a western orientated culture pattern in the Surinam coastal area has been described in Chapter IV § 6). Their protest against the development project in particular, as has been pointed out in the course of the case history, may be briefly recapitulated as follows:

1 The fact that the development project was forced upon the Paramount Chief, his prominent tribesmen and their subjects without any previous consultation resulted in their withholding their cooperation during the first years, and giving it only grudgingly afterwards.

2 Because the division of the community (into above- and below-stream Djukas) was implicated in the development project, controversies were sharpened, so that the project came to be regarded as a source of conflicts.

3 The religious system of the Djuka society is aimed at giving protection against both natural and supernatural dangers. An encroachment upon this system, so it is believed, can have harmful results for the community as well as for the individual. It was feared that the ultimate intention of the development project was to overthrow this religious system. Van Lier succeeded only to a very slight degree in removing this fear. The reason was that he himself followed an ambiguous policy: on the one hand he assured the Djukas that he had no intention of giving their children a Christian education , on the other hand he propagated western civilization, which, in his view (and in theirs!) was irrevocably bound up with Christianity.

4 The division of dwelling-places and land depends on kinship relations. Thus efforts to bring about changes in this connection also encounter resistance.

5 Administrative relationships are marked by a situation of incomplete ascendency[13], so the balance of power is apt to undergo fluctuations resulting from political manoeuvres. Outside interference, that is by non-Djukas, is firmly repulsed. Van Lier's attempts to exert some influence on these internal machinations when they threatened to harm his development work did not succeed.

e The influence of 'chance events'

Two important 'chance events' occurred in the case-history in question, one of which influenced the development work favourably, the other unfavourably.

1 The strike

This strike (Chapter v § 2d), instigated by the Paramount Chief and involving the freight carriers on the Tapanahoni, had, in addition to a number of unfavourable results, also an unexpectedly favourable effect on the development work. As a result of the strike Granman Amakti was summoned to the city and given a reprimand. The promise he was forced to sign contained the clause that he would henceforth, contrary to his previous attitude, give his active support to the development work and especially to the cause of education. Although the result of this promise did not come up to expectation, at any rate he no longer openly opposed the school.

The second important result was that a Head Chief was now appointed next to the Paramount Chief with full co-responsibility, namely the High Priest Kanapé, who was on the side of the postholder and supported him as much as possible.

2 The death of Chief Popo and other chance events

Chief Popo died after a struggle for power against High Priest Kanapé (Chapter VI § 2). According to Djuka concepts it was an irrefutable fact that Kanapé was responsible for his death. Since the friendship between Kanapé and Van Lier was well-known (and not approved of) the postholder came in for his share of suspicion. A number of new accidental occurrences strengthened this view: a series of accidents, illnesses and deaths in the vicinity of Van Lier and Kanapé. In the eyes of the Djukas these happenings were by no means a matter of chance: they were the work of Popo's spirit of revenge (or *kunu*). Another unhappy circumstance was that the postholder was accused of evil magical practices (or *wisi*) and was consequently shunned. It cost much time, events that contradicted the above suspicions, and power of persuasion before the Djukas regained confidence in the benevolent intentions of the postholder. Naturally the development work was hampered by this situation.

f Final assessment

Van Lier's enterprise had proved a failure. The Djuka society had not achieved development, a process of social change had not been launched. I have indicated the reasons for this. Now, after some fifty years, the failure does not surprise us either. But the man who, despite his lack of technical knowledge needed for the development of a primitive community still did his utmost to carry out the project single-handed, commands admiration. For many years Van Lier held out, notwithstanding opposition of the colonial as well as the primitive community, terribly isolated, without proper means of communication, without comfort, pursuing his work in the face of constant adversity. He was able to do this because of his idealism, his devotion, his perseverance, his interest in his fellow human beings and his desire to gain insight into the Djuka society. Van Lier had his strong and his weak points: "The Brutus of the play is neither the purely noble hero nor a blundering and unwordly idealist led by trickery."[14]

NOTES

[1] Data from archives of the *Secretariaat der Suriname Missie*, Amsterdam.
[2] Bonne, 1920, p. 39, et seq.; Ratelband, 1944, p. 193 et seq.; Gonggrijp, 1960, p. 63 et seq.
[3] Pater F. Morssink, De Volksmissionaris, 1919-1920, pp. 312 and 346.
[4] Unfortunately this treatise, like those on the Saramaccaners, the Paramaccaners, the Bonnis and the Matuaris, was never published.
[5] Drs. Ch. H. Eersel, Director of the Language Bureau in Paramaribo, went over the translation with me.
[6] The word 'river' is used to designate both the tribal territory and its population.
[7] Da Kodjo Kanapé is referring here to the situation as it was in 1925. Previously (2nd and 3rd period, Chapters V and VI), Amakti had made efforts to have the school in Drietabbetje.
[8] De Schlippe (1962, p. 85) remarks that "the term was finally consecrated at the 9th session of the Economic and Social Council of the United Nations (E/2437). But long before that it was used in British African dependencies".
[9] Kater, 1967, p. 102: "In many cases, however, this reality by no means conforms with the ideal put forward in the publications of the United Nations."
[10] The principles mentioned were drawn up by the United Nations and may be found in the U.N. Charter of 1966, and in the 'guiding principles' of the U.N. Economic and Social Councils E/1553, 1969, and E/2931, 1957. Cf. also Margaret Mead, 1955, p. 303 et seq.
[11] Cleveland, Mangone and Adams, 1963, p. 377 et seq.
[12] Cleveland, Mangone and Adams, 1963, p. 124. Their study is relevant to Americans who go and work abroad, without specifying the type of work they do. Goodenough (1963, p. 344 et seq.) applies these elements in the description of the ideal executor of a development project.
[13] Thoden van Velzen, 1966, p. 267 et seq.
[14] Sanders, 1967, p. 18.

LIST OF WORKS CONSULTED

Abbreviations used:

w.i.g.: West-Indische Gids
n.w.i.g.: Nieuwe West-Indische Gids
b.t.l.v.: Bijdragen Taal-, Land- en Volkenkunde
v.t.l.v.: Verhandelingen Taal-, Land- en Volkenkunde
t.k.n.a.g.: Tijdschrift van het Koninklijk Nederlands Aardrijkskundig Genootschap.

AHRENSBERG, CONRAD M. and ARTHUR H. NIEHOFF, 1964, Introducing Social Change, Aldine Publishing Company, Chicago.
BAAL, J. VAN, 1967, Mensen in verandering, N.V. De Arbeiderspers, Amsterdam.
BAKKER, J. P., 1955, "Over ontstaan en vervorming van de laaggelegen landbouwgronden der bosnegers langs de grote rivieren van Suriname", in: Gedenkboek Fahrenfort, Groningen.
BATTEN, T. R., 1964[4], Communities and their Development, Oxford University Press, London.
BENJAMINS, H. D., AND JOH. F. SNELLEMANS, eds. 1914/1917, Encyclopaedie van Nederlandsch West-Indië, Martinus Nijhoff, 's-Gravenhage and E.J. Brill, Leiden.
BENJAMINS, H. D., 1920/1, Review of: W.F. van Lier, 1919, w.i.g. 2, 163-72.
BENJAMINS, H. D., 1923/4, "Bevolkingscijfers van Britsch-Guiana en Suriname", w.i.g. 5, 197-215.
BENJAMINS, H. D., 1929/30, "'Sneki-koti'. Inenting tegen den beet van vergiftige slangen", w.i.g. 11, 497-512; 1931/2, 13, 3-24; 317-483.
BONNE, C., 1920/1, "Het Boschnegerschrift van Afaka", w.i.g. 2, 391-6.
BOONACKER J., 1916, "Politieke contracten met de Boschnegers in Suriname", b.t.l.v. 71, 371-411.
BRONS, J.C., 1952, Het rijksdeel Suriname, De erven F. Bohn n.v., Haarlem.
BUREAU VOLKSLECTUUR, 1961, Woordenlijst van het Sranan-Tongo, Glossary of the Surinam Vernacular, N.V. Varekamp & Co., Paramaribo.
BUSIA, K.A., 1960[3], "The Ashanti of the Gold Coast", in Daryll Forde, ed., African Worlds, Studies in the Cosmological Ideas and Social Values of African Peoples, Oxford University Press, Oxford, 190-210.

BUVE, R. TH. J., 1963, "Surinaamse slaven en vrije negers in Amsterdam gedurende de achttiende eeuw", B.T.L.V. 119, 8-17.
CLEVELAND, HARLAN, GERARD J. MANGONE AND JOHN CLARKE ADAMS, 1960, The overseas Americans, McGraw-Hill Book Company Inc., New York.
COSTER, A.M., 1866, "De Boschnegers in de kolonie Suriname, hun leven, zeden en gewoonten", B.T.L.V. I, 1-36.
CURRIE, A., 1948, Nota inzake bestuurszorg voor Boschnegers en Indianen. M.S.
DARK, PHILIP J. C., 1954, Bush Negro Art. An African Art in the Americas, Alec Tiranti Ltd., London.
DOORNBOS, LIEUWE, 1966, Kinderjaren aan de Tapanahony, Van Denderen, Groningen.
DUSSELDORP, D.B.W.M., 1963, "Geografische mobilitiet en de ontwikkeling van Suriname", B.T.L.V. 119, 18-50.
ESSED, F.E., ed., 1965, Nationaal Ontwikkelingsplan Suriname, Stichting Planbureau Suriname, Paramaribo.
EXODUS, ABRAHAM (M.H. DUCROO), n.d. Het land van bij-ons-buiten, etc., N.V. Leiter-Nypels, Maastricht.
FERMIN, PHILIPPE, 1789, Description Générale, Géographique et Physique de la Colonie de Surinam, etc., E. van Harrevelt, Amsterdam, 2 vol.
FOSTER, GEORGE M., 1962, Traditional Cultures: and the Impact of Technological change, Harper & Row, New York.
FURNIVALL, J.S., 1956, Colonial Policy and Practice. A comparative study of Burma and Netherlands India, New York, University Press, New York.
FRANSSEN HERDERSCHEE, A., 1905a, "Verslag van de Gonini-expeditie", T.K.N.A.G., 1-174.
FRANSSEN HERDERSCHEE, A., 1905b, "Verslag der Tapanahoni-expeditie", T.K.N.A.G., 847-1032.
GEYSKES, D.C., 1954/5, "De Landbouw bij de Boschnegers van de Marowijne", W.I.G. 30, 135-53.
GLUCKMAN, M. 1967, "Introduction" in A.L. Epstein, ed., The Craft of Social Anthropology, Tavistock Publications, London, I-XX.
GONGGRIJP, J.W., 1961, "The evolution of a Djuka-script in Surinam", W.I.G. 40, 63-72.
GROOT, SILVIA W. DE, 1963, Van Isolatie naar integratie, V.T.L.V. 41, Martinus Nijhoff, 's-Gravenhage.
GROOT, SILVIA W. DE, 1965, "Migratiebewegingen der Djoekas in Suriname van 1845 tot 1863", N.W.I.G. 44, 133-51.
GOODENOUGH, WARD HUNT., 1963, Cooperation in Change. An anthropological approach to community development, Russell Sage Foundation, New York.
GOUVERNEMENTS RESOLUTIES, Centraal Archief Suriname.
HARTSINCK, JAN JACOB, 1770, Beschrijving van Guiana of de Wilde Kust in Zuid-America etc., Gerrit Tielenburg, Amsterdam, 2 vol.
HAYES, SAMUEL P., 1959[2], Measuring the Results of Development Projects, Unesco, Paris.
HEECKEREN, E.L. VAN, 1826, Aanteekeningen betrekkelijk de kolonie Suriname, C.A. Thieme, Arnhem.
H(ERLEIN), J.D., 1718, Beschryvinge van de volk-plantinge Zuriname, Meindert Injema, Leeuwarden.
HERSKOVITS, M.J. and F.S. HERSKOVITS, 1934, Rebel Destiny, Among the Bush Negroes of Dutch Guiana, McGraw-Hill Book Company, New York.
HERSKOVITS, M.J. and F.S. HERSKOVITS, 1936, Surinam Folklore, Columbia University Press, New York.
HERSKOVITS, MELVILLE J., 1946, "Problem, Method and Theory in Afroamerican studies", Phylon, The Atlanta University Review of Race and Culture 7, 337-54.

HOETINK, H. 1958, Het Patroon van de oude Curaçaose Samenleving, Van Gorcum en Comp. N.V., Assen.
HURAULT, JEAN, 1961, Les noirs refugiés Boni de la Guyane Française, Mémoires de l'Institut Français d'Afrique Noire (I.F.A.N.), Dakar.
JUNKER, L., 1922/3, "Eenige mededeelingen over de Saramaccaner boschnegers", W.I.G.4, 449-80.
JUNKER, L., 1923/4, "Over de afstamming der Boschnegers", W.I.G. 5, 310-17.
JUNKER, L., 1924/5, "Godsdienst, zeden en gebruiken der Boschnegers", W.I.G. 6, 73-81.
JUNKER, L., 1925/6, "De godsdienst der Boschnegers", W.I.G. 7, 81-95; 127-37; 153-64.
JUNKER, L., 1933/4, "Herinneringen aan het oerwoud. Uit mijn dagboek van 1921, W.I.G. 15, 177-90; 209-26.
KAHN, MORTON G., 1931, Djuka, The Bush Negroes of Dutch Guiana, The Viking Press, New York.
KAPPLER, A., 1854, Zes jaren in Suriname, W.F. Dannenfelser, Utrecht.
KAPPLER, A., 1881, Holländisch-Guiana, etc., W. Kohlhammer, Stuttgart.
KATER, ADRIANUS, 1967, Community Development in Marokko, Thesis Amsterdam, Groningen.
KESLER, C.K., 1940, "Slavenopstanden in de West", W.I.G. 22, 257-70; 289-302.
KÖBBEN, A.J.F., 1964, Van primitieven tot medeburgers, Van Gorcum en Comp. N.V., Assen.
KÖBBEN, A.J.F., 1967a, "Participation and Quantification" in: D.G. Jongmans and P.C.W. Gutkind, ed., Anthropologists in the fields, Van Gorcum, Assen, 35-56.
KÖBBEN, A.J.F., 1967b, "Unity and Disunity. Cottica Djuka society as a kinship system", B.T.L.V. 123, 10-52.
KÖBBEN, A.J.F., 1968a, "Continuity in Change", B.T.L.V. 124, 56-89.
KÖBBEN, A.J.F., 1968b, "Law at the Village Level" (MS).
KOL, H. VAN, 1901, Een noodlijdende kolonie, Masereeuw & Bouten, Amsterdam-Rotterdam.
KOL, H. VAN, 1919/1, "De Koloniale Staten", W.I.G. 1, 5-23.
KRUIJER, G.J., 1951, Suriname en zijn buurlanden, J.A. Boom en Zn., Meppel.
KUYP, E. VAN DER, 1962, "Literatuuroverzicht betreffende de voeding en de voedingsgewoonten van de Boslandcreool in Suriname", W.I.G. 41, 205-72.
LAMUR, H.E., 1965, "De levensomstandigheden van de in Paramaribo werkende Aukaner arbeiders", N.W.I.G. 44, 119-33.
LICHTVELD, L., 1930/1, "Een Afrikaansch bijgeloof: snetji-koti", W.I.G. 13, 49-52.
LIER, R.A.J. VAN, 1949, Samenleving in een Grensgebied, Martinus Nijhoff, 's-Gravenhage.
LINDBLOM, G., 1924, Afrikanische Relikte und Indianische Entlehungenn in der Kultur der Buschnegers Surinams, Wettergren & Kerben, Göteborg.
LINTON, RALPH, 1936, The Study of Man, an Introduction, Appleton-Century-Crofts, Inc., New York.
LOTH, I.E., 1910, "Aanteekeningen over de Djoeka's (Aucaner Boschnegers) in Suriname", T.K.N.A.G. 27, 339-46.
MEAD, MARGARET, 1955, Cultural Patterns and Technical Change, The New American Library, New York.
MERTON, ROBERT, K., 1966, Social Theory and Social Structure, revised and enlarged edition, The Free Press, New York, Collier - MacMillan Ltd., London.
MORSSINK, F., 1918, "Iets over de Boschnegers in de Boven Marowijne door W.F. van Lier", De Surinamer, 22 Dec.
MORSSINK, F., 1919/20, "Bezoek aan den zwarten koning der wouden", De Volksmissionaris, 312-346.

MORSSINK, F., 1932, De Evangeliseering der Djoekas, MS.
MORSSINK, F., 1934, Boschnegeriana. Derde afdeling: Djoekas of Aucaners, MS.
MORSSINK, F., 1934/5, "Nogmaals de dood van Jankoeso en: nog niet het einde van een dynastie", W.I.G., 16, 91-105.
NASSY, DAVID DE IS. COHEN, 1788, Essai historique sur la colonie de Surinam, etc., Paramaribo (Unchanged reprint S. Emmering, Amsterdam, 1968).
NATIONAAL ONTWIKKELINGSPLAN SURINAME 1965, Ed. F.E. Essed, Stichting Planbureau Suriname, Paramaribo.
NETSCHER, P.M., 1888, Geschiedenis van de koloniën Essequebo, Demerary en Berbice, van de vestiging der Nederlanders aldaar tot op onzen tijd, Martinus Nijhoff, 's-Gravenhage.
NEWBURY, C.W., 1961, The Western Slave Coast and its Rulers, European trade and administration among the Yoruba and Adja-speaking peoples of south-western Nigeria, Southern Dahomey and Togo, Clarendon Press, Oxford.
OOFT, C.D., 1963, De Staten, Geschiedenis, rechtskarakter en samenstelling, Paramaribo.
OUDSCHANS DENTZ, FRED. 1938. Cornelis van Aerssen van Sommelsdijck, P.N. van Kampen en Zn., Amsterdam.
OUDSCHANS DENTZ, FRED. 1948, "De afzetting van het Groot-opperhoofd der Saramaccaners, Koffy in 1835 en de politieke contracten met de Boschnegers in Suriname", B.T.L.V. 104, 33-43.
OUDSCHANS DENTZ, FRED., 1949, Geschiedkundige tijdtafel van Suriname, J.H. de Bussy, Amsterdam.
PANHUYS, L. C., VAN, 1908, "Iets over de Marowijne rivier en hare geschiedenis", Bull. van het Koloniaal Museum, no. 12.
PARRINDER, GEOFFREY, 1961², West African Religion. A Study of the Beliefs and Practices of Akan, Ewe, Yoruba, Ibo and Kindered Peoples, The Epworth Press, London.
PISTORIUS, THOMAS, 1763, Korte en zakelyke beschryvinge van de colonie van Zuriname, Theodorus Crajenschot, Amsterdam.
PLANTE FEBURE. J.M., 1918, West-Indië in het Parlement, 1897-1917, Martinus Nijhoff, 's-Gravenhage.
QUINTUS BOSZ, A.J.A., 1954, Drie eeuwen grondpolitiek in Suriname, Van Gorcum, Assen.
RAPPORT, 1911, De economische en financiële toestand der kolonie Suriname. Rapport der Commissie benoemd bij besluit van zijne excellentie den minister van koloniën van 11 Maart 1911, Afd. B., No. 56, Martinus Nijhoff, 's-Gravenhage.
RAPPORT, 1920, Suriname Studie-Syndicaat. Rapport der Studie-commissie naar aanleiding van haar bezoek aan Suriname, Gebr. Tuinzing, Rotterdam.
RATELBAND, K., 1944/5, "Een Boschnegerschrift van West-Afrikaanschen oorsprong", W.I.G. 26, 193-205.
SANDERS, N., 1967, "Introduction" to Julius Caesar, New Penguin Shakespeare, Penguin Books Ltd., Harmondsworth, Middlesex.
SECRETARIS-AGENDAS, CENTRAAL ARCHIEF SURINAME.
SCHLIPPE, PIERRE DE, 1962, "Theory of Community Development", in: J.A. Ponsioen ed., Social Welfare Policy First collection. Contributions to Theory, Mouton & Co., 's-Gravenhage, 85-107.
SCHMIDGALL, F.L., 1961, Community Development. Verslag van een literatuur-studie, Landbouwhogeschool, Wageningen, stencilled ed.
SPALBURG, J.G., 1899, De Marowijne en hare bewoners, H.B. Heyde, Paramaribo.
STAAL, G.J., 1921/2, "Het voorspel der installatie van den posthouder bij de Aucaners", W.I.G. 3, 630-6.

STAAL, G.J., 1922/3, "Overeenkomst met de Aucaner Boschnegers", W.I.G. 4, 48-52.
STAHEL, G., 1933/4, "De cultuurwaarde van Suriname", W.I.G. 15, 158-62.
STEDMAN, J.G., 1796, Narrative, of a five years' expedition, against the Revolted Negroes of Surinam, in Guiana, etc., J. Johnson and J. Edwards, London, 2 Vol.
SURINAME STUDIE SYNDICAAT, 1920, Rapport der Studie-commissie naar aanleiding van haar bezoek aan Suriname, Gebr. Tuinzing, Rotterdam.
SYPESTEYN, C.A. VAN, 1854, Beschrijving van Suriname, historisch, geographisch en statistisch overzigt, uit officiële bronnen bijeengebragt, De Gebroeders van Cleef, 's-Gravenhage.
TEENSTRA, M.D., 1835, De landbouw in de kolonie Suriname, H. Eekhoff, Groningen, 2 Vol.
TEENSTRA, M.D., 1842, De Negerslaven in de kolonie Suriname, H. Lagerweij, Dordrecht
THODEN VAN VELZEN, H.U.E., 1966a, Politieke beheersing in de Djuka maatschappij. Een studie van een onvolledig machtsoverwicht, Thesis Amsterdam, Afrika-Studiecentrum, Leiden, 2 Vol.
THODEN VAN VELZEN, H.U.E., 1966b ,"Het geloof in wraakgeesten: bindmiddel en splijtzwam van de Djuka-matri-lineage", N.W.I.G. 45, 45-52.
TICHELMAN, F., 1967, "De S.D.A.P. en Indonesië, 1897-1907, enkele gegevens en problemen", De Nieuwe Stem, 683-723.
VELSEN, J. VAN, 1967, "The Extended-Case Method and Situational Analysis", in A.L. Epstein, ed., The Craft of Social Anthropology, Tavistock Publications, London, 129-149.
VERDOORN, J.A., 1965, Volksgezondheid en sociale ontwikkeling, Het Spectrum N.V., Utrecht - Antwerpen.
VERHANDELINGEN DER KOLONIALE STATEN, Centraal Archief Suriname.
VERKADE-CARTIER VAN DISSEL, E.F., 1937, De mogelijkheid van landbouwkolonisatie voor blanken in Suriname, H.J. Paris, Amsterdam.
VOORHOEVE, J., 1960, "De handschriften van Mr. Adriaan François Lammens", N.W.I.G. 28-49.
VRAAGBAAK, DE, 1925, Almanak voor Suriname, Erven H. van Ommeren, Paramaribo.
WERTHEIM, W.F., 1964, East-West Parallels. Sociological approaches to modern Asia, W. van Hoeve, The Hague.
WERTHEIM, W.F., 1967, "Ontwikkelingshulp als neo-kolonialisme", De Nieuwe Stem, 22, 461-83.
WETERING, W. VAN, 1966, "Conflicten tussen co-vrouwen bij de Djuka", N.W.I.G. 45, 52-60.
WETERING, W. VAN, Djuka Witchcraft Beliefs, a Sociological Approach (Thesis Amsterdam, forthcoming).
WOLBERS, J., 1861, Geschiedenis van Suriname, A .de Hoogh, Amsterdam.
WONG, E., 1936, "Hoofdenverkiezing, stamverdeeling en stamverspreiding der Boschnegers van Suriname in de 18e en 19e eeuw", B.T.L.V., 97, 295-362.
WIJNHOLT, M.R., 1965, Strafrecht in Suriname, N.V. Uitgeversmaatschappij AE.E. Kluwer, Deventer.

BIBLIOGRAPHY OF WILLEM FREDERIK VAN LIER'S WRITINGS

(English translation of titles)

1.	1918	Some facts about the Bush Negroes in the Upper Marowijne, Journal *Suriname*, 5 Febr. 1918-7 Jan. 1919.
2.	1919	Some facts about the Bush Negroes in the Upper Marowijne, Brochure containing articles from *Suriname* and two lectures. H. van Ommeren, Paramaribo.
3.	1921	Among the Aucaners I, *West Indische Gids*, Vol. III, 1921.
4.	1922	Among the Aucaners II, III, *West-Indische Gids*, Vol. IV 1922-1923.
5.	1926	How Boni met his end, Weekly *De Periscoop*, No. 93.
6.	1927a	Some facts about the influence of Christianity on the Matuarians, Lecture 13 Jan. *Christelijke Jongelieden Vereeniging Paulus*.
7.	1927b	Country and Ethnography, Weekly *De Persicoop*, No. 165.
8.	1930a	Some facts about the legal conceptions of the Aucaners, *De Emancipatie Courant*, 1 July, No. 5.
9.	1930b	Some facts about the concept of *wisi* among the Bush Negroes, Offprint from Newspaper *De Surinamer* (see 20).
10.	1938a	Kandu *De Emancipatie*, 1938 (see 13, 14, 15)
11.	1938b	Symbols among the Bush Negroes (see 17), Talk to the Freemason Lodge Concordia.
12.	1940a	Notes on the spiritual life and the society of the Djukas in Suriname, *Bijdragen Taal- Land en Volkenkunde* Part 99, 2.
13.	1940b	Kina, Monthly *De Surinaamse Politie* (sequel to Kandu, 1938, see 10).
14.	1943a	Kina, *De Emancipatie*, June (sequel to Kandu 1938) (see 10).
15.	1943b	Kandu-Kina-Mula, Offprint from *De Emancipatie* (see 10, 13, 14).
16.	1943c	A supplement to Mula, Offprint from *De Surinamer* 18 Sept. (see 15).
17.	1943d	Symbols among the Bush Negroes, Monthly *Suriname Zending* No. 3, 4/5, etc. (see 27).
18	1944a	Orthodoxy and Modernism among the Aucaner Bush Negroes, Offprint from *Het Protestantenblad*, 26 Aug. and 2 Sept.
19.	1944b	Mission Work, *Suriname Zending*, No. 8.
20.	1944c	Some facts concerning the concept of *wisi* among the Bush Negroes, *Suriname Zending*, No. 3, 4, 5/6 (see 9).

21.	1945	New Year's Celebrations among the Aucaners, *Het Nieuws*, 31 Dec.
22.	1947	Some facts about *kunu* (Fate), *Het Nieuws*, 4 Jan.
23.	1948	Some facts about the religion of the Aucaners and the Matuarians, broadcast talk, 18 Aug.
24.	1949	Kantamasi, Lecture 19 July.
25.	1950	Some facts about life in the interior (as it used to be), *De West*, 6 July. (also in broadcast talks 22.3. '45 and 21.8.'47).
26.	1951a	Busi-mama, *De West*, 13 April.
27.	1951b	Symbols among the Bush Negroes, *Protestantenblad*, 10 Febr.
28.	1951c	Some facts about *afkodrai*, *De West*, 4 May
29.	undated a	Some facts about *afkodrai*, *wisi*, *bakru*, *jorka*, etc., brochure, previously partly published in *Suriname*.
30.	undated b	Some facts about animism among the Bush Negroes (typescript).
31.	undated c	How a Djuka dies and is buried (typescript).

GLOSSARY OF DJUKA WORDS APPEARING IN THE TEXT

Akrekuna	– name of a god, also of a village on the upper Tapanahoni.
afkodrei	– idolatry, i.e. worship of African gods and, in general, rituals belonging to this religion. (Dutch: afgoderij).
Anansi	– spider, principal trickster of the animal tales (Twi).
– tori	– stories, tales about Anansi, also generic name for tales.
bakra	– foreigner, inhabitant of the coastal plain of Surinam, white and coloured; uninitiated in the way of life and religion of the Bush Negroes.
basi	– master, boss, the best one.
Bassia	– minor chief. Name derived from Bastiaan: overseer of the slaves on the plantations.
béré	– matrilineage, subdivision of a *lo*: clan. (English: belly).
bilo	– below (here: lower Tapanahoni).
– ningre	– below-Negroes: living along the lower part of the Tapanahoni.
Blakadjakti	– black jacket. name for the vice village chief derived from the colour of his uniform.
broko-dé	– ritual mourning feast.
bumbi	– poisonous root (*Theprosia-toxiana syn*) used to poison fishing water.
Busi-kaptèn	– bush captain (minor chief).
corjari	– dug-out. (Dutch: corjaal).
Da	– form of address toward a higher placed or older person (male).
datra	– doctor
Djibri	– name of a god.
dresie	– medicine, to cure, to dress.
fon tjifunga	– part of mourning feast: driving out evil spirits from the village.
fufuru	– to steal, to cheat.

Gedeunsu	– Oracle god, 'brought along' from Africa (Dahomey).
Granfiskari	– derived from Grand-Fiscal, a judicial function in the colonial administration before 1863. Here: deputy Granman, for the exercise of secular, especially legal, authority.
Gran Gadu	– Great God.
Granjorka	– spirit of prominent ancestor.
Gran-kaptèn	– head-captain (village chief).
Gran-krutu	– general council.
Granman	– Paramount chief, also used for the Governor of Surinam.
Gran Tata, Gran Gadu, Sweli Gadu, Gwangwella	– Great God (Tata: father; Sweli: oath; Gwangwella: sacral name of the Great God) Oracle god, 'brought along' from Africa.
heru	– responsibility.
jorka	– spirit of deceased, ghost.
kankantri	– sacred tree (silk-cotton tree).
kandu	– object with magic power to keep off thieves (Loango).
kapewerie	– brushwood, undergrowth, tall weeds.
Kaptèn	– captain: village chief.
kina	– taboo (Loango).
kisiman	– coffin-makers (category of priests).
kondré	– country, abode, town.
koti	– popular remedy against bites or stings of poisonous animals (Ewe?).
kré-oso	– 'cry house'. Here every corpse lies in state until it is buried.
Kromanti	– sacred language, also name of a god and of a category of gods, derived from Coromantin, ancient Gold Coast kingdom.
krutu	– council, counsel, court of law.
kunu	– avenging god or spirit. Power of revenge exercized by god or spirit (means 'death' in Ewe).
kwak	– cassava-meal.
Lanti	– 1 Djuka government 2 State government.
lanti-siki	– epidemic, lit.: country-sickness,
Ledidjakti	– red-jacket: name for the village chief, derived from the colour of the coat trimmings of his uniform.
leriman	– missionary teacher.
lo	– clan (Joruba or Ibo).
lowe-ten	– period of escape (from slavery).
lukuman	– see *obiaman*. Lukuman is a word used in the coastal area of Surinam.
masra	– mister, sir, master.
massanga	– storage hut.
misie (missie)	– madam, mistress, also queen (with name).

mula	– ceremony performed at the transference of supernatural knowledge from one person to another.
Nana, Nana Kediampon, Nijankapon	– Supreme God, Sky God (Ashanti).
neku	– poisonous liana (*lonchocarpus sp.*) used to poison fishing water.
obia	– charm; supernatural force with healing and protecting magic power (Ibo).
– man	– medicine-man, maker of charms.
ogri sani	– evil (supernatural) force, lit.: bad, ugly things.
opo	– upper (here: upper Tapanahoni).
– ningre	– upper-Negroes: living along the upper part of the Tapanahoni.
oroman	– gravediggers (category of priests).
ponsu	– fishing with poison. A special event, in which the surrounding villages take part. The poison (*neku*) is dropped in a damned up part of the river. (A method used in West Africa).
sneki	– snake.
spari	– sting-ray (*potamotrygon reticulatus Gthr*).
sula	– rapid, cascade, cataract.
sweri (sweli)	– oath, also trial by 'poison'.
tabiki (tabbetje)	– island in a river.
tafia	– kind of rum.
winti	– supernatural force, god or spirit who can 'take possession' of a person, bring him (or her) in state of trance.
– man	– he (or she) who, while in state of trance, acts as medium of a *winti* and is supposed to give medical advice under influence of the supernatural force.
wisi	– black magic, poison.
– man	– witch; he (or she) who has the power to use black magic ('poison') against others.
– wasi	– nonsense, madness.

MAPS

Upper and Lower Tapanahoni
Taken over from orientation maps drawn up by District Commissioner J. Michels, used during official journeys.

Suriname
Winkler Prins Atlas 6th edition.
With some alterations by me taken over from the New Winkler Prins Atlas, 6th edition 1963, published by the Publishing Firm Elsevier Ltd. Amsterdam.

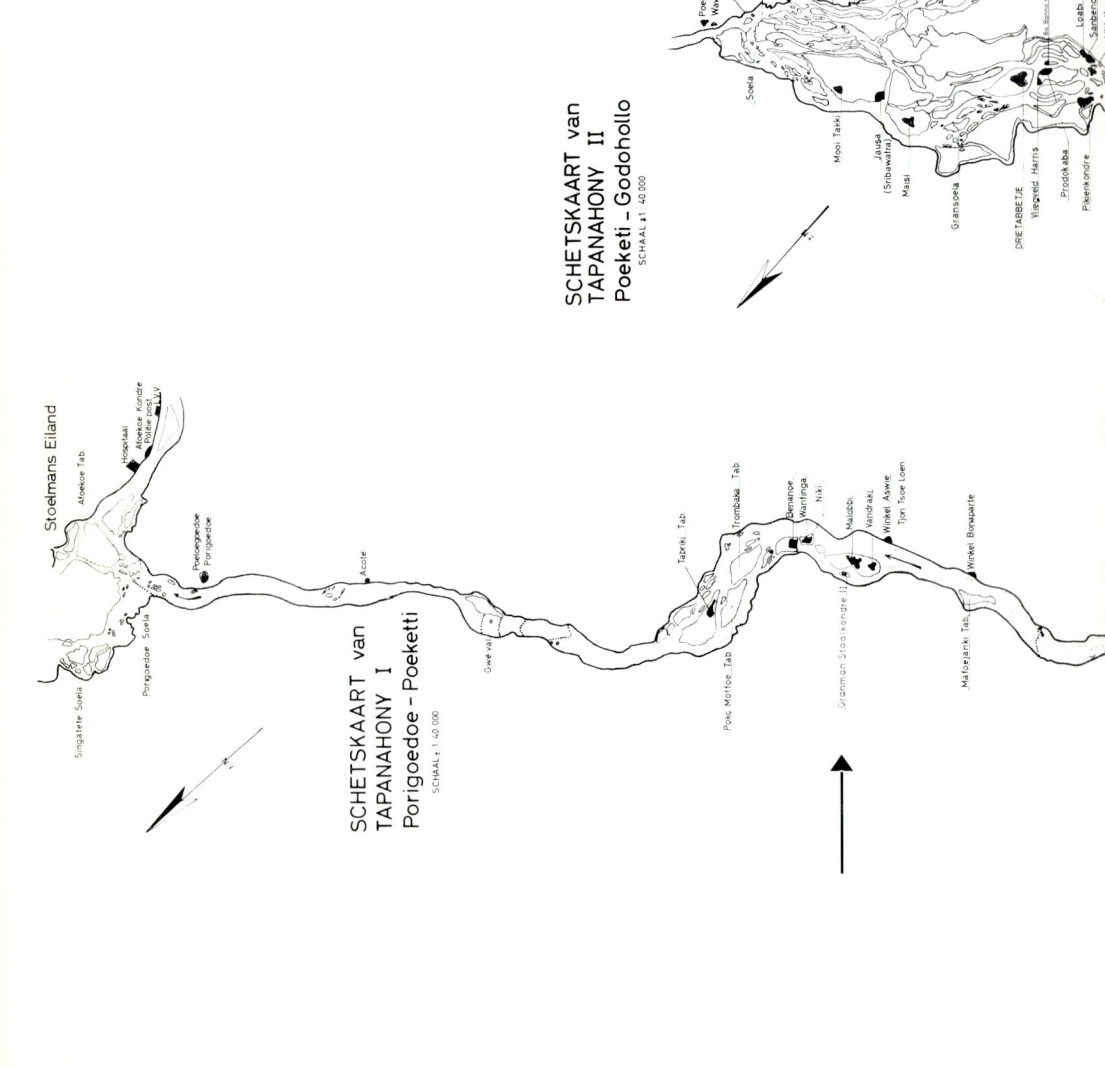

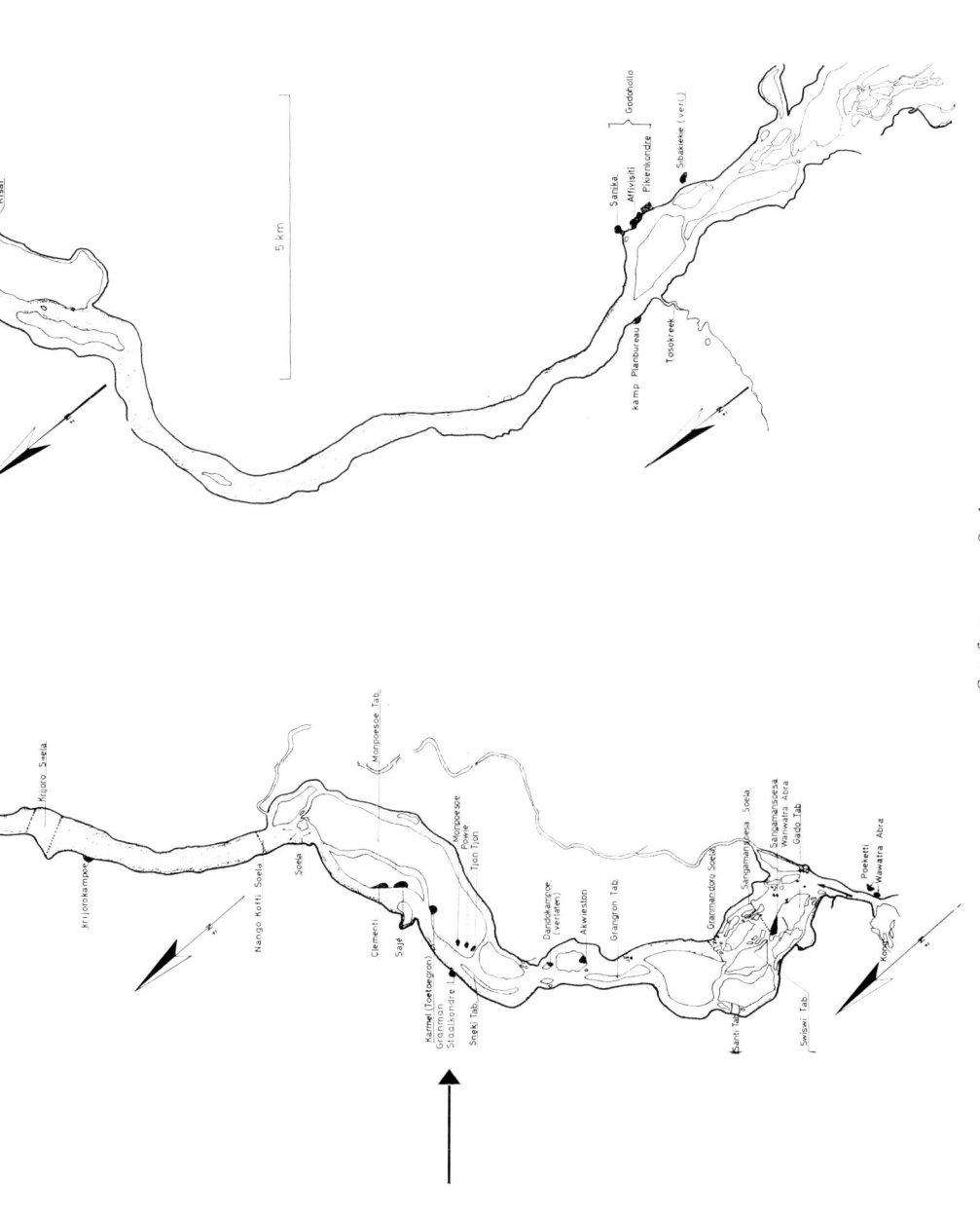

See frame map Surinam

Taken over from orientation maps drawn up by District Commissioner J. Michels, used official journeys

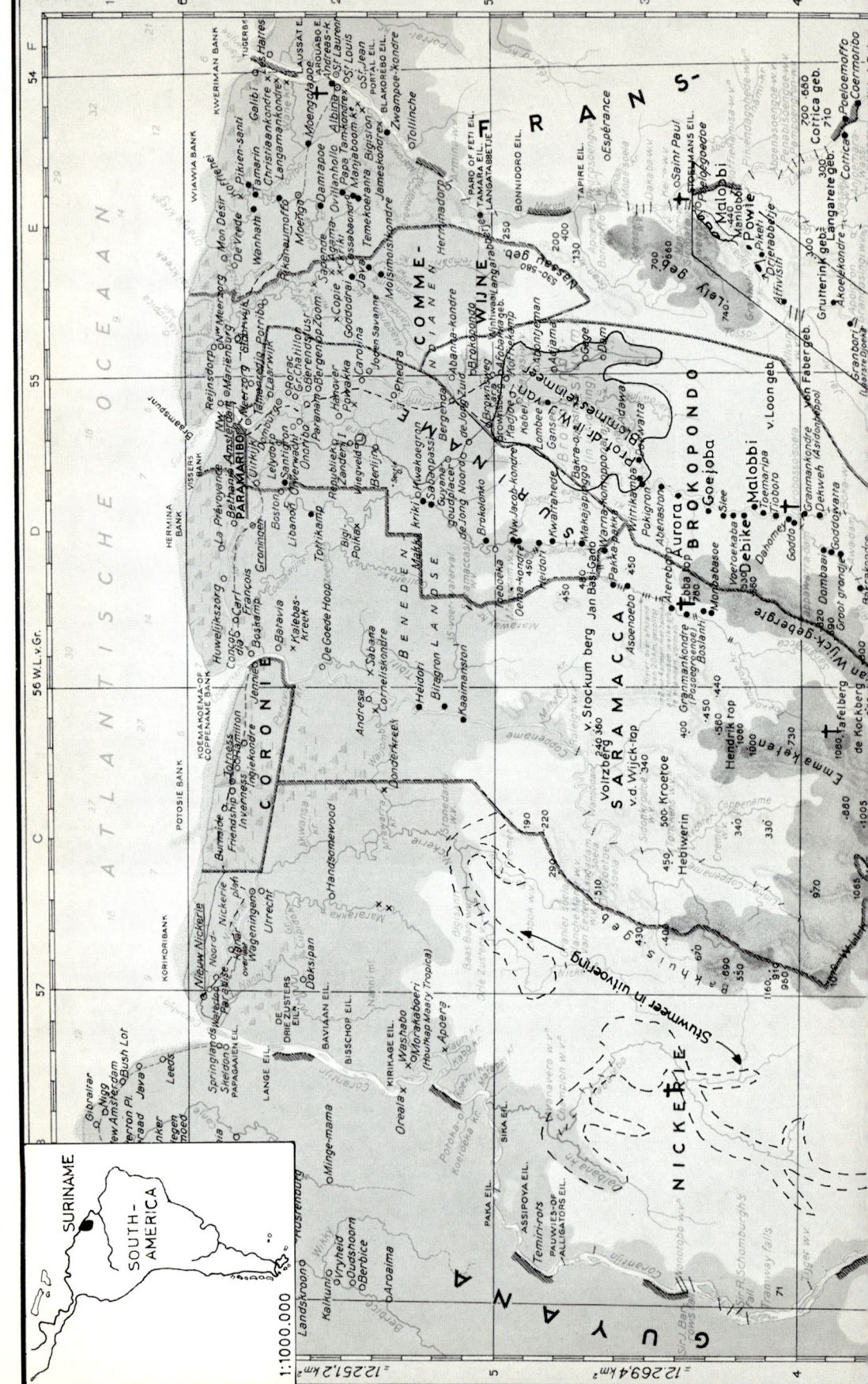

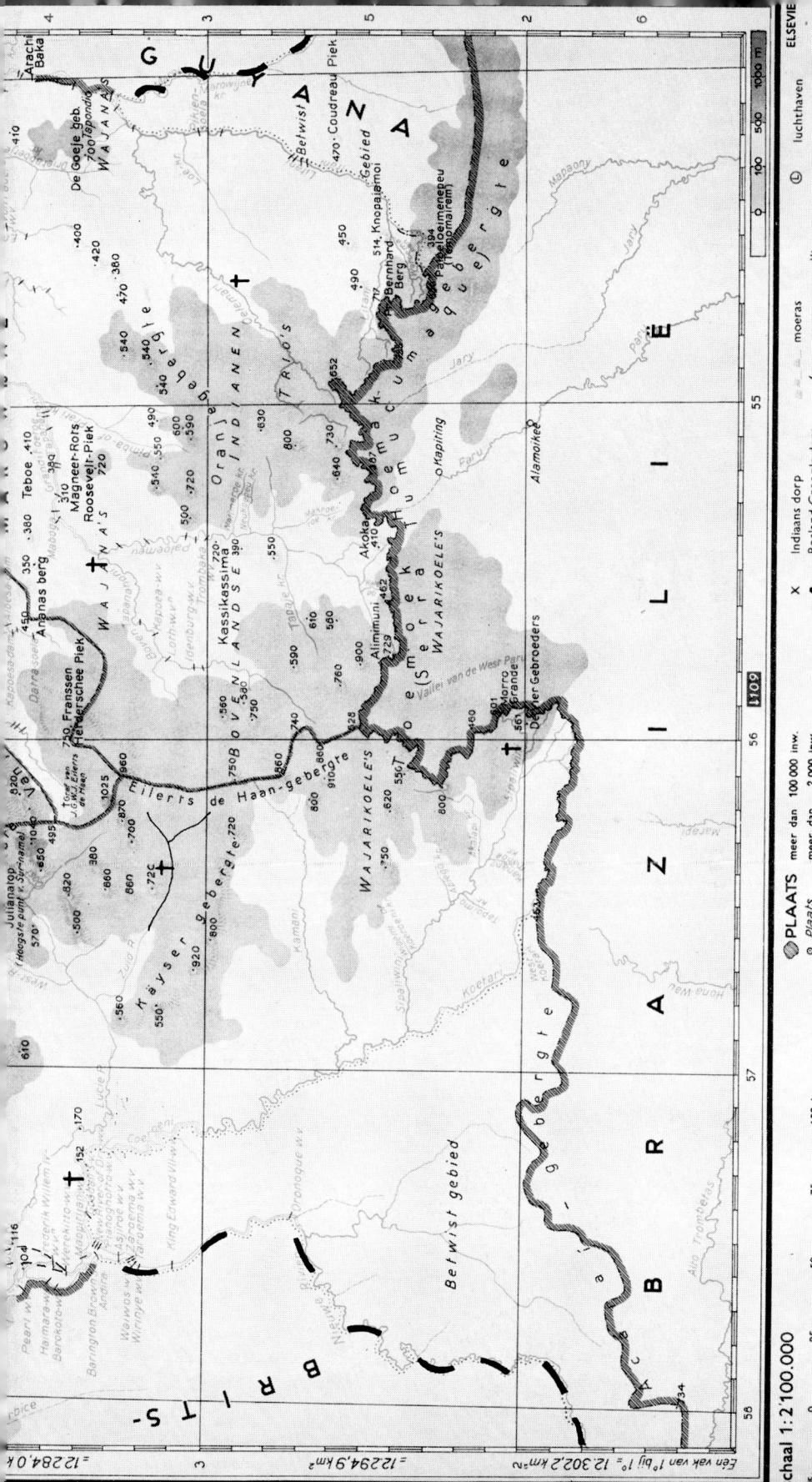

With some alterations by me taken over from the New Winkler Prins Atlas, 6th edition 1963, published by the Publishing Firm Elsevier Ltd. Amsterdam

WITHDRAWN BY
WHITMAN COLLEGE LIBRARY